Great Labor

Quotations

Sourcebook and Reader

Peter Bollen: Great **Labor Quotations** Sourcebook and Reader

Great Labor Quotations

Sourcebook and Reader

Peter Bollen

Red Eye Reference
a division of

Red Eye Press, Inc.
Los Angeles • California

Great **Labor Quotations** Sourcebook and Reader
© 2000, Peter Bollen, All rights reserved.

Published by
Red Eye Reference
P.O. Box 65751
Los Angeles, CA 90065
United States of America

Design by Red Eye Press and C.C.S. Graphics Associate
Typesetting by Cristina C. Santos, C.C.S. Graphics Associate, Whittier, CA
Edited by James J. Goodwin
Back cover photograph courtesy Lynn Historical Society
Back cover cartoon ©Huck/Konopacki Labor Cartoons

Library of Congress Cataloging-in-Publication Data

Great labor quotations : sourcebook and reader / [compiled by] Peter Bollen.
    p. cm.
  Includes bibliographical references and indexes.
  ISBN 0-929349-06-7 (pbk.)
  1. Labor--United States--Quotations, maxims, etc.

HD8066.G74 2000
331--dc21

                     00-034462

First printing August, 2000

99, 98, 97, 96.   6, 5, 4, 3, 2, 1

Printed and bound in the United States of America
by Castle Lithograph, Inc.

 330

Dedicated
to my mother,
Frances Lillian Bailin Bollen (1924-1992)
and
to my father,
James William Bollen (1917-)

Frances Bollen, a shipyard worker and rank and file union organizer during World War II.

Table of Contents

Table of Contents

Foreword

by Jim Green

I am very pleased to write the **Foreword** to Peter Bollen's new *Great Labor Quotations: Sourcebook and Reader*. As a labor historian, history teacher, and labor educator, I have found this compendium to be enlightening and thought-provoking. Bollen's compiling by chapters, and ordering within, gives the reader a sense of working people's struggles and the progression of organized labor, as well as the inspiration of their words. As I read over this wonderful collection of wit and wisdom, the words uttered by the champions of working people, by their union leaders and by the toilers themselves, I am struck by a number of things.

First, in the great tradition of Thomas Paine, we read the words of men and women who used "common sense" to speak to the great issues of the day. In the euphemistic age of "spin-doctors" and "newspeak," it is exciting to read these honest words, spoken directly, conveyed in plain English. I'd venture that today, labor spokespersons are still more direct and less equivocal than those who speak for capital, for "the law," and for the government. I hope the voices of labor remain true to the rhetorical tradition reflected in this book and don't give themselves over to the spin-doctors.

Second, we are reminded in this proletarian equivalent of *Bartlett's Familiar Quotations* that the voice of labor has been absolutely essential to the chorus of democracy, even when, or especially when, it struck discordant notes in the symphony performed to celebrate the American success story. There are countless reminders in this volume of how eloquent speakers and writers helped make "the labor question" (often understood as the class question) a central public issue in the United States between 1877 and 1937. In his biography of Sidney Hillman, Steve Fraser suggests that with the brilliant leader's death after World War II, this question ceased to be of interest to most of our citizens.

I however, can see in the words collected here that the labor question presses itself on society once again, even while our political, business and cultural leaders want to focus on other questions, questions about consumption, not about production. It is good that we hear so much from the American Federation of Labor's pragmatic chieftains: from Sam Gompers and

George Meany who never minced any words about the realities of economic life under capitalism. They may be out of favor now, and we may see in their words a limited vision that no longer serves the movement well as it enters a new century; but we may still hear in their words the wisdom that comes from working people living lives of struggle.

I am glad that Peter Bollen has updated and reworked his original *Handbook*. We can now hear from a brilliant new generation of labor leaders who will not allow America to ignore the issues and problems of wage-earning people that remain, in some respects, unchanged after a century of capitalism in our nation. Our citizens need to hear the voices of working people again; and now the union movement has new voices that cannot be silenced or ignored.

Do we not hear in these new voices of organized labor an echo of those radical and progressive voices that shout out from these pages? Do we not hear in those who carry on the struggle today some of the moral fervor of the eloquent Frederick Douglass, the passionate Eugene Debs, the visionary Henry George, the courageous Mother Jones, the defiant Rose Schneiderman, the pugnacious Walter Reuther, the martyred Joe Hill? Some of us may, as Earl Robinson sang, still dream that we saw Joe Hill last night, "just as live as he could be." But if we aren't so fortunate as dreamers, we can be fortunate readers as we peruse the poetic words of the Wobbly bard in this book.

In closing, I must say how useful this new work has been to me in my current work as a labor historian and educator. The *Sourcebook* will be of even more use as a research tool for writers, teachers, public speakers, and rank-and-file workers looking for words of wisdom. This volume also brings the critical insights of labor history to bear on the questions of the day. Many quotations in Bollen's collection illustrate the character of labor's heroes and heroines: they spoke the truth to power in their day; they spoke with voices that still deserve a hearing; they spoke with words that still inspire us to complete the tasks that lie ahead.

Jim Green, a professor of history and labor studies at the Labor Resource Center, University of Massachusetts at Boston, authored *The World of the Worker: Labor in Twentieth Century America*, soon to be published in a revised, updated form by the University of Illinois Press. He co-authored *Commonwealth of Toil: Chapters from the History of Massachusetts Workers and their Unions*. His acclaimed latest work, *Taking History to Heart: The Power of the Past in Building Social Movements*, published by the University of Massachusetts Press, blends autobiography and history.

Introduction

American liberty, in all its ennobling forms, is perhaps best illustrated by a study of American labor history. In the words of historian William Cahn, "The history of America has been largely created by the deeds of its working people and their organizations—there is scarcely an issue that is not influenced by labor's organized efforts or lack of them." The story of labor—organized and unorganized, skilled and unskilled, of men and women, elderly and young, native and foreign born, blue collar and white collar—is, by and large, the story of America. This collection of primarily American labor quotations encompasses what I feel reflects the best of past and present labor thoughts through the brightest voices—the advocates, activists, movers and shakers, as well as the foes of the American labor movement.

Historically, labor's opponents have regarded the trade union movement as subversive. Borne as a result of employer tyranny, union organizing flowered during the New Deal years of the 1930s as the Great Depression darkened the American Dream. The fruit of these seminal years of strife, upheaval, and industrial growth were the hard-fought gains of the labor movement: child labor legislation, fair labor wage and law standards, health and safety standards, unemployment and injury compensation, Social Security legislation, and the legal sanctioning of collective bargaining.

The violent conflicts of the past have largely given way to the new challenges of competition within a global economy, workplace changes because of innovative high technology, and a more service-oriented economy. But many of labor's themes are timeless, always speaking to the challenge of improving the quality of life in America. Eugene Debs once declared, "No strike has ever been lost and there can be no defeat for the labor movement." American history gives credence to his maxims.

The voices heard through this sourcebook range from the unemployed rank and filer to the silver-tongued orator. There are martyrs such as Joe Hill and August Spies, and revolutionaries like Big Bill Haywood and Tom Mooney. There are inspirational passages from Martin Luther King, Jr. and Clarence Darrow, as well as the erudite chimes of defiance from John L. Lewis. Other great wits include renowned organizer Saul Alinsky, whose presence was banned from the city of Oakland; Mother Jones, who led and inspired workers well into her nineties; and Eugene Debs, who once ran for president and ran his Railway Workers union from his jail cell.

The voices bespeak the calls for dignity, freedom, and fairness that are at the core of American democracy. These are the voices of the defenders, the critics, the barons, the revolutionaries, the leaders, the organizers and, especially, the workers that give testimony to The American Labor Movement.

Author's Note

There are 1371 quotations categorized into 17 chapters. The first few quotations in each chapter introduce themes reflected by the quotations that follow. Within chapters, quotations form progressions of associated subjects. The intent was to produce an enlightening, enjoyable book as well as a worthwhile sourcebook.

The first chapter, **This Working Life**, introduces universal themes of work and labor with quotations centuries old to those from yesterday's news. **Bread and Butter** presents the basic issues, such as fair wages and working conditions, that spawned the labor movement. **Strife and Strike**, **Organizing and Unions**, and **Solidarity Forever** portray traditional and contemporary themes of unions and labor actions.

The Law, **Civil Rights**, **Economics**, and **Politics** depict the written and unwritten rules and forces that have governed working Americans. By following **Politics**, **Public Employment** mirrors the circumstances of public employees who often are subject to the dictates of politicians. The mostly damning quotations in **The Corporate World** and **The Media** typify labor's adversarial position toward corporations, and its perception that the media voice the views of corporate America. **Voices for Labor** resonates with the emotions and thoughts of primarily well-known labor leaders.

Contemporary themes common to all workers are found in **Unemployment**, which includes the new world of downsizing and job insecurity; **Brave New World**, an airing of the uncertainties of global competition; and **Team Concept**, an array of views about new experiments in labor-management cooperation. The last chapter, **The Sporting Life**, relates the sentiments of professional athletes in their unique positions as "workers," along with the words of sports commentators, team owners, and leaders.

Much of labor history is remembered through oral tradition and many of the quotations recounted here are well known. Other passages are selections from interviews, biographies, trade journals, letters, newspapers, collections, and recollections.

Authors frequently reused their quotations, and some quotations were recycled by new speakers, leading to erroneous attribution. Every attempt has been made to ensure the accuracy of each quotation, its original source, and its origination date. If readers should note any inaccuracies, they are welcome to write the publisher; corrections will be made in subsequent printings.

Editor's Note

When first introduced, the author of each quotation is identified by his or her profession or popular acclaim. Because some quotation dates were not known, the first entry for politicians and union officers includes their positions and terms in office. For authors no longer living, dates of birth and death are given. Fifteen **Biographical Briefs** should help familiarize readers new to the labor movement with prominent and oft-quoted labor leaders from the past.

For authors best known by a pen name or preferred version of their given name, the given name is bracketed, such as: [Frederick] Ray Marshall; the pen or preferred name is used for subsequent entries. Popular nicknames are set off by quotes, such as: Mary "Mother" Jones; the nickname is used thereafter. Organizations are first identified by their full names; subsequent entries are by acronyms. The **Acronym Glossary/Index** provides a quick reference guide.

Because many quotations could easily be housed in several chapters, the reader should use key words and the indexes when searching for a particular subject or quotation. The **Acronym**, **Author**, and **Word/Keyword** indexes provide avenues to particular topics, quotations, or authors; and the **Selected Bibliography** and **Resource Directory** facilitates further research. Last, the **List of Photographs, Drawings, and Biographical Briefs** help readers quickly return to specific images or historical figures.

Quotations are often ungrammatical, reflecting the vernacular of the speakers. Editorial corrections were limited to typographical errors. Bracketed words were inserted within quotations only to clarify the subject of the quotation, insert a missing letter or word, or identify an acronym.

Within the credits, the use of *in* before a book title indicates that the quotation author was quoted in that book. Titles not preceded by *in* indicate that the quotation author authored that book or work.

Acknowledgments

The completion of this volume is owed, in large part, to the assistance and encouragement of friends and colleagues.

The urging of my late mother, Frances Bollen, that I complete this work, was a driving force in life and in memory. She anguished through the vicissitudes and challenges of a labor-oriented family. Her efforts, along with those of my father, Jim Bollen—as life-long advocates for working people—served as lasting models for inspiration. My wife, Ellen, provided unwavering support, even while enduring the travails of an edgy writer facing deadlines.

I am especially grateful to the publisher, Jim Goodwin, who believed in this project. As my mentor and editor, Jim is chiefly responsible for making this book possible.

I also want to acknowledge those who gave their praise and support to my original *A Handbook of Great Labor Quotations*: former Secretary of Labor Ray Marshall; Studs Terkel; Ed Asner; Pete Seeger; labor press editor John Harvey; labor historian Jim Green, who also wrote the Foreword to this book; and the late Cesar Chavez, George Seldes, and American Postal Workers Union (APWU) business agent Jim Smyrnios. Thank you all for your dedication to the labor movement.

Too, I wish to applaud Moe Biller, the international president of the APWU and one of the seminal leaders of the Great Postal Strike of 1970. This was the first successful strike of government employees and resulted in the creation of the APWU with collective bargaining for postal employees.

The efforts of my friend, union organizer Tony Mastas, motivated me to persevere. Working with Tony has been an education in labor relations at the personal level. Also, the contacts he provided were invaluable in completing this book.

Barbara Beckwith of the National Writers Union (NWU) and Bob Chatell of the Boston NWU, both whom tirelessly advocate for writers' freedoms, also inspired me, as did Father Edward Boyle of the Boston Labor Guild.

For help in researching quotations, I want to thank the librarians at the Salem, Massachusetts Public Library, especially Susan Szpak; and Helen F. Bender of the Boston Public Library.

For their help with finding and selecting the photographs and drawings, my thanks go to Donald Spatz, Lee Sayrs, and Linda DeLoach at George Meany Center for Labor Studies; Ken Turino, Diane Shepherd, and Heather Johnson at Lynn, Massachusetts Historical Society; and Mary J. Wallace at Walter J. Reuther Archives at Wayne State University.

The contributions of Harry Petzold, talented artist and loyal friend, along with that of cartoonists Patrick Hardin, Gary Huck, and Mike Konopacki are much appreciated.

The manuscript might not have been completed if not for Alicia Gavalya, Jim Tournas, Jean Goodwin, Greg Dagoumas, and Linda Impemba, all of whom guided me through my computer learning, persevering until the manuscript was completed. Linda's guidance was invaluable throughout manuscript development.

Finally, I can't forget my friends and my family—the Bollens, the Plumers and the Keans—who tolerated me when I faced deadlines and who supported me through my battles with the government (*see* **About the Author**). Thank you all for continually sending me your well wishes, news clippings, and cartoons, and for sharing good conversation about our workday ordeals and our political prejudices. You made the process, as well as the project, all worthwhile.

Chapter 1

This Working Life

❖1❖

There is nothing better than that all should enjoy their work, for that is
their lot.

> Ecclesiastes 4.22, The Holy Bible, Containing the New and Old
> Testaments, New Revised Standard Version, 1989

❖2❖

The end of labor is to gain leisure.

> Aristotle (384-322 B.C.), philosopher, biologist,
> literary critic, teacher

❖3❖

[Work] Something made greater by ourselves and in turn makes us
greater.

> Maya Angelou, novelist, poet, actress, in *Black Scholar*,
> Jan.-Feb., 1977

❖4❖

Labor, I should say, is any painful exertion [of] mind or body undergone
partly or wholly with a view to future good.

> William Stanley Jevons (1835-1882),
> English economist, inventor

❖5❖

A man is worked upon by what he works on. He may carve out his
circumstances, but his circumstances will carve him out as well.

> Frederick Douglass (1817-1895), slave, abolitionist, orator,
> founder of *The North Star* newspaper, statesman,
> *The Life and Times of Frederick Douglass*, 1895

❖6❖

Ask not whether a man is useful in his work but whether the work is
useful to man.

> Pope John Paul II

❖7❖

Each person's work will be shown for what it is. On judgement day it will be brought to light. It will be put through fire. The fire will test how good everyone's work is.

I Corinthians 3:13, Holy Bible,
New International Reader's Version, 1995

❖8❖

Choose a job you love, and you will never have to work a day in your life.

Confucius (551-479 B.C.), teacher, philosopher,
author, source for Confucianism

❖9❖

If a man love the labour of his trade, apart from any suggestion of success or fame, the gods have called him.

Robert Louis Stevenson (1850-1894), novelist, poet

❖10❖

To find joy in work is to discover the fountain of youth.

Pearl Buck [Pearl Walsh née Sydenstricker] (1892-1973),
novelist, biographer, humanitarian, 1932 Pulitzer Prize
for fiction, 1938 Nobel Prize for literature,
The Joy of Children, 1964

❖11❖

When work is a pleasure, life is a joy! When work is a duty, life is slavery.

Maksim Gorky [Aleksei Maksimovich Peshkov]
(1868-1936), Russian novelist, dramatist, "the great proletarian
writer," *The Lower Depths*, 1902

❖12❖

To feel valued, to know, even if only once in a while, that you can do a job well is an absolutely marvelous feeling.

Barbara Walters, American Broadcasting Corporation (ABC)
television interviewer, broadcaster

❖13❖

The greatest analgesic, soporific, stimulant, tranquilizer, narcotic, and to some extent even antibiotic—in short, the closest thing to a genuine panacea—known to medical science is work.

Thomas Stephen Szasz, psychiatrist,
The Second Sin, "Medicine," 1973

First Labor Day Parade, 9/5/1882, New York City. From *Frank Leslie's Illustrated Newspaper*, 9/16/1882. The messages on the placards from 118 years ago remain familiar. Courtesy George Meany Memorial Archives.

❖14❖

No other technique for the conduct of life attaches the individual so firmly to reality as laying emphasis on work; for his work at least gives him a secure place in a portion of reality, in the human community.

> Sigmund Freud (1856-1939),
> founder of psychoanalysis, medical researcher

❖15❖

Work spares us from three great evils: boredom, vice, and need.

> Voltaire [Francois Marie Arouet] (1694-1778),
> French poet, dramatist, essayist, historian, philosopher,
> reformist leader, *Candide*, 1759

❖16❖

Labor, even the most humble and the most obscure, if it is well done, tends to beautify and embellish the world.

> Gabriele D'Annunzio (1863-1938), poet, author, soldier, political
> activist, 1920, in *Survey of Labor Relations*, 1987

❖17❖

Far and away the best prize that life has to offer is the chance to work hard at work worth doing.

> President Theodore Roosevelt (1901-1909), 1906 Nobel Peace
> Prize, Labor Day speech, Syracuse, N.Y., 9/7/1903

❖18❖

It is labour indeed that puts the difference on everything.

> John Locke (1632-1704), English empiricist philosopher,
> mercantilist, *An Essay Concerning Human Understanding*, 1690

❖19❖

Labor is the source of all wealth and all culture.

> Ferdinand Lassalle (1825-1864), German labor and political
> activist, preamble, *Arbiter-Programm*, 1862

❖20❖

Labor: One of the processes by which A acquires property of B.

> Ambrose Bierce (1842-1914), author, satirist,
> *The Devil's Dictionary*, 1906

→21←

No man will labor for himself who can make another labor for him.

Thomas Jefferson (1743-1826), slave owner, wrote Declaration of
Independence, President (1801-1809), father of the University of
Virginia, ambassador, architect, naturalist

→22←

The desire of one man to live on the fruits of another's labor is the
original sin of the world.

James Bronterre O'Brien (1805-1864), Irish Chartisp leader

→23←

Every man is dishonest who lives upon the unpaid labor of others, no
matter if he occupies a throne.

Robert G. Ingersoll (1833-1899), "The Great Agnostic,"
Republican politician, lawyer, orator, statesman, author

→24←

Where the whole man is involved there is no work. Work begins with the
division of labor.

Marshall McLuhan, communications theorist,
author, *Understanding Media*, 1964

→25←

When a man tells you that he got rich through hard work, ask him whose.

Donald Robert Perry Marquis (1878-1937), author, humorist,
columnist, *New York Sun* and *New York Tribune*

→26←

If hard work were such a wonderful thing, surely the rich would have kept
it all to themselves.

Lane Joseph Kirkland (1922-1999), president (1980-1995),
American Federation of Labor-Congress of Industrial
Organizations (AFL-CIO)

→27←

Unless people are independently wealthy, they're going to work; they're
going on welfare; or they're going to steal. There are no other alterna-
tives.

Bill Posey, Florida state representative, 1995

→28←

Let the thief no longer steal, but rather let him labor, doing honest labor with his hands, so that he may be able to give to those in need.

Ephesians 4:28, Holy Bible, Revised Standard Edition, 1953,
New Testament Section, 1946

→29←

It's true hard work never killed anybody, but I figure, why take the chance?

President Ronald Wilson Reagan (1981-1989), 4/22/1987

→30←

Personally, I have nothing against work, particularly when well performed, quietly and unobtrusively, by someone else. I just don't happen to think it's an appropriate subject for an "ethic."

Barbara Ehrenreich, political activist, biologist,
columnist, author, *The Worst Years of Our Lives,*
"Goodbye To The Work Ethic," 1990

→31←

Men do not shrink from work, but from slavery. The man who works primarily for the benefit of another does so only under compulsion, and work so done is the very essence of slavery.

Eugene Victor Debs (1855-1926), labor organizer, a founder and
president of American Railway Union (ARU),
Socialist presidential candidate

→32←

It is work, work that one delights in, that is the surest guarantor of happiness. But even here it is a work that has to be earned by labor in one's earlier years. One should labor so hard in youth that everything one does subsequently is easy by comparison.

Ashley [Montague Francis] Montagu (1905-1999),
anthropologist, educator, lecturer, prolific author

→33←

The surest prescription for starting an American boy toward understanding success is to let him go to work before he is fully grown.

The Saturday Evening Post, 1936

→34←

The most beautiful sight that we see is the child at labor. As early as he may get at labor the more beautiful, the more useful does his life get to be.

Asa Griggs Candler (1851-1929), founder of Coca-Cola, mayor of Atlanta (1917-1918)

→35←

Let us be grateful to Adam, our benefactor. He cut us out of the "blessing" of idleness and won for us the "curse" of labor.

Mark Twain [Samuel Langhorne Clemens] (1835-1910), author, humorist, lecturer, printer, *Following the Equator*, 1897

→ **Eugene Victor Debs**, 1855-1926, Terra Haute, Indiana

Eugene Debs worked briefly on a railroad when he was 14. Called home by his mother, he worked as a grocery clerk. He maintained interest in railroads and, at 20, helped organize a union local of the Brotherhood of Locomotive Firemen, for which he later became a national officer and the editor for its magazine. After failing to unify railroad brotherhoods, he founded and became president of the American Railway Union in 1893, which grew to be the country's largest union.

Debs became a socialist and a founder of the Social Democratic party (1897) and the Socialist Party of America (1901). He ran as the Socialist presidential candidate five times and amassed 915,000 votes in 1920 while simultaneously serving a prison sentence. In 1905 Debs helped found the Industrial Workers of the World, but left the organization in 1908 because of conflicts with his pacifist beliefs.

Eugene Victor Debs. Drawing courtesy ©Harry Petzold.

A great orator, union advocate, and moral leader, Debs was revered as a martyr. He was jailed 6 months for his role in the Pullman strike of 1894 and, in 1918, was sentenced to 10 years in prison for criticizing the government's Espionage Act of 1917; in 1921, President Harding pardoned him. One of the most prominent voices for laborers in the American Labor Movement, Debs championed unions as essential tools to confront organized business and to give working people a means to affect political, non-violent change. ←

✦36✦

Work is not a curse, it is the prerogative of intelligence, the only means to manhood, and the measure of civilization. Savages do not work.

President Calvin Coolidge (1923-1929)

✦37✦

Work is the curse of the drinking classes.

Oscar Fingal O'Flahertie Wills Wilde (1854-1900), dramatist, novelist, poet, in *Life of Oscar Wilde*, 1946

✦38✦

The human race is faced with a cruel choice: work or daytime television.

Unknown

✦39✦

Without work all life goes rotten.

Albert Camus (1913-1960), Algerian born existential philosopher, author, playwright, 1957 Nobel Prize for literature

✦40✦

Work is life, you know, and without it, there's nothing but fear and insecurity.

John Winston Lennon (1940-1980), songwriter, musician, member of Beatles band, in interview on BBC-TV, 12/15/1969

✦41✦

When people are serving, life is no longer meaningless.

John William Gardner, Secretary of Health, Education and Welfare (HEW, 1965-1968), Lyndon Johnson Administration, founder and chairman of Common Cause (1970-1977)

✦42✦

Work itself isn't humiliating if it gives you financial independence. There is dignity in that. The indignity comes when management perceives you as so many worker bees, not as contributing individuals.

Brian Kremer, auto worker, artist

→43←

What is the use of money if you have to work for it?

George Bernard Shaw (1856-1950), critic, essayist, novelist,
dramatist, socialist, philosopher, revolutionary evolutionist,
1925 Nobel Prize for literature

→44←

It is, of course, the supervised who produce the goods and do the work of the world, not the supervisors who stand and watch, and the proliferation of watchers seems to me an ominous and unhealthy development.

Lane Kirkland

→45←

I am the people—the mob—the crowd—the mass. Do you know that all the great work of the world is done through me?

I am the workingman, the inventor, the maker of the world's food and clothes.

Carl August Sandburg (1878-1967), poet, biographer,
reporter, novelist, 1940 Pulitzer Prize for history,
1951 Pulitzer Prize for poetry

→46←

Labor is one of the great elements of society—the great substantial interest on which we all stand ... but labor—intelligent, manly, independent, thinking and acting for himself, and earning its own wages, accumulating those wages for his capital, educating childhood, maintaining worship, claiming the right of the elective franchise and helping to uphold the great fabric of the state. That is American labor, and all my sympathies with it and my voice 'til I am dumb will be for it.'

Daniel Webster (1782-1852), Congressman (Federalist-N.H.,
1812-1816, National Republican-Mass., 1823-1927, Senator,
NR-Mass., 1827-1833), lawyer, statesman, orator

→47←

As I pass up and down [my city] streets I see in many places the work my own hands have wrought on her buildings and I feel that in a sense I am a part of our city. My strength and whatever skills I possess are woven into her material fabric that will remain when I am gone, for Labor is Life taking a permanent form.

Walter Stevenson, union carpenter, in *With Our Hands*, 1986

⇥48⇤

In my apron I carry nails and pliers, a heavy hammer, and pride.

Maria Bachman, tradeswoman

⇥49⇤

Since all human beings have a certain dignity purely because of their humanity, it is obvious that every laboring man is entitled to be treated as a dignified creature. But that is not what is commonly meant by those who speak of the dignity of labor. ... Who would seriously argue that there is dignity in cleaning out sewers, making beds in third-rate motels, working on a garbage truck, or sweeping floors and cleaning toilets in a house of prostitution?

Steve Valentine Patrick Allen, humorist, actor, television host, producer, singer, songwriter, author, *Reflections*, 1994

⇥50⇤

I cleaned toilets inside and out, emptied wastebaskets and scrubbed the restroom floors, urinals and sinks. I never felt burdened with any sense of stigma. It's a necessary job and when you do it well, you feel good about it.

Louis Oswald, former janitor and present owner of cleaning service firm

⇥51⇤

A little dignity. That's what the worker has, and that's what we have to raise up.

Editorial, *Boston Globe*, 9/10/1995

⇥52⇤

Originality and the feeling of one's own dignity are achieved only through work and struggle.

Fyodor Mikhailovich Dostoyevsky (1821-1881), Russian novelist, *A Diary of a Writer*, 1873

⇥53⇤

The single most important issue of the service sector is ... dignity.

Thomas Reilly Donahue, secretary-treasurer (1979-1995), interim president (1995), AFL-CIO

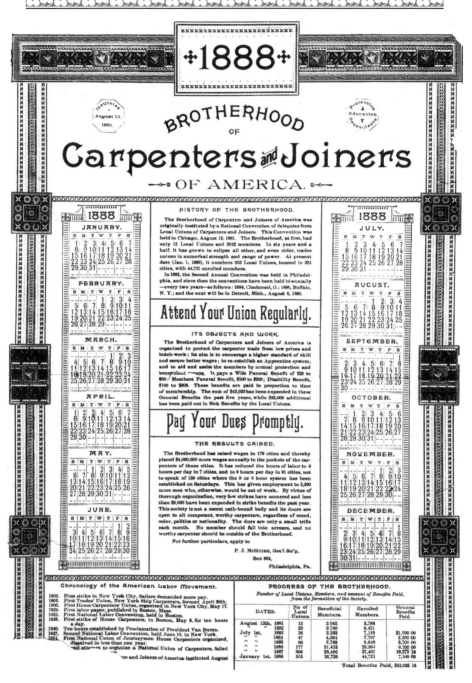

Brotherhood of Carpenters and Joiners of America calendar of 1888 (*see* details pages 74 and 118). Courtesy George Meany Memorial Archives.

✦54✦

If a man is called to be a street sweeper, he should sweep streets even as Michelangelo painted, or Beethoven composed music, or Shakespeare wrote poetry. He should sweep streets so well that all the hosts of heaven and earth will pause to say, here lived a great street sweeper who did his job well.

> Reverend Martin Luther King, Jr. (1929-1968), a principal leader
> of American non-violent civil rights movement, Baptist clergyman,
> 1964 Nobel Peace Prize

✦55✦

No race can prosper 'til it learns there is as much dignity in tilling a field as in writing a poem.

> Booker Taliaferro Washington (1856-1915), educator, activist,
> orator, first principal of Tuskegee Institute, in address to the
> Atlanta Exposition, 9/18/1895

✦56✦

Yes, you need the water. Yes, you need the sun. But that alone won't give you the plant. You need the working hands to give it life.

> Adrian Alvarez, gardener, on the pride in his work, 3/21/1999,
> *Los Angeles Times*

✦57✦

Those who labor in the earth are the chosen people of God, if ever He had a chosen people.

> Thomas Jefferson

✦58✦

The farmer who goes forth in the morning and toils all day is as much of a businessman as the man who goes upon the board and bets upon the price of grain.

> William Jennings Bryan (1860-1925), Congressman (D-Neb.,
> 1891-1894) political orator, presidential candidate, editor, lawyer,
> Secretary of State (1913-1915), Wilson Administration

✦59✦

You can't eat for eight hours a day nor drink for eight hours a day nor make love for eight hours a day—all you can do for eight hours is work.

> William Faulkner (1897-1962), novelist, poet, 1949 Nobel Prize
> for literature, 1954 and 1962 Pulitzer Prizes for fiction,
> in *Writers at Work: First Series*, 1958

❧60❧

Eight hours for work.
Eight hours for rest.
Eight hours for what you will.

> Banners at the Tompkins Square Rally for the Eight-Hour Day,
> 1874; last lines from song sung by Knights of Labor and
> supporters of the eight-hour day, c. 1886

❧61❧

Eight Hours For Work,
Eight Hours For Recreation,
Eight Hours For Sleep.

> Slogan of American Federation of Labor (AFL), under leadership
> of its first president, Samuel Gompers, c. 1886,
> in *Work and the Nature of Man*, 1966

❧62❧

I go on working for the same reason that a hen goes on laying eggs.

> [Henry Louis] H. L. Mencken (1880-1956),
> editor, essayist, author, literary and social critic, journalist,
> in *On the Meaning of Life*, 1932

❧63❧

The reason I write about work is that that's just about damn near all I've ever done.

> William Pancoast, General Motors (GM) worker, novelist

❧64❧

One man wins success by his words; another gets his due reward by the work of his hands.

> Proverbs 12:14, Holy Bible, Revised Standard Edition, 1953,
> Old Testament Section, 1952

❧65❧

All there is said for work as opposed to dancing is that it is so much easier.

> Heywood Broun (1888-1939), journalist, columnist, first
> president of American Newspaper Guild, *Pieces of Hate: and Other
> Enthusiasms*, 1922

❧66❧

Labor [work] is the curse of the world, and nobody can meddle with it without becoming proportionately brutified.

> Nathaniel Hawthorne (1804-1864), novelist, 8/12/1841, in
> *Passages from the American Notebook*, 1868

✦67✦

Work is not a curse, but drudgery is.

> Henry Ward Beecher (1813-1887), clergyman, author,
> abolitionist, *Proverbs from the Plymouth Pulpit*, 1887

✦68✦

Hard work is damn near as overrated as monogamy.

> Huey "the Kingfish" Pierce Long (1893-1935) Governor (D-La.,
> 1928-1932) and Senator (D-La., 1932-1935)

✦69✦

Nobody works as hard for his money as the man who marries it.

> Kin Hubbard (1868-1930), caricaturist, humorist

✦70✦

I never knew an early rising, hard-working prudent man, careful of his earnings, and strictly honest who complained of bad luck.

> Henry Ward Beecher

✦71✦

We are more ready to strive and work for superfluities than for necessities. People who are clear-sighted, undeluded, and sober-minded, will not go on working once their reasonable needs are satisfied. ... Yet it is well to keep in mind that both children and artists need luxuries more than they need necessities.

> Eric Hoffer (1902-1983), longshoreman, philosopher, writer, in
> *Overcoming Middle Class Rage*, 1971

✦72✦

Most men, even in this comparatively free country, through mere ignorance and mistake, are so occupied with the factitious cares and superfluously coarse labors of life that its finer fruits cannot be plucked by them. Their fingers, from excessive toils, are too clumsy and tremble too much for that.

> Henry David Thoreau (1817-1862), naturalist, transcendentalist,
> writer, advocate of peaceful civil disobedience, *Walden*, 1854

✦73✦

Work and play are words used to describe the same thing under differing conditions.

> Mark Twain

→ **Samuel Gompers**, 1850-1924, London, England

Samuel Gompers immigrated to the United States in 1863 and began working as a cigar maker in New York City. He joined the cigar makers union in 1864 and became the local's president (1874-1881). Regarded as the first great labor leader in America, Gompers helped found the Federation of Trade and Labor Unions in 1881. In 1886 the Federation was realigned with craft unions into the American Federation of Labor (AFL), an association of 150 unions, with Gompers as its first president. Under his leadership workers won higher wages, shorter hours, better working conditions, and more respect for organized labor. Renowned and highly regarded for his integrity, Gompers became the labor movement's leading spokesman. He advocated strong unions that could bargain with employers and his national union grew to become a model for others.

Samuel Gompers. Drawing courtesy ©Harry Petzold.

Many activists considered Gompers too conservative because he opposed political union activity and the inclusion of blacks, women, and unskilled workers. He served as president of the AFL (except for 1895) until his death in 1924. His memoirs, *Seventy Years of Life and Labor*, were published in 1925. ←

→74←

Work expands so as to fill the time available for its completion.

Cyril Northcote Parkinson (1909-1993), British political
scientist, *Parkinson's Law*, 1958

→75←

The sum of wisdom is that the time is never lost that is devoted to work.

Ralph Waldo Emerson (1803-1882), essayist, poet,
"Success," Society and Solitude, 1870

→76←

Any man can do any amount of work, provided it isn't the work he's supposed to be doing.

Robert Benchley (1889-1945), author, humorist, actor, critic, in
The Algonquin Wits, 1968

❖77❖

The average man won't really do a day's work unless he is caught and cannot get out of it.

Henry Ford (1863-1947), founder of the Ford Motor Company,
pioneer of assembly line production, *Detroit News*, 10/20/1931,
in *The Legend of Henry Ford*, 1948

❖78❖

Laziness results either from special privileges, or physical and mental abnormalities. Our present insane system of production fosters both, and the most astounding phenomenon is that people should want to work at all now.

Emma Goldman (1869-1940), anarchist, social activist

❖79❖

There is no expedient to which a man will not go to avoid the real labor of thinking.

Thomas Alva Edison (1847-1931), inventor

❖80❖

The work of the individual still remains the spark that moves mankind ahead even more than teamwork.

Igor Sikorsky (1889-1972),
Russian aeronautical engineer, inventor

❖81❖

I never did anything worth doing by accident; nor did any of my inventions come by accident; they came by work.

Thomas Edison

❖82❖

The 'work ethic' holds that labor is good in itself; that a man or woman becomes a better person by virtue of the act of working. America's competitive spirit, the 'work ethic' of this people, is alive and well on Labor Day, 1971.

President Richard Milhous Nixon (1969-1974), in *Working*, 1974

❖83❖

Labor is life.

Thomas Carlyle (1795-1881), Scottish essayist and historian

✦84✦

Labor is the fruit of civilization, not the basis of it.

Alexander Crummell (1819-1898), clergyman,
educator, writer, 1881

✦85✦

Labor is the great producer of wealth: it moves all other causes.

Congressman Daniel Webster, 4/2/1824

✦86✦

Whatever there is of greatness in the United States or indeed in any other country, is due to labor. The laborer is the author of all greatness and wealth. Without labor there would be no government, and nothing to preserve.

President Ulysses Simpson Grant (1869-1877)

✦87✦

We recognize that labor dishonors no man.

President Ulysses S. Grant, 1877

✦88✦

Without labor nothing prospers.

Sophocles (c. 497-406 B.C.), dramatist, Athenian politician

✦89✦

Without Labor no one prospers.

Popular banner

✦90✦

The Christian community has always held suspect the tendency in America to scorn physical labor and the so-called blue-collar world. That type of elitism is contrary to the Gospel.

Father Edward F. Boyle, chaplain of archdiocese of Boston,
Catholic Labor Guild

✦91✦

God does not measure men's lives only by the amount of work, which is accomplished in them. He who gave the power to work may also withhold the power.

Benjamin Howett, passages from the *Theological Writings*

✈92✜

Men hang out their signs indicative
of their respective trades;
shoemakers hang out a gigantic
shoe; jewelers a monster watch;
and the dentist hangs out a gold
tooth; but up in the mountains
of New Hampshire, God Almighty
has hung out a sign to show
that there he makes men.

> Daniel Webster, referring to the Old Man in the Mountain, a
> granite outcropping naturally shaped as a man's profile on a New
> Hampshire mountainside

✈93✜

The students react to my praise of toil with great applause and loud
demands for a holiday from work.

> John Kenneth Galbraith, economist, author, lecturer, administrator

✈94✜

Few men ever drop dead from overwork, but many quietly curl up and die
because of undersatisfaction.

> Sydney J. Harris, columnist

✈95✜

It is not labor that kills, but the small attritions of daily routine that wear
us down.

> Roy Bedicheck, writer

✈96✜

I don't think anybody yet has invented a pastime that's as much fun, or
keeps you as young, as a good job.

> Frederick Hudson Ecker, chairman, Metropolitan Life

✈97✜

If you keep working you'll last longer and I just want to keep vertical. ...
I'd hate to spend the rest of my life trying to outwit an 18-inch fish.

> Harold Sydney Geneen (1910-1997), executive of International
> Telephone & Telegraph Corp. (IT&T, 1959-1978)

✦98✦

What sustains me is work.

Actress Bette [Ruth Elizabeth] Davis' (1908-1989) response to
Barbara Walters' question, 'What sustains you?' (in five words or
less), ABC television interview, 1988

✦99✦

People say, 'Why don't you retire? You've worked all your adult life, and
you've more than given back to the community.' I say, 'If I retired, I would
undo all the good things I've done.'

Zelda David, elder citizen, 1980

✦100✦

Retirement can be a wonderful thing. You can suck in your stomach just
so long.

Burt Reynolds, actor

✦101✦

Retirement is the dirtiest word in the American language.

George Seldes (1890-1995), journalist, press critic, author, on his
97th birthday, as his latest book reached the best-seller lists

✦102✦

You can never retire from the working class. If you want to eat, live
decently, have a nice house and help your children and grandchildren, the
struggle has to go on.

Albert Fitzgerald, past president, United Electrical, Radio and
Machine Workers of America (UE)

✦103✦

We lift their spirits, we clean their bodies, and oftentimes we're the last
smiling face they see before they leave here.

Declaration of Nurses Aides campaign, Service Employees
International Union (SEIU), Michigan, 1995

✦104✦

One cannot walk through a mass-production factory and not feel that one
is in hell.

[Wystan Hugh] W. H. Auden (1907-1973), poet, critic,
1948 Pulitzer Prize for poetry

⇾105↤

Any executive who thinks the ultimate in busyness consists of having two important phone calls on hold and a major deadline in 20 minutes, should try facing six tables full of clients simultaneously demanding that you give them their check, fresh coffee, a baby seat, and a warm, spontaneous smile. ... 'Success' means surviving the shift.

Barbara Ehrenreich, *The Worst Years of Our Lives*, 1990

⇾106↤

'Raises, not roses,' is the motto of secretaries, most of them women in low-paying jobs. A good secretary must have the patience of Job, the hide of an elephant, the manners of Emily Post and the fingers of Houdini.

Bella English, columnist

⇾107↤

On the evening bus, the tense, pinched faces of young file clerks and elderly secretaries tell us more than we care to know.

Studs [Louis] Terkel, author, oral historian, radio host, social commentator, 1985 Pulitzer Prize for nonfiction

Chapter 2

Bread and Butter

✢108✦

The history of America has been largely created by the deeds of its working people and their organizations. Nor has this contribution been confined to raising wages and bettering work conditions; it has been fundamental to almost every effort to extend and strengthen our democracy.

William Cahn, labor authority and historian

✢109✦

Like green plants hunting for sunlight, working people will always seek a better life. This is a basic urge of the human spirit.

Anonymous

✢110✦

The test of our progress is ... not whether we add more to the abundance of those who have too much, it is whether we provide enough for those who have too little.

President Franklin Delano Roosevelt (FDR, 1933-1945)

✢111✦

Take not from the mouth of labor the bread it has earned.

President Thomas Jefferson, Inaugural Address, 3/4/1801, in
Survey of Labor Relations, 1987

✢112✦

Food for the body must come before food for the soul. Moses knew that. Jesus knew that. And the good union leader, the good union member—as well as the good employer, the good politician, the good citizen—they all know that.

John Cort, Catholic writer

✢113✦

Not by bread alone.

> Official slogan of International Ladies Garment
> Workers Union (ILGWU)

✢114✦

We want bread and roses too.

> Famed sign of women picketing at
> Lawrence Mill (or Textile) Strike, 1912

✢115✦

Yes, it is bread we fight for—but we fight for roses too.

> Final stanza—*Bread and Roses*, strike poem

✢116✦

Mankind has been and is divided into three parts: the Haves, the Have-Nots, and the Have-a-Little, Want Mores.

> Saul Alinsky, labor official, organizer, author

Marching mill workers from the International Workers of the World, 1906. Courtesy George Meany Memorial Archives.

✥117✥

The way to honor work, which we all claim to do, is first of all to pay for it.

Barbara Ehrenreich

✥118✥

We pay best, those men who destroy us—Generals. Second, those who cheat us—Politicians. Third, those who amuse us—Singers and Dancers. And, last of all, those who instruct us—Teachers.

Horace Mann (1796-1859), U.S. Representative (Whig-Mass.,
1848-1853), Christian statesman, educator, founder of the Public
School System, Commonwealth of Massachusetts

✥119✥

Give to every man the fruit of his own labor—the labor of his hand and of his brain.

Robert G. Ingersoll

✥120✥

Nature has her own laws, and this is one—a fair day's wages for a fair day's work.

Vivian Grey, activist

✥121✥

All we ask is an honest day's wages for an honest day's work, and we are willing to be considerate and just.

Eugene Debs, 1886 speech

✥122✥

Give us our share and the devil take the hindmost!

Familiar slogan

✥123✥

Americans cannot eat or live on platitudes or musical phrases—they want buying power.

John Llewellyn Lewis (1880-1969), labor organizer, president
United Mineworkers of America (UMWA, 1920-1960), a founder
of Congress of Industrial Organizations (CIO)

→124←

The workman demands an adequate wage, sufficient to permit him to live in comfort, unhampered by the fear of poverty and want in his old age. He demands the right to work amid sanitary surroundings, both in home and in workshop, and the right to provide for his children's wants in the matter of health and education. It is his desire to make the conditions of his life and the lives of those dear to him tolerable and easy to bear.

President [born Thomas] Woodrow Wilson (1913-1921),
1919 Nobel Peace Prize

→ ←

→ John Llewellyn Lewis, 1880-1969, Lucas County, Iowa

John L. Lewis dropped out of school at 12 and became a coal miner when he was 17. Self-educated, Lewis became a leader of coal miners and, by 1920, was elected president of the United Mineworkers of America (UMWA). Lewis grew to become a forceful and eloquent leader during the most turbulent times of unionization. In 1935, wanting to organize mass production industries, he broke away from the American Federation of Labor and joined the Committee for Industrial Organizations, which later became the Congress of Industrial Organizations (CIO). In 1942, the UMWA split from the CIO, partly because of antagonism between Lewis and the CIO's new president, Philip Murray, that grew out of Lewis's support of presidential candidate Wendell Willkie, who ran against Franklin D. Roosevelt.

John L. Lewis. Courtesy George Meany Memorial Archives.

In retaining the loyalty of the miners, Lewis ignored unions' no-strike World War II policies, politicians' pleas, and public sentiment. He led strikes during and following the war that won substantial medical and retirement benefits for his miners. Lewis was famous for his flaming oratory, often quoting Shakespeare and the Bible. He retired in 1960 after serving 40 years as president of the UMWA. ←

✦125✦

Just grin, keep on working.

> Charles Michael Schwab (1862-1939), president,
> Bethlehem Steel, 1929

✦126✦

Do you mind, first inflating the stomachs of my members?

> John L. Lewis, in response to a senate investigative committee
> on inflationary matters

✦127✦

If you want to enrich the job, enrich the paycheck.

> William "Wimpy" Winpisinger (1924-1997), international
> president (1977-1989), International Association of Machinists
> and Aerospace Workers (IAM)

✦ **William "Wimpy" Winpisinger**, 1924-1997, Cleveland, Ohio

William Winpisinger quit high school to enter the navy during World War II. He learned the trade of diesel mechanic, joining the International Association of Machinists and Aerospace Workers (IAM) after his military service. Exercising leadership qualities as early as age 26, he rose in prominence and eventually became International President of the IAM in 1977 and was named a vice president of the AFL-CIO.

Serving three terms as IAM president, Winpisinger was flamboyant, aggressive, radical, and outspoken. He was often sought by the media and asked to testify to Congress on legislation affecting working people. Under his bold leadership, the IAM filed a lawsuit against the Organization of Petroleum Exporting Countries (OPEC), the international oil cartel, for price fixing and denying his union members the right to work. Winpisinger's legacy was imaginative leadership and serving the nation's oppressed and underprivileged. ✦

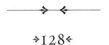

✦128✦

We want a better America, an America that will give its citizens, first of all, a higher and higher standard of living so that no child will cry for food in the midst of plenty.

> Sidney Hillman (1887-1946), first president (1914-1946) of
> Amalgamated Clothing Workers of America (ACWA), Textile
> Workers Union of America (TWUA), predecessors to Union of
> Needlecrafts, Industrial & Textile Employees (UNITE)

↘129↙

The role of a labor union is to ensure that the balance is not tipped in favor of the employer when employees do not receive wages and benefits commensurate with their contribution.

William Burrus, vice president,
American Postal Workers Union (APWU)

↘130↙

Employers and employees alike have learned that in union there is strength, that a coordination of individual effort means an elimination of waste, a bettering of living conditions, and is, in fact, the father of prosperity.

Governor Franklin D. Roosevelt (D-N.Y., 1929-1932), in address
before the New York Women's Trade Union League, 6/8/1929

—————→ ←—————

↘ **Sidney Hillman**, 1887-1946, Lithuania

Sidney Hillman immigrated to the United States in 1907. He began working in the garment industry, where his labor activism started during a clothing worker's strike in 1910. By 1914, he had risen from union ranks to president of the Amalgamated Clothing Workers, a position he held until 1946. Under his stewardship came some of labor's greatest gains. Hillman pioneered such reforms as the 40-hour workweek and the setting of wage scale standards. He promoted union-management cooperation and such novel ideas as cooperative housing and banking.

Hillman was also a co-founder and vice president (1935-1940) of the Congress of Industrial Organizations (CIO) and the chairman of the powerful CIO Political Action Committee (1943-1946). As an influential advisor to President Franklin D. Roosevelt, Hillman enjoyed

Sydney Hillman. Courtesy George Meany Memorial Archives.

such political clout that "Clear it with Sidney" became a presidential catch phrase during the 1944 presidential campaign and later would become a catchall phrase regarding labor issues. Hillman also co-founded the American Labor party (1945) and the World Federation of Trade Unions. ↙

→131←

The next time you wonder what the union does for you, take a look at the car you drive, the house you own, the standard of living you have, and realize that the union got these for you and that management is hell bent on driving your standard of living into the ground.

Tom Kelly, president, APWU local

→132←

It is time that all Americans realized that the place of labor is side by side with the businessman and with the farmer, and not one-degree lower.

President Harry S. Truman (1945-1953), 1948

→133←

The Labor Movement—
The Folks That Brought You
The Weekend

Bumper sticker

→134←

More.

The philosophy of Samuel Gompers (1850-1924), first president
of the AFL, for the American Labor Movement

→135←

More, more, here and now.

Samuel Gompers' pragmatic program

→136←

Most teachers join our union because we have a contract, we process their grievances, and we manage a welfare fund, and we get them salary increases.

Albert Shanker (1928-1997), president (1974-1997), American
Federation of Teachers (AFT), 1973

→137←

We have no immediate ends. We are going from day to day. We are fighting for immediate objects.

Adolph Strasser, a founder of the AFL, 1883

⇥138⇤

The working class and the employing class have nothing in common. There can be no peace so long as hunger and want are found among millions of working people and the few, who make up the employing class, have all the good things in life.

> Industrial Workers of the World (IWW)
> constitution preamble, 1908

⇥139⇤

The best answer is for the people to cut down on their extravagance. They should eat less.

> President Herbert Clark Hoover (1929-1933), giving advice
> during the Great Depression, in *High Treason*, 1950

⇥140⇤

Hunger is not debatable.

> Harry Hopkins (1890-1946), Secretary of Commerce (1939-
> 1940), Federal Relief Administrator, Franklin D. Roosevelt
> Administration

⇥141⇤

There is no America without labor, and to fleece the one is to rob the other.

> President Abraham Lincoln (1861-1865)

⇥142⇤

If a man tells you he loves America, yet hates labor, he is a liar!

> President Abraham Lincoln

⇥143⇤

It has come to these poor miners to bear this cross ... that the human race may be lifted up to a higher and broader plane than it has ever known before.

> Clarence Seward Darrow (1857-1938), attorney, orator, author,
> defending national UMWA walkout of 100,000 miners for living
> wage increases, 2/13/1903

⇥144⇤

75 and 10 or hit the bricks.

> Richard Frankensteen, United Automobile, Aerospace and
> Agricultural Implement Workers of America (UAW) leader, calling
> for 75¢ minimum and a 10¢ general raise, 1941

✦145✦

If you make $2.58 an hour, they give you a pension, but if you make $1.65 an hour, they say you don't need it, you're not entitled to it, and furthermore, it's socialistic.

> Walter Philip Reuther (1907-1970), president of UAW, 1970
> negotiations, in *The Brothers Reuther*, 1976

✦146✦

They don't suffer. They can't even speak English.

> George Frederick Baer (1842-1914), railroad industrialist/
> operator, legal counsel for J.P. Morgan, responding to reporters'
> questions about starving miners

✦ **Clarence Seward Darrow**, 1857-1938, near Kinsman, Ohio

Clarence Darrow was admitted to the Ohio bar in 1878, moved to Chicago in 1888, and worked as a railroad corporate counsel until 1894. That year he resigned to defend (unsuccessfully) Eugene Debs and other Pullman Strike defendants. He renounced his earlier lucrative, corporate practice, becoming a defender of the underdog. From 1895 to the 1930s, Darrow took on the major cases and controversies of his day. As a staunch opponent of capital punishment, he defended in 50 murder cases, losing only one client to execution. He won an acquittal for IWW leader Big Bill Haywood in the famous frame-up case of the murder of former Governor Steunenberg of Idaho.

Clarence Darrow. 1925. *Detroit News* Collection, Walter P. Reuther Library, Wayne State University.

A great orator, Darrow also championed such causes as freedom of expression and the closed shop for unions. Often his clients were unpopular and their alleged crimes seemingly indefensible. He is best remembered for the trial of accused child-killers Leopold and Loeb and the Scopes trial, in which he defended a teacher's right to teach evolution in a public school. Darrow wrote several books, including *The Story of My Life*, 1932. ✦

✦147✦

When employers in this country say labor costs are too high, what they're really saying to you is, you have it too good. What they're really saying to you is, all you need is enough to get you into the plant and work.

Boris Block, UE general secretary-treasurer, 1982

✦148✦

We're willing to sacrifice, but only if there's an equality of sacrifice—if every segment of the economy sacrifices equally. We've been saying for a long time that there is not a wage-price spiral at all now but a price-wage spiral.

Douglas Andrew Fraser, president (1977-1983), UAW, 1978

✦ **Walter Philip Reuther**, 1907-1970, Wheeling, West Virginia

Walter Reuther began his union career as a tool-and-die maker at a Ford Motor Company assembly plant in Detroit. He became shop foreman before being fired for union activism in 1932. Along with his brother Victor, he was a founder of the United Auto Workers of America (UAWA) and led actions such as the famous sit-down strikes to unionize the plant at the Ford Motor complex in Dearborn, Michigan. At 30, Reuther gained national fame after 40 Ford-hired thugs specifically targeted Reuther and other union organizers, beating and chasing them from the Rouge plant when they attempted to pass out union leaflets. But reporters witnessed the beatings and chronicled the bloody injuries to 9 men and 7 women. Newspaper stories and graphic photographs (*see* photograph page 50) turned public opinion in favor of the unions and made Reuther a hero, but also a target.

Walter Reuther, 1946. Walter P. Reuther Library, Wayne State University.

He survived a 1938 kidnapping attempt and a 1948 assassination attempt in which his right arm was permanently disabled by a shotgun blast.

Elected president of the UAWA in 1946, he negotiated innovative contracts, winning cost-of-living raises, health and pension benefits, paid vacations, and raises based on productivity. Through imaginative and skillful negotiation, he brought blue-collar workers into the middle class with newfound job security. Because of his persuasive leadership in dealing with General Motors, auto executive George Romney called him "the most dangerous man in Detroit."

Reuther also was president of the Congress of Industrial Organizations (CIO) from 1952 to 1955 and backed the merger with the AFL, becoming the AFL-CIO's first vice president (1955-1967). Reuther withdrew the UAWA from the AFL-CIO in 1968 because of conflicts with George Meany's conservatism. Reuther believed that unions needed to take an active role in promoting social programs. He lobbied for civil rights legislation and consulted on War on Poverty programs. Under his direction, the UAW financed the 1963 March on Washington for civil rights and, with logistics and capital, assisted fledgling unions such as the United Farm Workers. Reuther died in an airplane crash in 1970. ❖

❖149❖

Whether you work by piece or work by day,
Decreasing the hours increases the pay.

Slogan used in push for the eight-hour day

❖150❖

For labor a short day is better than a short dollar.

President William McKinley (1897-1901), in a letter to Henry
Cabot Lodge, 9/8/1900

❖151❖

The time has come to give our members steady work and wages every week and every year. Not just steady work and wages 30 or 35 weeks a year. But steady work and wages 52 weeks a year.

I. W. [Iorwith Wilbur] Abel (1908-1987), president (1965-
1977), United Steelworkers of America (USA), calling for a
guaranteed annual wage, 1976

❖153❖

The most important thing to a worker with a family is 52 paychecks a year.

Donald Cox, employee/director,
Saratoga Knitting Mills, New York

→154←

As sure as I'm standing here, the American worker is going to have a four-day workweek without a cut in pay. I strongly believe the U.S. economy is capable of performing in that fashion. But it's going to be a struggle, and the battle is going to be won on the picket lines and the bargaining tables and not in the halls of Congress.

Douglas Fraser, 1978

→155←

I'm not sure there is a line to be drawn; I'm not sure there is bad taste, when it comes to protecting your family, or trying to raise your standard of living.

Domenic Bozzotto, president, Hotel and Restaurant Employees
and Bartenders Union, Boston

→156←

For every dollar the boss has and didn't work for, one of us worked for a dollar and didn't get it.

William Dudley "Big Bill" Haywood (1869-1928), U.S.
communist and labor leader, co-founder, IWW

→157←

There are three ways by which an individual can get wealth—by work, by gift, and by theft. And clearly, the reason why the workers get so little is that the beggars and thieves get so much.

Henry George (1839-1897), economist, *Social Problems,*
new edition, 1931

———— → ← ————

→ **William "Big Bill" Dudley Haywood**, 1869-1928, Salt Lake City, Utah

Big Bill Haywood began working in the mines as a young child. He joined the newly formed Western Federation of Miners in 1896 and, through union activism, became the union's secretary-treasurer in 1900. In 1905 he co-founded the Industrial Workers of the World (IWW) with the goal of uniting the workers of the world into "one big union."

A controversial labor leader known for militarism, Haywood was accused in 1905 of murdering Frank Steunenberg, an anti-labor former governor of Idaho. Clarence Darrow defended Haywood, who was acquitted and became a labor hero. Haywood advocated class struggle and no compromise, IWW doctrines that contrasted with the AFL's less militant policies. He was a leader of the Lawrence and Paterson mill strikes in 1912 and 1913. He opposed America's entry into the World War and was arrested for sedition. After being convicted in 1918 along with 165 other IWW leaders, he jumped bail in 1921 while awaiting a new trial and fled to the Soviet Union. Haywood's autobiography, *Bill Haywood's Book*, was published in 1929. ←

✣158✣

We insist that labor is entitled to as much respect as property. But our workers with hand and brain deserve more than respect for their labor. They deserve practical protection in the opportunity to use their labor at a return adequate to support them at a decent and constantly rising standard of living, and to accumulate a margin of security against the inevitable vicissitudes of life.

President Franklin D. Roosevelt, fireside chat, 1936

✣159✣

The union miner cannot agree to the acceptance of a wage principle which will permit his annual earnings and his living standards to be determined by the hungriest unfortunates whom the non-union operators can employ.

John L. Lewis, 1927, in *Labor Baron*
—A Portrait of John L. Lewis, 1944

✣160✣

Labor is not fighting for a larger slice of the national pie—labor is fighting for a larger pie.

Walter Reuther, 1945

✣161✣

When government social programs are blamed for all our economic ills, we cannot retreat into amnesia, conveniently forgetting the grim conditions that gave birth to those programs.

Lane Kirkland, Chicago, 8/1981

✣162✣

We have tried you good people of the public—and we have found you wanting. ... I can't talk fellowship to you who are gathered here. Too much blood has been spilled. I know from my experience it is up to the working people to save themselves.

Rose Schneiderman (1884-1972), labor leader, suffragist, in speech to public on enforcing safety rules after the tragic Triangle Shirtwaist Factory fire resulted in 146 deaths, 3/25/1911, in *All For One*, 1967 (This tragedy became the impetus for a host of commissions investigating working conditions that would lead to reforms governing worker safety. Many reforms came under Governor Al Smith and the reformation continued under Governor Franklin D. Roosevelt.)

✦163✦

It is to the real advantage of every producer, every manufacturer and every merchant to cooperate in the improvement of working conditions, because the best customer of American industry is the well-paid worker.

President Franklin D. Roosevelt, Cleveland, 10/16/36

✦164✦

Even 'good employers' didn't do very much about cutting down noise or abating chemical fumes, or providing effective safety devices, until they were prodded into it by the union and by requirements of a government agency truly dedicated to enforcing the law.

Harold Buoy, president, Boilermakers Union,
on Occupational Safety & Health Administration (OSHA) laws,
(Occupational Safety and Health Act, 1970)

✦165✦

Does anybody really think that auto plants or steel mills or coal mines would be better places to work today if there were no unions? Does anybody think their own employer, be it a retail store or a factory or an insurance company or even a state highway department, wouldn't try to cut corners if it meant making or saving a few dollars more?

Richard J. Perry, labor editor

166✦

I verily believe there are a large number of operatives in our cotton mills who have too much spare time now. (To reduce working hours) would increase crime, suffering, wickedness and pauperism.

Mill owner, fighting against the 10 hour day, 1845,
in *Women and the American Labor Movement*, 1982

✦167✦

There is such a thing as too much education for working people some-times. ... I have seen cases where young people were spoiled for labor by being educated to a little too much refinement.

Thomas L. Livermore, manager of Amoskeag Mills in Manchester,
N.H., answering a Senate investigating committee, 1883

✦168✦

The Golf links are so near the mill
That almost every day,
The laboring children can look out
And see the men at play.

Sarah Norcliffe Cleghorn (1876-1959), poet, in Franklin Adams'
column *The Conning Tower, New York Tribune*, 1919

Children demonstrating during the Lawrence Mill strike, 1912. Courtesy George Meany Memorial Archives.

+169+

I regard my workpeople just as I regard my machinery.

Mill owner at Lawrence Mill Strike, 1912,
in *The Lawrence Strike of 1912*, 1980

+170+

Some day the workers will take possession of your city hall, and when we do, no child will be sacrificed on the altar of profit.

Mary Harris "Mother" Jones (1830-1930), labor activist, in *The Lawrence Strike of 1912*, 1980

+171+

As the Company has gone to the expense and trouble of establishing a store, butcher shop, and saloon for the accommodation and convenience of its employees, all employees will be expected to patronize these places to the exclusion of all other similar establishments.

Work rules of the Northern Pacific Coal Company, on developing the "Company Store," 1885

✦172✦

The miner knows that he digs death as well as coal, and the death tonnage is appalling.

Saul Alinsky, *John L. Lewis: An Unauthorized Biography*, 1949

✦173✦

If we die and are sent to hell, at least we won't burn.

Claude Messier, president, Asbestos Miners Union, Quebec

✦174✦

Cotton Breathes But We Can't

Cotton workers' brown lung disease placard, 1978

✦ **Mary Harris "Mother" Jones**, 1830-1930, Cork, Ireland

After emigrating from Ireland, Mother Jones worked as a teacher and dressmaker. She lost her husband and four children in the yellow fever epidemic of 1867 and then lost her dressmaking business in the famous Chicago fire of 1871. She committed herself to labor activism and to fighting worker oppression, becoming a fearless leader of strikes, boycotts, unionization drives, and public rallies. A dynamic public speaker, Mother Jones became a symbol of labor's call for the rights to decent wages and living conditions. She tirelessly traveled the country, championing legislation to ban child labor and helping to organize miners, garment workers, and streetcar workers.

Jones was a founder of the Social Democratic party (1898) and the Industrial Workers of the World (1905). In 1913 she was convicted

Mother Jones, from the cover of *The Autobiography of Mother Jones, Pittston Strike Commemorative Edition*, 1990. Courtesy Charles H. Kerr Co., Chicago.

of conspiracy to commit murder; authorities blamed her for contributing to violence that occurred during coal miner organizing drives in Virginia. Her sentence was commuted in 1914, and she continued with her activism, which lasted over half a century. Jones was 101 when she died in 1930. She authored two labor books, *The New Right*, 1899, and *Letters of Love and Labor*, 1900-1901; and an autobiography, first published in 1925. ✦

❧175❧
You'll get pie in the sky when you die.

Line from song written for the Spokane Free Speech Fight, 1910,
by Joe Hill [Joel Emmanuel Hagglung] (1879-1915), labor
agitator, IWW organizer, songwriter, labor movement martyr
(*see* photograph page 204)

❧176❧
Fifty-three years ago the ILG was officially organized to war against the
sweatshop. Today the garment workers return to their place of origin. We
have wiped out the sweatshop. Now we return to wipe out the slum.

David Dubinsky (1892-1982), labor leader, helped oust corrupt
union officials, organizer of Liberal party and American Labor
party, president (1932-1966) of ILGWU, in his groundbreaking
Address of Cooperative inspired under ILGWU auspices, 1953

David Dubinsky addresses ILGWU members at Madison Square Garden, New York, on
his 25th anniversary as their president, 6/22/1957. Courtesy George Meany Memorial
Archives.

✦177✦

Fifty years ago, few enterprises carried safety devices to protect workers' limbs and lives. Some protested that adoption of such devices would increase costs. Yet few firms today plead that they cannot afford to introduce safety devices. Is meaningfulness in work any less important?

Daniel Bell, journalist, essayist, sociologist, labor editor, in *Upton Sinclair—American Rebel*, 1975

✦178✦

Food isn't unionized, remember that.

William Winpisinger, in explaining that the rise in the prices of food was not due to wage increases, 1982

✦179✦

The growers don't care about people, and they never will. Their improvements, their labor-saving devices are all for their own benefit, not for ours.

Cesar Estrada Chavez (1927-1993), labor organizer, founder and first president, United Farm Workers of America (UFW)

✦ **Cesar Estrada Chavez**, 1927-1993, Yuma, Arizona (*see* photograph 130)

Cesar Chavez, born to a migrant worker family, began working in the fields at age 10, picking every crop possible in southern California and Arizona. He left school in the eighth grade and was a U. S. Navy veteran of WWII. While in his 20s, he worked for the Community Service Organization founded by Saul Alinsky, becoming Director in 1958. He started organizing farm workers in 1962, forming the National Farm Workers Association; later, he established the first successful union of farm workers in U.S. history, the United Farm Workers Union of America (UFW). Chavez advocated fasts, pickets, and marches to bring attention to farm workers' strikes. As UFW president, he led a five-year strike-boycott against California wine-grape growers, enlisting nationwide support from millions of Americans. The successful boycott led to binding contracts with the major grape growers. In 1972, the UFW became a member of the AFL-CIO.

Chavez renewed efforts to unionize all California vegetable pickers, but a dispute with the International Brotherhood of Teamsters led to the loss of UFW membership. His leadership and principles of non-violence in the tradition of Martin Luther King, Jr. and Mahatma Ghandi, prompted Senator Robert Kennedy to call Chavez "one of the heroic figures of our time." Chavez was honored posthumously in 1994 with the Presidential Medal of Freedom. ✦

Fieldwork with the short handled hoe, c. 1960s. Walter P. Reuther Library, Wayne State University.

⇥180⇤

If I had enough money, I would take busloads of people out to the fields and into the labor camps. Then they'd know how that fine salad got on their table.

Roberto Acuna, farm worker

⇥181⇤

It is not required that greater attention must be given to safety and health measures than to increased output—where that increase is achieved by diluting those measures?

Thomas Donahue, 1982

⇥182⇤

We can only say that we regard the welfare of the town as highly as anyone can do; and that we consider it to consist, not in the aggrandizement of a few individuals, but in the general prosperity and the welfare of the industrious and laboring classes.

Female Society of Lynn, insisting on a wage week for shoebinders, which led to the first organized women's strike, Lynn, Mass., 1883, in *Women and the American Labor Movement*, 1982

❧183❧

The needs and interests of union members are inseparable from those of the rest of American society.

Ray Denison, AFL-CIO legislative director

❧184❧

We shall realize and hold on to our gains only by making progress with the community and not at the expense of the community.

Walter Reuther, in *The Brothers Reuther*, 1976

❧185❧

The answer to our problems is not to put more burdens on the workers, the real answer is national health insurance.

Walter J. Butler, service employee

❧186❧

No social issue has a higher priority to the labor movement than enactment of national health insurance.

Lane Kirkland, secretary-treasurer AFL-CIO (1969-1979),
Labor Day, 1978

❧187❧

If the unions were not there to argue your case for national health care, for rebuilding America, for public education, for fair taxes—we would all be the poorer for it.

Reverend Jesse Louis Jackson, Baptist minister, civil rights leader,
founder of People United to Save Humanity (PUSH),
president, Rainbow Coalition

❧188❧

You cannot get to (Health Care) universal coverage without a police state.

Congressman Newton Leroy Gingrich (R-Ga., 1979-1999),
ABC interview, 8/14/1994

❧189❧

I had the pleasure of going to that high school. ... They asked for a trade union leader. I told those kids I got a son who's a doctor. He was able to borrow $50,000 from the government to go to school in order to be a doctor. How do you think this happened? It's because we in the trade unions fought for all these grants. We fought for all the gravy, all the good things that students got.

Frank Lumpkin, unemployed steelworker, in *The Great Divide*, 1988

❧190❧

It is one of the enduring triumphs of the labor movement that not only have you worked for yourselves, but you have not forgotten the rest of America. When you work for a minimum wage law, most of organized labor is not really affected, but you are affected in the sense that you are helping millions of others who have no way to express themselves.

Benjamin Lawson Hooks, clergyman, lawyer, civil rights leader,
Federal Communications Commission (1972-), director (1977-
1993), National Association for the Advancement of Colored
People (NAACP)

❧191❧

There is a direct correlation between the decline in our quality of life and the decline of unionization. A significant portion of the drop in American wages and our standard of living during the 1980s, for example, is due to the steep loss of union membership. The hardest hit have been minorities, blue collar workers and workers without college degrees.

Richard Trumka, president (1982-1995), UMWA,
secretary-treasurer (1995-) AFL-CIO

Chapter 3

Strife and Strike

✦192✦

Those who profess to favor freedom and yet deprecate agitation are men who want crops without plowing up the ground. They want rain without thunder and lightning.

Frederick Douglass, 1857

✦193✦

Find out what people will submit to and you have found out the exact amount of injustice and wrong, which will be imposed upon them.

Frederick Douglass

✦194✦

The only people whose names are recorded in history are those who did something. The peaceful and indifferent are forgotten; they never know the fighting joy of living.

Elizabeth Gurley Flynn, "The Rebel Girl" (1890-1964), IWW organizer, rights activist, a founder of American Civil Liberties Union, U.S. Communist Party leader, Seattle, 1/28/1917

✦195✦

Is it not much better to even die fighting for something than to have lived an uneventful life, never gotten anything and leaving conditions the same or worse than they were and to have future generations go through the same misery and poverty and degradation?

Elizabeth Gurley Flynn

✦196✦

Who struggles can fail. Who doesn't struggle has already failed!

Bertolt Brecht (1898-1956), German dramatist, poet, Marxist

✦197✦

You more likely regret that you hadn't spoken up—than what you said.

Ronald J. Neroda, 10/1997

✦198✦

If you think by hanging us you can stamp out the labor movement ... the movement from which the downtrodden millions, the millions who toil in want and misery, expect salvation, if this is your opinion, then hang us!

August Spies (1855-1887), orator, labor agitator,
leader of Haymarket gathering, martyr, after being sentenced to
death in the eight-hour day frame-up in Chicago, 1886,
in *Labor's Untold Story*, 1955

✦199✦

If nobody quits until I do, there will be no quitting!

John R. Lawson, UMWA organizer, after being sentenced to life
imprisonment for murder after frame-up trial, 1915

✦200✦

There will come a time when our silence will be more powerful than the voices you are strangling today.

August Spies

✦201✦

The men who perished upon the scaffold as felons were labor leaders, the first martyrs to the class struggle in the United States.

Eugene Debs, on the Molly Maguires (1860s-1870s), in *Appeal to
Reason*, 11/23/1907

✦202✦

Aye, gentlemen, if the jails could have put down insurrection and rebellion, then you and I would not be living in America today. ... If it was in my power tomorrow to provoke another strike in this city that I would succeed I would do it, even though the jail opened to receive me.

Clarence Darrow, defending union organizer Thomas I. Kidd in
Oshkosh Conspiracy case, in *Attorney for the Damned*, 1957

✦203✦

Don't waste any time mourning. Organize!

Telegraph sent to Big Bill Haywood and the Wobblies from Joe
Hill before his execution, 11/19/1915, after a dubious murder
conviction on circumstantial evidence

✦204✦

Jails were made for men who fight for their rights. My spirit was never in jail. They can jail us, but they can never jail the cause.

Cesar Chavez

❧205❧

It's very evident we're very happy to be here because this is the best way to win the struggle. This kind of spirit can't be jailed.

Jailed farm worker Juanita Escarano to Cesar Chavez and workers,
in *Cesar Chavez, Autobiography of La Causa*, 1975

❧206❧

The only rights we have are the rights others give us. We are not born with rights. All rights are conditional. They are not absolute. You have to earn your rights or fight for them.

Lawrence Sullivan, secretary, Greater Boston Labor Council

❧207❧

To the extent that the working class has power based upon class-consciousness, force is unnecessary; to the extent that power is lacking, force can only result in harm.

Eugene Debs

❧208❧

It is one of our proudest boasts that the American working class has, generally speaking, the highest standard of living of any working class in the world. How did our workingmen achieve this position? Only through struggle, intense struggle against bitter opposition and especially through the struggle of organized labor.

Rockwell Kent (1882-1971), illustrator, painter, 1948,
in *High Treason*, 1950

❧209❧

No gains without pains.

Benjamin Franklin (1706-1790), printer, statesman, inventor,
author, philosopher

❧210❧

It's time to raise less corn and more hell.

Mary Ellen "Yellin" Clyens Lease (1850-1933), lawyer,
populist political leader, 1880

❧211❧

No conflict with legitimate enterprise, no antagonism to necessary capital.

Slogan of original Noble Order of the Knights of Labor, c. 1869

✦212✦

Power concedes nothing without a demand. It never did and it never will.

Frederick Douglass

✦213✦

If there is no struggle, there can be no progress.

Frederick Douglass

✦214✦

That is the only language that a lot of employers ever understand—the language of force.

William Green (1873-1952), miner, miners organizer, president
of AFL (1924-1952), 1933, in *Toil and Trouble*, 1964

✦215✦

You only make progress by fighting for progress.

George Meany (1894-1980), first president
(1955-1980) of AFL-CIO

✦216✦

They are smiting me hip and thigh. Right merrily I shall return their blows.

John L. Lewis, in *Men Who Lead Labor*, 1937

✦ **George Meany, 1894-1980**, New York, New York
(*see* photograph page 132)

George Meany, a plumber from age 16, devoted himself full time to union activities after he was elected business agent for his union local in 1922. He developed as a leader in the trade union movement, becoming president of the New York State Federation of Labor (1934-1939). An astute lobbyist, he helped promote 72 pro-labor bills in the New York legislature. Meany was elected secretary-treasurer of the American Federation of Labor, serving from 1940 to 1952. He succeeded as president of the AFL, continuing as president during the historic AFL-CIO merger in 1955 until he retired in 1979.

Meany was a powerful and effective leader during a time when labor made some of its greatest gains. He actively promoted civil rights in union policy and in federal legislation, but he also alienated many unionists in the 1950s by using the anti-communist hysteria of the times to influence union elections and destroy rivals with the government's help. In the late 1960s and early 1970s, Meany alienated union "doves" by his unwavering support of the Vietnam War, which culminated in the 1972 presidential campaign when he refused to support George McGovern, thus breaking the AFL-CIO tradition of always supporting the Democratic presidential candidate. He was awarded the Presidential Medal of Freedom in 1963. ✦

❖217❖

Those who chant their praises of democracy but who lost no chance to drive their knives into labor's defenseless back must feel the weight of labor's woe even as its open adversaries must ever feel the thrust of labor's power.

> John L. Lewis, Labor Day speech, 9/3/1937, in *John L. Lewis: An Unauthorized Biography*, 1949

❖218❖

If we don't survive we don't do anything else.

> John Sinclair, author

❖219❖

Peaceably If We Can: Forcibly If We Must

> Popular banners during the Eight-hour Movement of the 1870s

❖220❖

I live in the United States, but I do not know exactly where. My address is wherever there is a fight against oppression. My address is like my shoes; it travels with me. I abide where there is a fight against wrong.

> Mother Jones

❖221❖

Pray for the dead and fight like hell for the living.

> Mother Jones

❖222❖

But I'll fight them as a woman, not a lady.

> From a woman's calendar, *The Liberated Woman's Appointment Calendar*, quote c. late 1970s

❖223❖

I do not doubt your ability to call out your soldiers and shoot the members of our union out of those plants, but let me say that when you issue that order I shall leave this conference and I shall enter one of those plants with my own people ... and the militia will have the pleasure of shooting me out of the plants with them.

> John L. Lewis, to Governor Frank Murphy (D-Mich., 1937-1938), in *The Brothers Reuther*, 1976

Sriking coal miners face state militia near Evarts, Kentucky, 1931. Courtesy Archives of Labor and Urban Affairs, Wayne State University.

❧224❧

Tanks can threaten and massacre us, but they will never be able to force us to work.

Lech Walesa, Polish Solidarity leader, later became President of
Poland (1990-1995), 1983 Nobel Peace Prize

❧225❧

A little bloodletting is sometimes necessary in desperate cases.

William H. Sylvis, president, National Labor Union (NLU),
1869, in *History of the Working Class*, 1927

❧226❧

We had to teach our employees a lesson, and we have taught them one they will never forget.

From a letter to Andrew Carnegie, president of Carnegie Steel,
from partner and plant manager Henry Clay Frick (1849-1919),
coke and steel industrialist, after Frick broke the last union,
the Amalgamated Association of Iron, Steel, and
Tin Workers at Homestead, Pa., 1892
(*see* Great Battle of Homestead page 137)

❧227❧

We'll drive them goddamned sons-of-bitches into the river and drown them. We'll starve them. We'll kill every damned man of them …

Judge Davis, speaking of the Wobblies (Industrial Workers of the
World), Minot, N.D., 1912

❧228❧

No tin-hat brigade of goose-stepping vigilantes or bubble-babbling mob of blackguarding and corporation-paid scoundrels will prevent the onward march of labor.

John L. Lewis, *Time* magazine, 9/9/1937

❧229❧

Survival of the fittest … What do you think industry does? What do you think the police do? Police broke our heads every day of the week. Ford Motors? They cracked heads all over the lot. Unless you were able to take care of yourself, they'd crack your head where it'd kill you. I survived.

James Riddle "Jimmy" Hoffa (1913-1975?), president (1957-
1971), International Brotherhood of Teamsters (IBT), discussing
his rise to power in the Teamsters Union

Members of the Ford Service Department attacking UAW official Richard Frankenstein during the Battle of the Overpass next to the Ford Motor Company's Rouge factory complex, Dearborn, Michigan, 5/26/1937. Courtesy Archives of Labor and Union Affairs, Wayne State University.

Don't complain. Don't explain.

Henry Ford II (1917-1987), president, Ford Motor Company

→231←

Did you know that Boss spelled backward is Double S-O-B?

Jim Hightower, syndicated radio host, political agitator,
public speaker, author

→232←

Sore and sad as I am by the illness, the killing, the maiming of so many of my fellow workers, I would rather see that go on for years and years, minimized and mitigated by the organized labor movement, than give up one jot of the freedom of the workers to strive and struggle for their own emancipation through their own efforts.

Samuel Gompers, in *With Our Hands*, 1986

→233←

You can't mine coal without machine guns.

Richard B. Mellon (1899-1970), banker,
Congressional testimony, 1937

→234←

The labor problem cannot be quenched by a fire hose. ... Our strength rests on our unity.

Joseph J. Ettor, IWW leader

→235←

They say in Harlan County
There are no neutrals there.
You'll either be a union man,
Or a thug for J.H. Blair.

Florence Reese song, *Which Side Are You On?*, 1932

→236←

I write songs to fan the flames of discontent.

Joe Hill (*Casey Jones* and *The Union Scab* are two of
his better known songs)

→237←

I favor shutting her down.

C.D. Leslie, sit-down striker, made this comment that began first
historic sit-down strike, Goodyear plant, Akron, Ohio, 1936, in
Labor's New Millions, 1938

⇥238⇤

The sit-down idea spread so rapidly because it dramatized a simple powerful act, that no social institution can run without the cooperation of those whose activity make it up.

Jeremy Brecher, in his book, *Strike!*, 1983

⇥239⇤

The right to a man's job transcends the right of private property. The CIO stands squarely behind these sit-downs.

John L. Lewis, defending auto workers' sit-down strikes

⇥240⇤

When the speedup comes, just twiddle your thumbs.
Sit down! Sit down!
And, when the boss won't talk, don't take a walk.
Sit down! Sit down!

UAW sit-down chants. Lyrics by a union lawyer, in *Walter Reuther, Labor's Rugged Individualist*, 1972

⇥241⇤

For 75 years big business had been sitting down on the American people.

Upton Beall Sinclair (1878-1968), novelist, playwright, muckraker, socialist, 1943 Pulitzer Prize for fiction, 1937

⇥242⇤

Take This Job And Shove It

Title of a song by Johnny Paycheck

⇥243⇤

The only thing workers have to bargain with is their skill or their labor. Denied the right to withhold it as a last resort, they become powerless. The strike is therefore not a breakdown of collective bargaining—it is the indispensable cornerstone of that process.

Paul Clark, *Changing Labor's Image*, a study guide by Pennsylvania AFL-CIO, 1989

⇥244⇤

I know the trials and woes of working men and I have always felt for them. I know that in almost every case of strikes, the men have a just cause for complaint.

President Abraham Lincoln, to delegation from the Machinists' and Blacksmiths' Union, 1863

⟿245⟽

Labor cannot on any terms surrender the right to strike.

> Louis Dembitz Brandeis (1856-1941), Supreme Court Justice
> (1916-1939), pioneered use of economic and sociological data in
> legal decisions, 1913

⟿246⟽

Neither common law nor the Fourteenth Amendment confers the absolute right to strike.

> Justice Louis Brandeis, for the Supreme Court, *Dorchy v. Kansas*,
> 1926

⟿247⟽

Show me the country that has no strikes and I'll show you the country in which there is no liberty.

> Samuel Gompers, 1925

⟿248⟽

If we had any doubts about the importance of the right to strike in a democratic society, the experience of Poland during the past decade should serve as a useful lesson. Members of the Polish solidarity union can testify that their union may have lingered under authoritarian rule if not for the willingness of the rank and file to put down their tools, and leave their factories.

> Monsignor George G. Higgins, *Organized Labor and the Church*, 1993

⟿249⟽

There simply does not exist a situation where workers engage in a strike except under extreme pressure. When we strike, we live on minimal strike benefits, and we are nearly always up against long odds. Ask a striking worker why they are on strike, and they will tell you, without exception, not money or benefits, but for justice.

> Jeff Crosby, local president, International Union of Electronics,
> Electrical Salaried & Machine Workers of America (IUE)

⟿250⟽

It [the strike] frees you in ways you never have been freed before. Yes, we've been liberated from our paychecks, but we've been liberated from fear too.

> Susan Watson, striking newspaper columnist on the *Detroit News/*
> *Free Press* strike, 1995

❖251❖

Do not strike in haste and repent at your leisure.

Samuel Gompers

❖252❖

The worker can't take out his frustration by punching his boss in the nose, but he can picket. Sometimes, it's healthy. It has a cleansing effect.

Alexander MacMillan, of Massachusetts State Labor Commission

❖253❖

You can hope for no success on any policy of violence. ... Violence necessarily means the loss of the strike.

Joseph Ettor

❖254❖

First you get a whip and then when everyone knows you have it, put it in the refrigerator.

David Dubinsky

❖255❖

A strike is a practical protest, or a revolt, frequently successful, against wrongs that may be unendurable. It is resorted to only when rendered necessary by the oppressive action of capital, exercised against the strikers or against any portion of their brethren with whom they have interests or sympathies in common.

John Swinton, labor journalist, 1880, in *The Bending Cross*, 1949

❖256❖

The strike is a weapon of the oppressed, of men capable of appreciating justice and having the courage to resist wrong and contend for principle.

Eugene Debs

❖257❖

One of the great reasons for the popularity of strikes is that they give the suppressed self a sense of power. For once the human tool knows itself a man, able to stand up and speak a word or strike a blow.

Charles Horton Cooley (1864-1929), sociologist, *Human Nature and the Social Order*, 1902

→258←

This is not a fight we want, this is not a fight we picked, this is not a fight we will walk away from.

Edward J. Doherty, Boston Teachers Union president,
on calling for a strike, 1993

→259←

Labor never quits. We never give up the fight—no matter how tough the odds, no matter how long it takes.

George Meany

→260←

The story of coal is always the same. It is a dark story. For a second's more sunlight, men must fight like tigers. For privilege of seeing the color of their children's eyes by the light of the sun, fathers must fight as beasts in the jungle. That life may have something of decency, something of beauty—a picture, a new dress ... for this, men who work down in the mines must struggle and lose, struggle and win.

Mother Jones, *The Autobiography of Mother Jones*, 1925

→261←

What is a strike? The answer is war. And what is a war? Resistance to wrong. Such is the history of war in the United States. ... Who is the craven that would have the Constitution of the United States so amended that Congress should never declare war?

Eugene Debs, in *The Bending Cross*, 1949

→262←

No More Talk—We Mean Business

Protest signs from Shorter Work-Week Movement

→263←

I have never order a strike; and I have never decreed a strike, and I have never had the power to call off a strike when it was once inaugurated.

Samuel Gompers

→264←

I will never advocate a strike, unless it be a strike at the ballot box, or such a one as was proclaimed to the world by the unmistakable sound of the strikers' guns on the field of Lexington.

Terence Vincent Powderly (1849-1924), president (1872-1874)
of Machinists' and Blacksmiths' Union, president (1879-1893) of
the Noble Order of the Knights of Labor, 1872, in *Strike!*, 1983

Terence Powderly, president, Knights of Labor. Courtesy George Meany
Memorial Archives

→ **Terence Vincent Powderly**, 1849-1924, Carbondale, Pennsylvania

Terence Powderly, a railroad worker and machinist, rose to the presidency of the Machinists' and Blacksmiths' National Union in 1872. Powderly's ideal was non-confrontational leadership, preferring management-labor cooperation. In 1879 he became the leader of the secretive Noble Order of the Knights of Labor. Founded in 1869, it was the first American organization to try to bring all workers into one centralized union. The Knights' idealistic goals included the 8-hour day, abolition of child and convict labor, equal pay laws, and cooperation with management.

During his presidency, the Knights of Labor abandoned secrecy and their ranks swelled from 10,000 to more than 700,000 by 1886. But the rival American Federation of Labor under the leadership of Samuel Gompers soon replaced the Knights as the foremost coalition of unions. Knights' leaders were unwilling to advocate strikes at a time when union activism was growing. Additionally, the press falsely blamed the Knights for the 1886 Haymarket Square Riot where 11 people were killed and, coupled with dissension over policies and mismanagement by its bureaucracy, the Knights rapidly lost membership. By 1893, membership had dwindled to about 70,000, mostly in Boston area unions of longshoremen and railroad freight handlers. Powderly, a charismatic leader, served as mayor of Scranton, Pennsylvania (1878-1884) and became a lawyer in 1894. He also served as Commissioner of Immigration (1897-1902) and in the Bureau of Immigration (1907-1921). ✦

→265←

Keep your sermons; give us your proxies.

Banner used to galvanize local churches in Kodak union drive

→266←

No Contract, No Work!

Original slogan of striking miners during World War II

→267←

The strike is the only weapon labor has.

Harry Bridges (1901-1990), founder and former president
(1937-1977), International Longshoremen's and Warehousemen's
Union (ILWU), 1978

→268←

Big business has thrown off its mask in the Lawrence strike.

Judge Ben Lindsey of Denver

→269←

Open the jail gates or we will shut the mill gates.

Slogan, Lawrence Mill Strike, 1912

Lawrence strikers march peacefully through Lawrence, Massachusetts, 1912. Courtesy George Meany Memorial Archives.

❖270❖

But they cannot weave cloth with bayonets, by all means make this strike as peaceful as possible. In the last analysis, all the blood spilled will be your blood.

> Lawrence Mayor Michael Scanlon, addressing strikers at the
> Lawrence Mill Strike, 1912

❖271❖

When they looked at ministers, priests, nuns, and bishops standing up with them, they realized that they were morally right—legally incorrect but morally right.

> Cecil Roberts, UMWA official, commenting on the support of the
> religious community in their successful 14-month strike, 1991

❖272❖

Thank God we have a system of labor where there can be a strike. Whatever the pressure, there is a point where the working man may stop.

> Abraham Lincoln, Hartford, Conn. speech, 3/6/1860, in *A Pictorial
> History of American Labor*, 1972

❖273❖

We have come too far, struggled too long, sacrificed too much, and have too much left to do, to allow that [which] we have achieved for the good of all to be swept away without a fight. And we have not forgotten how to fight.

> Lane Kirkland, Solidarity Day, 1981

❖274❖

When enough people begin to feel that they are less important than property, a state has the beginning of a revolutionary movement; and such movements are less fomented by agitators than they are inspired by the very elements who are trying to preserve the status quo.

> Sydney J. Harris

❖275❖

> 'tis the night before Christmas
> And all through GE
> Not a wheel will be turning
> Until the Unions agree!

> *UE Strike Report*, Christmas, 1969, in *Them and Us*, 1974

✦276✦

Esau was a traitor to himself; Judas Iscariot was a traitor to his God; Benedict Arnold was a traitor to his country; a strikebreaker is a traitor to his God, his country, his wife, his family and his class.

Jack [John Griffith] London (1876-1916), author, socialist,
adventurer, *The Definition of a Scab*

✦277✦

Even if we or our families were not directly involved, we had heard and read about pickets being beaten, jailed, sometimes killed. Honoring a picket line was the least we could do. It still is.

Sydney Lens, author

✦278✦

It wasn't a precept that required discussion or debate. It made no difference which union was on strike, or what it was demanding. Good people didn't cross picket lines. Ever.

Sydney Lens

✦279✦

The vanishing sanctity of the picket line is as valid an indicator as any of our political disarray and decay. We'll have a functioning movement when the old rule is in full force again: Never cross a picket line.

Sydney Lens

✦280✦

We will not eat the bread of our oppressors.

Reverend Timothy Mitchell, uniting homeless men with
boycotting bakery workers

✦281✦

I couldn't ever cross a picket line, even to film.

Barbara Kopple, Oscar-winning film maker

✦282✦

What kind of a job is it where you take the bread and butter off a fellow worker's table? Colonial is getting its few strikebreakers by paying Judas money to a few no-nothings to bring in their friends. Tell them you don't want their dirty thirty pieces of silver.

Advertisement in Boston newspapers protesting strikebreakers
hiring practices by Colonial Provision Company and Boston
Sausage Company, 1955

Daily Evening Item.

VOL. LL. NO. 38   LYNN, MASS., WEDNESDAY, JANUARY 21, 1903.   PRICE TWO CENTS.

STILL BRINGING IN CUTTERS FROM OUT OF TOWN.

Boot and Shoe Workers' Union Lands Another Batch of Workmen—Said to Have Come From Chicago.

SIX SHOPS ARE GIVEN WORKMEN TO-DAY.

G. W. Belonga Turn Workmen Locked Out—Stock Fitters Organize In Knights of Labor —B. & S. W. Union of Cutters Formed With 75 Members—Board of Health Enforcing Vaccination Regulations—General Melee on Andrew Street Tuesday Evening—Hooting, Jeering Crowds Followed B. and S. W. Union Cutters From Strike Factories—Little Excitement This Morning When Strike Breaking Cutters Were Escorted to Work.

Police Bringing the Mob to a Stop at the Entrance to Andrew Street.

Bitter conflict over strikebreakers has been ongoing for well over a century. Detail of *Lynn Item* newspaper front page, 1/21/1903. Courtesy Lynn Historical Society.

⇢283⇠

A strikebreaker who steals our job during this strike is like a robber who steals a prize milk cow or tractor from your farm. ... The strikebreakers are only hurting the chances for an early settlement of the strike and they are greatly damaging the future prosperity of our community.

> Strike bulletin, Kohler Company, 1954, in *Kohler on Strike*, 1967

⇢284⇠

Individualism is for scabs. This country is set up for scabs. Crossing a picket line, making your own deal. America is the land of opportunity. And a strike, if nothing else, creates lots of opportunities.

> Thomas Geoghegan, labor lawyer, author,
> *Which Side Are You On?*, 1991

⇢285⇠

Don't scab for the bosses,
Don't listen to their lies,
Us poor folks haven't got a chance,
Unless we organize.

> Florence Reese song, *Which Side Are You On?*

⇢286⇠

A scab in labor unions is the same as a traitor to his country.

> Eugene Debs

✦287✦

We wove the flag; we dyed the flag; we live under the flag; but we won't scab under the flag!

> Rallying cry appearing on a huge American flag hung by striking
> flag-makers during IWW Mill Workers' Strike, Paterson, N. J.,
> after employers, using a ploy of patriotism, hung American flags
> with signs appealing for a return to work, 3/17/1913

✦288✦

The scab is powerless under terrorism. As a rule, he is not so good nor so gritty a man as the men he is displacing, and he lacks their fighting organization.

> Jack London, from a speech, *The Scab*, Oakland, Calif., 4/5/1903
> and from essay in *Atlantic Monthly, Vol. XCIII*, 1904

✦289✦

There is nothing lower than a SCAB.

> Jack London

✦290✦

The scab is a man who goes in to take the place of his fellow man who is working for better conditions.

> Clarence Darrow, 1903, in *Attorney for the Damned*, 1957

✦291✦

We have heard a great deal in this country of late about the scab. ... As a class, this body of men, as has been shown in this case, has always been ready to take the benefits that flow from organized labor, and never been willing to fight to obtain them.

> Clarence Darrow, 1903, in *Attorney for the Damned*, 1957

✦292✦

In America, it's mostly legal to go on strike. It's simply illegal to win one. Exercise your right to strike and the boss can immediately hire replacement workers—popularly known as scabs.

> Alexander Cockburn, columnist

✦293✦

The truth is workers in the U.S.A. have, in theory, the right to strike, but we don't have the right to win a strike.

> George Kourpias, president, IAM,
> commenting on employers' right to replace workers

Scene from The Great Shoemaker's Strike of 1860, Central Square, Lynn, Massachusetts. Frank Leslie illustration, courtesy Lynn Historical Society.

State militia oversees strikers and demonstrators. The banner reads "American ladies will not be slaves. Give us fair compensation and we labour cheerfully." Frank Leslie illustration, courtesy Lynn Historical Society (*see also* Elvira Hall page 121).

❖294❖

Divide and conquer. As long as some people have commanded the work of others, this has been management's basic principle.

Peter Rachleff, labor historian

❖295❖

They've been trying to tell us there are three separate groups in GE [General Electric]: the company, the employees, and the union. That's what they've based themselves on. We have to show them they're wrong. The UE represents the workers. The workers are the union. We have to show them there are not three groups but just two: the company and the union. Them and us.

Young worker, UE Local 924, Decatur, Ill., in *Them and Us*, 1974

❖296❖

If you don't come in on Sunday, you needn't come in on Monday.

Sign on elevator threatening garment workers at Triangle Shirtwaist Company, 1901

❖297❖

It's like sending up a pinch hitter to the plate without a bat, or asking a man at the blast furnace to make steel without iron ore.

David McDonald (1902-1979), former president (1952-1965), United Steelworkers of America, on giving up the use of the strike

❖298❖

To expect that one dependent upon his daily wage for the necessities of life will stand by peaceably and see a new man employed in his stead is to expect much.

Andrew Carnegie (1835-1919), steel industrialist, president, Carnegie Steel, philanthropist, in *Toil and Trouble*, 1964

❖299❖

Some argue that employers need to offer permanent status in order to attract replacement workers. Almost 60 years of industrial history in this country has shown this isn't the case.

Congressman William Lacy Clay, Sr. (D-Mo. 1969-), 1991

❖300❖

The right to strike has become no more than the right to quit.

Senator Howard Morton Metzenbaum (D-Ohio, 1974, 1976-1995), before the Senate, on the argument for the right to strike, 1991

✣301✣

Organized labor does not place its reliance upon reason and justice but on strikes, boycotts, and coercion. ... It denies to those outside its ranks the individual right to dispose of their labor as they see fit—a right that is one of the most sacred and fundamental of American liberty.

David M. Parry, National Association of Manufacturers

✣302✣

It is common sense that permanently replaced strikers means trading experienced, skilled employees for inexperienced ones. Inexperienced replacement workers start at the bottom of the learning curve, a circumstance that can sometimes have grave circumstances. We wouldn't have wanted rookies, for instance, assembling the tanks used by American soldiers fighting in Desert Storm.

Senator Herb H. Kohl (D-Wis., 1989-)

✣303✣

Permanent replacement (of strikers) is the equivalent of a nuclear first strike. One side is encouraged to believe it will prevail by wiping out the other side. In fact, both sides lose.

Congressman William Clay

✣304✣

I think we're going to see a lot more violence unless we bring in some kind of anti-scab law.

Elaine Bernard, director, Harvard Trade Union Program, on Supreme Court ruling favoring strikebreakers

✣305✣

Hold The Line

Popular union refrain, used also by President Franklin D. Roosevelt

✣306✣

Fight labor's demands to the last ditch and there will come a time when it seizes the whole of power, makes itself sovereign and takes what it used to ask.

Walter Lippmann (1889-1974), journalist, *New York Herald Tribune* columnist, author, 1958 Pulitzer Prize for lifetime achievement, 1962 Pulitzer Prize for international journalism

✦307✦

Sidney, this is strike number two, one more and you're out!

> Tom Kiernan, striking meatpacker, yelling at a boss after strikers
> were decertified. The union drive proved successful, and the strike
> was won, in *The Colonial Strike*, 1955

✦308✦

Yale is full of Schmidt—Cut the Schmidt

> Placards from worker-student strike at Yale University, referring to
> Yale President Benno Schmidt, 1991

✦309✦

Well, Mr. Lewis, you beat us, but I'm not going to forget it. I just want to tell you that one of these days we'll come back and give you the kind of a whipping that you and your people will never forget.

> General Motors' John Thomas Smith to John L.
> Lewis after defeat by sit-down strikers, 1937, in *John L. Lewis:
> An Unauthorized Biography*, 1949

✦310✦

The establishment can accept being screwed, but not being laughed at.

> Saul Alinsky

✦311✦

One must be careful never to destroy one's opposition. You may defeat them, but your goal should always be to convert them, never to destroy them.

> Walter Reuther, in *The Brothers Reuther*, 1976

✦312✦

For the past four and a half years the United States has been in the throes of a major labor upheaval which can fairly be described as one of the greatest mass movements in our history.

> *Fortune* magazine, 1937

✦313✦

In fact, strikes are a much less disruptive influence in the workplace than many other factors. Statistics suggest that the common cold, for instance, causes more worker absence than strikes.

> Paul Clark, citing a Dept. of Labor study of the years 1980-1988

⇒314⇐

Sometimes a bad settlement hurts the public worse than a strike.

> Willard Wirtz, Secretary of Labor (1962-1969),
> Kennedy and Johnson Administrations

⇒315⇐

While strikes have their part and all that and we certainly have advocated for years that you have got to have the right to strike—we find more and more that strikes really don't settle a thing.

> George Meany

⇒316⇐

[President] White said I was absolutely right and talked about how gains have been made when workers have taken things in their own hands, legally or illegally. The way I read that was to go ahead and take over the plant, so I did.

> Joe Albanese, Canadian Auto Workers vice president, reviving
> tactics of early 1980s, bringing management back to the
> bargaining table

⇒317⇐

Without the right to strike, the progress that has been made in achieving decent wages and working conditions during the past 50 years would be severely endangered. ... Every other industrial nation except South Africa protects the right of labor to strike.

> Coretta Scott King, civil rights activist, columnist, widow of
> Reverend Martin Luther King, Jr. (*see* photograph page 130)

⇒318⇐

The right to strike is an essential part of collective bargaining in our democratic society. Without the real possibility of a strike, there is little incentive for management to negotiate a fair settlement with labor.

> Coretta Scott King

⇒319⇐

In most countries, non-government workers can strike and expect to get their jobs back when the labor action ends. In South Africa and the United States, though, you can walk out for what you believe is right only to find that someone else has placed a photo of his kids on your desk.

> Alfred Lubrano, reporter on strike

❖320❖

The Gospel demands sensitivity to the voices of the poor and the power-less. Without the right to legally withhold labor, working men and women become powerless and oftentimes impoverished.

Sister Pat Drydyk, director, National Farm Workers Ministry

❖321❖

I just cannot see the abandonment of the strike as a weapon of last resort.

Leonard Freel Woodcock, president (1970-1977) of UAW, U.S.
ambassador to People's Republic of China (1979-1981), 1976

❖322❖

To such open declaration by the Marion businessmen that they will assist capital to choke Labor can there, on the part of workers, be any conceiv-able answer save the most militant and universal and immediate organiza-tion of trade unions? Can there be any conceivable policy for neutrals save hearty assistance to that labor organization with sympathy, with pen, and with money? This nation cannot survive half slave and half free.

Sinclair Lewis (1885-1951), prolific novelist, playwright, 1926
Pulitzer Prize, 1930 Nobel Prize for literature, on the aftermath
of the violent textile strike at Marion, N.C., 1929

❖323❖

I come from a very dirty business. ... The enemy was the collective spirit. I got hold of that spirit while it was still a seedling. I poisoned it, choked it, bludgeoned it if I had to, anything to be sure it would never blossom into a united work force.

Martin Jay Levitt, professional union buster, consultant,
Confessions of a Union Buster, 1993

❖324❖

Union busting is a field populated by bullies and built on deceit. A cam-paign against a union is an assault on individuals and a war on the truth. The only way to bust a union is to lie, distort, manipulate, threaten and always attack. ... The consultants are terrorists.

Martin Jay Levitt, *Confessions of a Union Buster*, 1993

❖325❖

We think any effort to bust a union should be fought back, in this town or any town. We don't think union-busting should be legal in America.

Paul Massaron, UAW official, on the Detroit newspaper strike

Reprinted with permission, courtesy ©Gary Huck.

✢326✣

They can take away the building, but they can't take away the union.

> Richard Trumka, attributed, in the face of a contractual dispute
> and heavy fines threatening the loss of a union building

✢327✣

If it is the workers who desire a less-forceful labor movement, why is it employers hire anti-union consultants to the tune of $100 million a year?

> Arthur Osborne, president, Massachusetts AFL-CIO

✢328✣

The company has more money, and it has a big, overstaffed personnel department. It can outspend, outbrief, and outman the union in any case, if it wants. It can do all the urinalysis it wants, and then, after two and a half years, it clobbers us in arbitration. Then it goes out and tells the public how labor is running the company.

> Thomas Geoghegan, *Which Side Are You On?*, 1991

✢329✣

They have the money.
But we have the people.

> Slogan—union leaflet

→330←

Unfortunately, our collective bargaining law is one-sided. It encourages employers to play brinkmanship with teachers rather than work cooperatively toward a settlement. Teachers are left with two bad choices. If we accept deteriorating working conditions and salaries, we lose our self-respect. If we take a stand against unfair employers and for economic dignity, we're called greedy and disrespectful lawbreakers.

Robert J. Murphy, president,
Massachusetts Teachers Association (MTA)

→331←

Striking teachers do not take away education from students; they only postpone it. It is a school committee and/or superintendent that deprives students of an education by calling a day of baby-sitting a day of education. ... No teacher wants to go on strike. Teachers are forced to strike when all other legal avenues have failed to bring about a fair contract.

Philip Katz, teacher

→332←

We know where you live. ... If you want to stay alive, vote NO.

From a letter to strikers by the Diamond Walnut Growers, Inc.,
1991, in *United Association of Journeymen or Apprentices
of the Plumbing and Pipe Fitting Industry of the United States and
Canada (UA) Journal,* 5/1994

→333←

If I were a weather forecaster, I'd say there's a 100 percent chance of a strike Tuesday. But weather forecasters have been known to be wrong.

Ted Kirsch, Teachers Union local president

→334←

I abhor strikes, as you know.

John L. Lewis, when asked if a strike impended in the steel
industry, in *Labor Baron—A Portrait of John L. Lewis,* 1944

→335←

There is a small group of nurses who believe that it is unprofessional to strike or even picket. I believe it's the most professional thing a nurse can do. It's far less professional to just accept changes we know have a devastating impact on the quality of care.

Kathleen Sperrazza, chairwoman,
Massachusetts Nurses Association (MNA)

❖336❖

Money and benefits are the obvious complaints, but more important is the fact that nurses are the lifeblood of any hospital. That is what is not being recognized.

Denise Sullivan, of MNA., during Hyannis strike

❖337❖

The balance of power in the marketplace has tilted so far toward insurers and their shareholders and away from the interests of their patients that it has placed our patients and physicians in a very dangerous position.

Dr. Randolph Smoak, chairman of
American Medical Association (AMA) board of trustees,
3/2/1999, *Los Angeles Times*

❖338❖

I can see the time coming when we're not simply independent business owners … but just workers.

Dr. Lawrence Koning, 3/2/1999, *Los Angeles Times*

❖339❖

I found that national organizations I used to belong to, like the AMA, won't go to bat for you or your patients.

Dr. Charles Goodman, on why he joined the Union of American
Physicians Dentists (UAPD), after fighting managed care
organizations, 3/2/1999, *Los Angeles Times*

❖340❖

The doctors are very demoralized. And it can't be good for the health of the system.

Joe Bader, union official, UAPD, on successful efforts to unionize
doctors, 3/1/1999 *Los Angeles Times*

❖341❖

Today is the day we physicians begin the process to take back the practice of health care in Los Angeles County.

Dr. Janice Nelson, after Los Angeles County doctors voted to join
the UAPD, 5/28/1999, *Los Angeles Times*

❧342❧

It's just scandalous. You just cannot accept having this kind of wage paid to anyone working on full-time patient care.

> Gary Guthman, of the Joint Council of Interns and Residents,
> commenting after doctors doing their one-year residencies at
> California College of Podiatry, picketed County-University of
> Southern California (USC) Medical Center over their $10,000
> per year stipend, which amounts to less than minimum wage,
> *Los Angeles Times*, 6/17/1999

❧343❧

Interns, residents and fellows … while they may be students learning their chosen craft, are also 'employees' …

> National Labor Relations Board (NLRB) overturning a 23-year
> precedent that had classified doctors-in-training as students,
> denying them collective bargaining rights, 11/26/1999

❧344❧

The labor movement was not built on a bed of roses. It was built against fierce employer and political resistance, by hard work and sacrifice. No one is going to make it easy to rebuild our movement. But rebuild it we must, if we hope to maintain the hard-won victories of our past.

> Henry Bayer, president, American Federation of State, County and
> Municipal Employees (AFSCME), 1995

❧345❧

No strike has ever been lost and there can be no defeat for the labor movement.

> Eugene Debs, American Railway Union president, after defeat of
> the Pullman Strike, which focused attention on the application of
> anti-trust laws to labor unions, 1894

❧346❧

We are blessed and strengthened by one piece of sure and certain knowledge: that there are no lost causes for us; that the fight is never over; that as long as we stand together and the blood is in us there can be no final defeat on any battleground.

> Lane Kirkland, 1969

Chapter 4

Organizing and Unions

✦347✦

Unions originated as working-class instruments of industrial warfare;
intended to resist the aggressions of employers and improve conditions
immediately incident to work.

Labor Unions—Encyclopedia Americana, 1980

✦348✦

Long ago we stated the reason for labor organizations. We said that they
were organized out of the necessities of the situation: that a single
employee was helpless in dealing with an employer; ... that union was
essential to give the laborers opportunity to deal on equality with their
employer.

Chief Justice Charles Evans Hughes (1862-1948) for the U.S.
Supreme Court (1930-1941), in *NLRB v. Jones & Laughlin Steel
Corp., 301 1 at 33,* 1937

✦349✦

With all their faults, trade unions have done more for humanity than any
other organization that ever existed. They have done more for decency,
for honesty, for education, for the betterment of the race, for the developing of character in man, than any other association of men.

Clarence Darrow, *The Railroad Trainman,* 1909

✦350✦

The working people of America are, of course, the backbone of the nation.

Woodrow Wilson, 1912

✦351✦

If I were a worker in a factory, the first thing I would do would be to join
a union.

President Franklin D. Roosevelt

Chronology of the American Labor Movement.

1803. First strike in New York City, Sailors demanded more pay.
1803. First Trades' Union, New York Ship Carpenters, formed April 30th.
1806. First House Carpenters' Union, organized in New York City, May 17.
1829. First labor paper, published in Boston, Mass.
1832. First National Labor Convention, held in Boston.
1835. First strike of House Carpenters, in Boston, May 8, for ten hours a day.
1840. Ten hours established by Proclamation of President Van Buren.
1847. Second National Labor Convention, held June 10, in New York.
1854. First National Union of Journeymen House Carpenters organized, dissolved in less than one year.
     ...nd attempt to organize a National Union of Carpenters, failed

...rs and Joiners of America instituted August

PROGRESS OF THE BROTHERHOOD.

Number of Local Unions, Members, and amount of Benefits Paid, from the formation of the Society.

DATES.	No of Local Unions	Beneficial Members.	Enrolled Members.	General Benefits Paid
August 12th, 1881	12	2,042	3,788	
" " 1882	23	3,780	6,421	
July 1st, 1883	26	3,293	7,119	$1,500 00
" " 1884	47	4,364	7,797	2,250 00
" " 1885	80	5,789	9,648	5,700 00
" " 1886	177	21,423	29,365	9,200 00
" " 1887	306	25,466	37,487	16,275 16
January 1st, 1888	353	26,738	44,721	7,100 00

Total Benefits Paid, $42,025 16

Details from 1888 union calendar with chronology (part missing) of American Labor Movement and Progress of the Brotherhood of Carpenters and Joiners of America (*see* page 11). Courtesy George Meany Memorial Archives.

→352←

The labor movement is people. Our unions have brought millions of men and women together, made them members one of another, and given them common tools for common goals. Their goals are goals for all America—and their enemies are the enemies for progress. The two cannot be separated.

> President John Fitzgerald Kennedy (1961-1963),
> 1957 Pulitzer Prize for biography

→353←

Many join unions for selfish reasons, and well they might. Whatever their faults, over the years unions have raised wages, shortened hours, secured vacations, pensions and other benefits. And the good ones have given workers, above all, a sense of independence and self-worth—dignity—the ability to stand up to the boss.

> John Cort

❧354❧

We have the most wealth of any nation because our workers have the skill to create it. We have the best products because they know how to make them. We have the most democratic system because of the values our trade unions have to sustain it.

Vice President Walter Frederick Mondale (1977-1981),
Carter Administration, 1981

❧355❧

I think American labor unions get a large share of the credit for making us a middle-class country.

George Frederick Will, editor, author, columnist, news and
political commentator, 1977 Pulitzer Prize for commentary

❧356❧

We created the middle-class. We redistributed the wealth of America in peaceful fashion.

Scott Molloy, labor educator, 1966

❧357❧

All that is necessary for the forces of evil to win in the world is for good men to do nothing.

Edmund Burke (1729-1797), English essayist, philosopher,
politician, attributed

❧358❧

Why should we get involved? Why should my child learn about what happened to workers a hundred years ago? If these children don't under-stand and appreciate the struggles of their parents, grandparents and great-grandparents, they may be doomed to fight the same battles over again.

Fred Kaltenstein, labor educator

❧359❧

The history of the labor movements needs to be taught in every school in this land. ... America is a living testimonial to what free men and women, organized in free democratic trade unions can do to make a better life. ... We ought to be proud of it!

Vice President Hubert Horatio Humphrey, Jr. (1965-1969),
Lyndon Johnson Administration

❖360❖

Our cause is a common one. It is war between poverty and wealth. ... This moneyed power is fast eating up the substance of the people. We have made war upon it, and we mean to win it. If we can, we will win through the ballot box; if not, then we shall resort to sterner means.

William Sylvis, in *History of the American Working Class*, 1927

❖361❖

Here you will tread upon a spark, but there and there, behind you and in front of you, and everywhere, flames blaze up. It is a subterranean fire. You cannot put it out.

August Spies

❖362❖

All great reforms, great movements, come from the bottom and not the top.

Governor John Peter Altgeld (D-Ill., 1892-1896), 1892

❖363❖

The trade-union movement is the only class movement in the country or the world.

Samuel Gompers, 1894 speech

❖364❖

As with any body of thought facing opposition, the words may die on the lips should arms not be raised together in action.

Marc Worthington, writer

❖365❖

People don't get opportunity or freedom or equality or dignity as an act of charity; they have to fight for it, force it out of the establishment.

Saul Alinsky

❖366❖

As sure as a man will raise his hand by some instinct, to shield himself against a blow, so surely will workingmen, instinctively, periodically, gather into unions. The Union is the arm that Labor instinctively throws up to screen its head.

Daniel DeLeon, Socialist Labor Party leader,
in *The Bending Cross*, 1949

→367←

Small fry are no longer small when they begin to organize. They take on purpose and power.

Heywood Broun, in *Men Who Lead Labor*, 1937

→368←

Stripped to its essentials, what the labor movement is all about is power, the power for workers to confront management at the job site, across the bargaining table or in the political arena on equal footing. And it is that fundamental of gaining power, a power workers have only achieved through collective action, that is the basis of the union movement.

Arthur Osborne

→369←

The business of collective bargaining is about power.

Mark Brooks, United Paperworkers International Union (UPIU)

→370←

If their union cannot help and protect them, their experience has been that no one else will.

John L. Lewis

→371←

Self-interest is the only principle upon which individuals or groups will act as if they are same.

[Asa] A. Philip Randolph (1889-1979),
founder and first president of the first successful black union, the
Brotherhood of Sleeping Car Porters, pioneer and activist of
civil rights movement, 1919

→372←

There is nothing fairer than workmen having unions for their mutual benefit.

Will Rogers (1879-1935), humorist, political commentator,
journalist, actor, 1934, in *Freedom of the Press*, 1935

→373←

The working millions, in all the ages, have been horses—were horses; all they needed was a capable leader to organize their strength and tell them how to use it, and they would in that moment be master.

Mark Twain, in speech, 3/22/1886

→374←

Speak up for people who cannot speak for themselves. Protect the rights of all who are helpless. Speak for them and be a righteous judge. Protect the rights of the poor and needy.

Proverbs 31: 8-9, Holy Bible, Revised Standard Edition, 1953,
Old Testament Section, 1952

→ **Asa Philip Randolph**, 1889-1979, Crescent City, Florida

A. Philip Randolph, a prominent African-American labor leader, tirelessly advocated for equality and fairness for black laborers. In 1917 he began *The Messenger*, a monthly magazine for railroad unions and black activism, and he organized a small union of New York City elevator operators. After several difficult years of fierce opposition from the Pullman Company, he founded the Brotherhood of Sleeping Car Porters (1925), the nation's first successful black trade union. With Randolph its first president (1925-1968), the union quickly won shorter hours and higher pay for the workers.

A. Philip Randolph, c. 1960s. Walter P. Reuther Library, Wayne State University.

In 1941, Randolph organized the March on Washington Movement to protest job discrimination. Although the march was never held, the movement helped to establish the federal Fair Employment Practices Committee. Under President Franklin D. Roosevelt, Randolph led the call to bar discrimination in the defense industries and was a driving force under President Truman to ban segregation in the armed forces. Randolph also was director of the 1963 March on Washington for Jobs and Freedom, which featured Martin Luther King, Jr. In 1955 he was appointed a vice president of the AFL-CIO and, in 1964, received the Presidential Medal of Freedom. The A. Philip Randolph Institute, of which he was a founder in 1964, helps promote understanding and cooperation between labor and the black community. ✦

✦375✦

An old fighter in the ranks of labor, a trade unionist from way back when the going was rough, who indoctrinated his boys when they were pretty young and told them the most important thing in the world to fight for was the other guy, the brotherhood of man, the golden rule.

Walter Reuther, on his father,
Val Reuther, in *The Brothers Reuther*, 1976

✦376✦

People didn't elect me to this job to be the master of ceremonies. People don't want Bert Parks to run the union; they want the Ayatollah Khomeini. When they get into a fight with management, they don't want Johnny Carson to show up, they want the toughest guy on the block to show up.

Domenic Bozzotto, 1988

✦377✦

The son-of-a-bitch from the Union Hall.

Introduction on the business card of Teamster
Vice President Doug Sims

✦378✦

Only when working people are organized into unions they control can they even decide what they want.

David Montgomery, worker, in *On Strike For Respect: The Clerical and
Technical Workers' Strike at Yale University, 1984-1985*, 1988

✦379✦

If you don't stand for something—you'll fall for anything.

Labor slogan found on T-shirts, placards

✦380✦

The bitterness with which employers oppose the organization of women furnishes the best evidence of their present value in supplying them with ignorant, unthinking and consequently cheap laborers.

Ida Van Etten, labor activist, suffragette, 1891, in *Women and the
American Labor Movement*, 1982

✦381✦

A woman's place is in her union.

Slogan of Coalition of Labor Union Women (CLUW)

✦382✦

Organize the Unorganized!

> Popular battle cry of the CIO, coined by John L. Lewis, 1935

✦383✦

I suppose the urge to serve the labor movement was born in me.

> Tom Mooney, militant IWW leader, in *Frame Up*, 1967

✦384✦

As an organizer I start from where the world is, as it is, not as I would like it to be.

> Saul Alinsky, *Rules for Radicals*, 1972

✦385✦

Perhaps because I've made more mistakes than anybody else, I've had a chance to learn more than anybody else. But still, the workers teach me every single day as I teach them.

> Cesar Chavez, in *Cesar Chavez: Autobiography of La Causa*, 1975

✦386✦

We also had some great victories in 1973 in the melons and tomatoes. They're obscure because people think in terms of signed contracts, but if they think in terms of organizing people and getting their response, they're good.

> Cesar Chavez, in *Cesar Chavez: Autobiography of La Causa*, 1975

✦387✦

Fear is a powerful force. In organizing, fear can be a negative force or it can be a powerful force for organizing [workers].

> Phil Primack, reporter

✦388✦

You take an immigrant who comes here. I leave my country, I go to America. I don't know the country, the language, the culture. I have to start a brand-new life in middle age and survive. Now, if I can do that, taking on the boss is a walk in the park.

> Domenic Bozzotto, 1988

✦389✦

Invariably right things get done for the wrong reasons. So the (labor) organizer looks for wrong reasons to get right things done.

> Saul Alinsky

→390←

They're sex workers, and they deserve the same treatment as other working people.

Sanda Steinbauer, SEIU organizer, on the successful union
organizing of strippers in a San Francisco club, 1996

→391←

Why should we worry about organizing groups of people who do not appear to want to be organized? If they prefer to have others speak for them and make the decisions which affect their lives without effective participation on their part, that is their right.

George Meany

→392←

I don't want to hear of apathy! It's your job to motivate the membership. We're the evangelists, we're the missionaries. ... We must elevate the understanding—to stand up to the bosses!

Moe Biller, president (1980-) American Postal Workers Union
(APWU), discussing the role of union officers and editors

→393←

Don't criticize ... organize!

T-shirt slogan

→394←

Don't Whine, Organize!

Saul Alinsky

→395←

If the strong combine, why should not the weak?

Peter McGuire (1852-1906), carpenter, founder and first
secretary of United Brotherhood of Carpenters and
Joiners Union (UBCJU), and a founder of AFL
(*see* 1888 calendar, pages 11, 74, 118)

→396←

The CIO has not opposed the craft unions, or their development, except in mass production industries where their jurisdictional claims are at best but theoretical. ... There is a place for both forms of trade unionism in a progressive and militant labor movement.

John L. Lewis, in advocating the merging of the AFL and CIO

❧397❧

All sinners belong in Church, all unions belong in the AFL-CIO.

Lane Kirkland

❧398❧

Intelligent discontent is the mainspring of civilization. It is agitation or stagnation. I have taken my choice.

Eugene Debs

❧399❧

What can Labor do for itself? The answer is not difficult. Labor can organize, it can unify; it can consolidate its forces. This done, it can demand and command.

Eugene Debs, in *The Bending Cross*, 1949

❧400❧

Let your watchword be: Union and progress, and until then, no surrender.

Samuel Gompers

❧401❧

But today I take it that every intelligent person who has investigated this question, outside of the counsel for the State, understands that working-men have the right to organize; understands that if laborers are not satisfied with their conditions, they may stop work; they may stop work singly or collectively, exactly as they please, and no court will say them nay.

Clarence Darrow, 1898, in *Attorney for the Damned*, 1957

❧402❧

The new self-interest (monopoly) will remain unenforced in business until we invent the forms by which the vast multitudes who have been gathered together in modern production can organize themselves into a people there as in government.

Henry Demarest Lloyd (1840-1937), journalist, lecturer, author,
Wealth Against Commonwealth, 1894, in *Critics and Crusaders*, 1948

❧403❧

To organize unions in the 80s, you're going to need unions that are attractive to the unorganized. That means having a union, which is democratic, aggressive and effectively responds to employees' needs on the job and in the community.

Nancy Mills, executive director, SEIU, Boston

❧404❦

As long as people work for a living, they will form unions.

George Meany

❧405❦

I believe in the union. I believe in people being organized. God meant the people to stick together.

Lucy Taylor, brown lung victim, who helped win
settlement against J.P. Stevens

❧406❦

There is no hope for workingmen outside of organization.

Peter McGuire, c.1880s

❧407❦

We must carry on the good work of organization until we have every man working at the trade within our ranks.

Frank Duffy (1901-1948), general secretary, Brotherhood of
Carpenters and Joiners of America (UBCJA)

❧408❦

Those of us who have been involved in organizing realize that it is costly, it is difficult, but certainly no more difficult than for our forefathers 100 years ago.

Richard Kilroy, Railway & Airline Clerks, 14th Convention, 1981

❧409❦

Once I'm elected, I'll run into that wall. We'll run into it again and again— and pretty soon we'll start splitting it.

Ron Carey, Teamsters for a Democratic Union (TDU) on fighting
internal corruption, 1992

❧410❦

If I were a factory employee, a workman on the railroads or a wage earner of any sort, I would undoubtedly join the union of my trade. If I disapproved of its policy, if the union leaders were dishonest, I would join in order to put them out. I believe in the union and I believe that all men who are benefited by the union are morally bound to help to the extent of their power in the common interests advanced by the union.

President Theodore Roosevelt

❖411❖

We're not a lynch mob.

> Lane Kirkland, when asked of acceptance of Teamsters Union into
> the AFL-CIO, despite charges of corruption

❖412❖

It's not easy being Number One.

> Teamsters' billboard, on their membership

❖413❖

If you're not big enough to lose, you're not big enough to win.

> Walter Reuther

❖414❖

Let's be guided by the sincere desire to place the union's welfare above
any personal consideration or any personal differences.

> Walter Reuther, victory speech, 1946

❖415❖

When people start seeking in a movement their own individual status in
life, it ceases to be a movement and starts to become an enterprise.

> Eric Hoffer

❖416❖

Now that we are becoming powerful, we should not adopt the vices which
organized labor has forced the employer to discard.

> Terence Powderly, on the Noble Order of the Knights of Labor,
> 1886, in *History of the Working Class*, 1927

❖417❖

We cannot get our members more involved unless we send strong signals
that the union belongs to them, not to a few officials at headquarters.

> Ron Carey, president (1992-1997), IBT

❖418❖

The labor movement must consist of trade unionists and be controlled by
them.

> Samuel Gompers

✦419✦

We need to reestablish the moral authority of unions. ... (unions) must learn, tolerate and even embrace controversy, and generate creative friction that promotes progressive social change.

Michael Eisenscher, *Organizing in the '90's*

✦420✦

Change means movement. Movement means friction. Only in the friction-less vacuum of a nonexistent abstract world can movement or change occur without that abrasive friction of conflict.

Saul Alinsky

✦421✦

The great scandal of the nineteenth century is that the Church lost the working class.

Pope Pius XI, as reported by the Abbie Cardijn, founder of Jeunesse Ouvriere Catholique (JOC) or "Young Catholic Workers"

✦422✦

The Church as employer has great influence with the workers it employs, and it has too often in the past used that influence to dissuade workers from choosing union representation.

Thomas Donahue, 1982

✦423✦

[Cesar Chavez's organizing efforts] were deeply rooted in his Catholic faith and inspired by the gospel and the church's social teachings.

Cardinal Roger M. Mahony, archbishop of Los Angeles, shortly after Chavez's death in 1993

✦424✦

The great struggling unknown masses of the men who are at the base of everything are the dynamic force that is lifting the levels of society. A nation is as great, and only as great, as her rank and file.

President Woodrow Wilson, New York, 1913, in *Labor's Untold Story*, 1955

✦425✦

The most important resource of a union is its rank and file.

Ray Rogers, labor organizer

⇥426⇤

Much of labor's leadership has lost touch with the rank and file. First, unions need to do more than address economics; it must become a cultural thing. I'd buy a couple of six packs, hire a blues band, and people would come together.

Ralph Fasanella (1914-1977),
retired organizer, artist of labor themes

⇥427⇤

Less Rank More File

Placard from picketers on national carhaul contract talks,
1979, in *A Troublemaker's Handbook*, 1991

⇥428⇤

Labor leadership, new or established, does not create movements. It is the other way around. Seeds for change in the labor movement are sown among rank-and-file workers by the conditions forced upon them. It is from this ground, from among these seeds, that new leadership springs to lead the struggle for change.

James J. Matles and James Higgins, *Them and Us*, 1974

⇥429⇤

Return the union to the rank and file.

Campaign slogan of United Steelworkers of America's (USWA)
Ed Sadlowski in Chicago election

⇥430⇤

[It is not reformers who will end oppression]; it is the obscure Bill Jones on the firing line, with stink in his clothes, rebellion in his brain, hope in his heart, determination in his eye and direct action in his gnarled fist.

Big Bill Haywood

⇥431⇤

Power is not in what the establishment has but in what you think it has.

Saul Alinsky, *Rules for Radicals, Tactics*, 1971

⇥432⇤

When ye be an anvil, lay ye still; when ye be a hammer, strike with all thy will.

John L. Lewis

✦433✦

The intellectuals had learned that they were powerless by themselves and that they could not accomplish anything unless they made an alliance with the working class.

> Malcolm Cowley (1898-1989), editor, literary critic, on forming
> alliances after the 1929 stock market crash

✦434✦

At the banquet of nature, there are no reserved seats. You get what you can take and you keep what you can hold. If you can't take anything, you won't get anything. And you can't take anything without organization.

> A. Philip Randolph

✦435✦

No issue can be negotiated unless you first have the clout to compel negotiation.

> Saul Alinsky

✦436✦

Power is a good thing; it's better than powerlessness.

> Albert Shanker

"Don't let it throw you — It's Just a negotiating tactic."

Reprinted with permission, courtesy ©Patrick Hardin.

Reprinted with permission, courtesy ©Gary Huck.

⇥437⇤

The selfish greed of "in-your-face capitalism" will not be stopped by relying on the altruism of CEOs. ... As can be seen in our history, the only answer to a powerful business leader is a powerful labor union.

Hilton M. Weiss

⇥438⇤

The only effective answer to organized greed is organized labor.

Thomas Donahue

⇥439⇤

If an employer doesn't treat its employees fairly and with dignity, that employer will be unionized no matter what. ... If nothing else, the union movement does deserve credit for being the alternative for an employer that isn't enlightened.

Fred Long, industrial relations manager

→440←

Effective labor unions are still by far the most powerful force in society for the protection of the laborer's rights and the improvement of his or her condition. No amount of employer benevolence, no diffusion of a sympathetic attitude on the part of the public, no increase of beneficial legislation, can adequately supply for the lack of organization among the workers themselves.

Monsignor John A. Ryan, in *Organized Labor and the Church*, 1993

→441←

All tactics means is doing what you can with what you have.

Saul Alinsky

→442←

It's not just a matter of organizing a confrontation; it's a matter of disorganizing your adversary.

Robert Wages, president, Oil, Chemical, and Atomic Workers International Union (OCAW)

→443←

One of the real serious mistakes being made by labor through this country is that they allow the strikes to fight from their doorsteps. We're going to move it to the doorsteps of the power base.

Ray Rogers

→444←

We have the intelligence, we have the desire, and we have the people to do the organizing job that's necessary. If we use the opportunity, we can overcome the consultants—we can overcome the loopholes in the NLRB [National Labor Relations Board].

William H. Wynn, president, United Food and Commercial Workers International Union (UFCW)

→445←

They say no businessman or politician can sit on a hot seat if it becomes hot enough. We are going to make it very hot.

Ray Rogers, on using the Corporate Campaign for a striking company

→446←

We were never meant to be business unionists. You were never going to confront power by trying to play their game, in their field, by their rules.

Robert Wages

⇥447⇤

The hospital strikers have demonstrated that you don't get a job done unless you show the Man you're not afraid. ... If you're not willing to pay that price then you don't deserve the rewards or benefits that go along with it.

> Malcolm X (born Malcolm Little, changed to Al-Hajj Malik El-Shabazz, 1925-1965), author, black activist, Muslim religious leader, speaking to striking hospital workers, Local 1199, at a New York City rally, 7/22/1962

⇥448⇤

It's not anti-Harvard to be pro-union.

> Slogan for successful organizing drive to unionize Harvard University office workers, 1989

⇥449⇤

Smith workers are not forming a union to make Smith College management angry. They're doing it to make the college better.

> Kristine Rondeau, organizer, Smith College clerical workers

⇥450⇤

Labor should become a social and political movement to transform the United States into a country in which the majority, rather than a corporate minority, controls people's destiny. ... Labor must stop behaving as an interest group and become an anti-establishment movement, calling for profound political and economic reforms that would benefit the entire working class and other popular forces of this country.

> Vincent Navarro, educator

⇥451⇤

Every professional organization group has an organization. Doctors have the AMA. Lawyers have the ABA. Business executives have any organization they want. No one would ever dream of trying to stop doctors, lawyers and business executives from organizing. But in this country, resistance to the organization of workers happens all the time.

> Monsignor George G. Higgins, *Organized Labor and the Church*, 1993

⇥452⇤

Labor brought about the country's great social changes, and we need people to carry the torch. Unions must work from the outside and encourage activists. Protesters get action, not people who go home and watch TV.

> Ralph Fasanella

✦453✦

Organizing new workers into unions has to be the primary goal of the labor movement today. Even in a shifting economy, there are millions of workers in all sectors of the economy who need, want and deserve union representation.

Governor Bill Clinton
(D-Ark., 1979-1981 and 1983-1993), 1992

✦454✦

With a union representing doctors so that they can concentrate on health care and what's best for patients, patients can rest easy.

Robert L. Weinmann, M.D., president of the physician's union,
after Los Angeles County doctors voted to join the UAPD,
5/28/1999, *Los Angeles Times*

✦455✦

Does labor have a part to play? It depends on whether working people can get their act together and rebuild the labor movement and turn it into a powerful force for both people's rights and democracy as it once was. It's going to have to be rebuilt from the bottom up.

Noam Chomsky, linguist, educator, historian,
Keeping the Rabble In Line, 1994

✦456✦

The themes dignity and social justice, the process of rank and file engagement and initiative, the instinct for daring and experimentation, the reliance on broad alliances, popular pressure, are all woven through the heritage of American working people.

The authors, in *On Strike For Respect, The Clerical and Technical Workers'
Strike at Yale University, 1984-1985*, 1988

✦457✦

The odds against labor seem formidable today just as they seemed to us over fifty years ago. But the instincts and talents of workers on the job should never be underestimated. It was a simple strategy devised by a Chevrolet plant worker in 1937 that forced General Motors, the world's largest corporation, to accept—unwillingly—the first United Auto Workers contract.

Genora Johnson Dollinger, 1991, referring to the Great GM Sit-
down Strike of 1937, in *A Troublemaker's Handbook*, 1991

AFL-CIO SEIU President John Sweeney with SEIU officers Gilbert Cedillo and David Baker (left to right), 1992. Photograph courtesy Johnny A. Knox, staff photographer, SEIU Local 660, Los Angeles.

⇢458⇠

Organizing a union these days is like breeding pandas in captivity. If everything goes right, it can be done. Miracles do happen. But it's so difficult, so risky, so fraught with frustration and disappointment that fewer and fewer people are willing to try.

Thomas Donahue, 1995

⇢459⇠

Our young people need to think of union careers as earnestly as they do of business careers and professions.

Martin Luther King, Jr.

⇢460⇠

Every successful social movement in history, including the civil-rights movement, was run by young people. If the labor movement is going to succeed and grow again, they need to be a big part of it.

Richard Bensinger, AFL-CIO educator

→461←

Our big need is more education of the membership and the millions who ought to be members. The thirties were a long time ago. Today's workers don't remember. We have to show them that our labor movement has a great track record. Our social stability is built on it. It is the heart of America.

Harry Kaiser, labor liaison for
National Consumer Cooperative Bank, 1981

→462←

I believe the history books will show that the triumph today will play as important a role in American history as the mass organizing drives of the 1930s.

John J. Sweeney, president, AFL-CIO, and former president
(1980-1995) of SEIU, commenting on the vote of 70,000 service
workers who voted 10 to 1 to join the SEIU, 2/25/1999

Chapter 5

Solidarity Forever

❧463❧

Alone we're nothing, together we're everything—it's the whole philosophy of Labor.

> Leon Davis, president, Local 1199, founder of a small union of
> drugstore workers in 1932, becoming America's largest
> organization of health care workers

❧464❧

All life is interrelated. All men are caught in an inescapable network of mutuality, tied in a single garment of destiny. Whatever affects one directly, affects all indirectly.

> Martin Luther King, Jr.

❧465❧

United We Bargain, Divided We Beg

> Slogan, song title, and SEIU Local 250
> Health Care Workers' union button

❧466❧

We must all hang together, or, most assuredly we shall all hang separately.

> Benjamin Franklin to John Hancock, July 4, 1776

❧467❧

Some day, there will come the brotherhood of man. Some day, industrial warfare, as well as warfare between nations, will be seen to be ridiculous and a waste of life and money. Some day, men will work together in a grand cooperative scheme. But until that day, the trade union must stand as the only safeguard of the working man; the only instrument by which he can maintain himself and his family.

> Clarence Darrow

♦468♦

Free societies and free trade unions go together. And it's not an accident that a lot of the fire for what happened in Eastern European countries came out of a trade union, *Solidarity*.

> George Shultz, businessman, educator, Secretary of State
> (1982-1989), Reagan Administration, Secretary of the Treasury
> (1972-1973) and Secretary of Labor (1969-1970),
> Nixon Administration

♦469♦

Whereas, a struggle is going on in all the nations of the civilized world between the capitalist and the laborer, which grows in intensity from year to year, and will work disastrous results to the toiling millions if they are not combined for mutual protection and benefit.

> Preamble of the AFL constitution, dropped from the AFL-CIO
> unity constitution in 1955

♦470♦

While American culture has idolized the 'self-made' man since the days of Horatio Alger, a harsh reality is again teaching working men and women that, as an old time motto put it, 'Each for himself is the boss's plea, unity of all is the workers' key.'

> Peter Rachleff

♦471♦

What a union representative should never forget is the power of the men behind him.

> Harry Bridges

♦472♦

Today, we say that when you pick a fight with any of us, you pick a fight with all of us! And that when you push us, we will push back.

> Richard Trumka, secretary-treasurer, AFL-CIO, 10/26/1995

♦473♦

The power of the capitalists is based on property, they have the laws, the army, everything! In spite of all that, the workers have something still more powerful. The workers' power ... is the common bond of solidarity.

> Joseph Ettor

✦ **Fannie Coralie "Frances" Perkins**, 1882-1965, Boston, Massachusetts

After graduating from Mount Holyoke College in 1902, Frances Perkins taught in Chicago. With a master's degree in social economics from Columbia University, she entered the field of social work and was appointed secretary of the New York Consumers League in 1910. Perkins became an authority on industrial hazards, hygiene, and working conditions. She investigated factory working conditions, particularly those of women and children, and lobbied for better working environments and shorter workweeks.

Secretary of Labor Frances Perkins stands behind President Franklin D. Roosevelt at the signing of the Social Security Act, 8/14/1935. Courtesy George Meany Memorial Archives.

Beginning in 1919 she served on industrial commissions, working in the administrations of New York Governors Al Smith and Franklin D. Roosevelt and, when Roosevelt became President in 1933, he appointed Perkins his Secretary of Labor. She was the first woman named to a U.S. Cabinet post, serving in all of Roosevelt's four terms. Her position allowed her to champion Social Security, the abolition of child labor, relief work programs, minimum wage and maximum-hour legislation, and the standardization of state industrial laws. Perkins was a member of the U.S. Civil Service Commission (1946-1952) and authored several books including *The Roosevelt I Knew*, 1946. ✦

✦474✦

... a solid bloc of people united to one another by unbreakable bonds which give them power and status to deal with their employers' terms.

Frances [Fannie Coralie] Perkins, pioneer of social security,
Secretary of Labor (1933-1945), Franklin D. Roosevelt
Administration, defining trade unions

✦475✦

Thank God, none of us know our place, and that the fight for equality and justice and workers' rights continues to go on. We are fueled daily by those who would take advantage of unorganized people without the strength of solidarity.

Eleanor C. Smeal, administrator, feminist, president, National
Organization for Women (NOW), president, Feminist
Foundation, 1981

✦476✦

To help organize in the best way, unions cannot be competing against one another. We need to act like Wobblies, as one big union.

Glennis Ter Wisscha, one of the Willmar 8, participants in a 1979
strike against the Willmar Bank, 1985

✦477✦

Teamwork in the Leadership and Solidarity in the Ranks

UAW slogan

✦478✦

Only organize and stand together. Claim something together, and at once; let the nation hear a united demand from the laboring voice, and then, when you have got that, go on after another; but get something.

Wendell Phillips (1811-1884), abolitionist leader, orator,
reformist, women's and labor rights advocate

✦479✦

Hold the fort for we are coming,
Union men be strong,
Side by side we battle onward,
Unity will come.

Knights of Labor song, 1885, in *The Great Divide*, 1988

Members of the Amalgamated Clothing Workers of America strike after their employer, Farah Company, imported clothing, threatening their jobs. Their call for demonstrators drew widespread union support. Placards in front of May Company, Los Angeles, identified such participating unions as: Broadcast Technicians; Communication Workers; Farm Workers; Federal Employees; Firefighters; Glass Bottle Blowers; Hotel and Restaurant Employees; Hatters and Millinery Workers; Insurance; Machinists and Aerospace; Masters, Mates and Pilots; Office Workers; Oil and Chemical; Railway Clerks; Rubber Workers; Seafarers; Service Employees; Sheet Metal; Steelworkers; Stereotypers; Stove and Furnace; and Transport Workers, 6/14/1973. Photograph by Cliff Kalick studio, courtesy Southern California Library for Social Studies and Research, Los Angeles.

❧480❧

It is a great mistake for any class of laborers to isolate itself and thus weaken the bond of brotherhood between those on whom the burdens and hardships of labor [fall].

Frederick Douglass, *Frederick Douglass*, 1991

❧481❧

Solidarity is necessary; division is the surest means to lose the strike. Remember always that you are workers with interests against those of the mill owners. ... There are but two races, the race of useful members of society and the race of useless ones.

Joseph Ettor, during Lawrence Mill Strike, 1912

❧482❧

When we put out a brochure, we may have a labor fight with a company, but we'll also talk about the company's environmental problems, their links to South Africa, their violations of equal rights, you name it. We hang out all the dirty linen, because we're helping to build allies and making people realize that this isn't only a labor struggle; it goes much further.

Ray Rogers

❧483❧

We are concerned with the welfare of all peoples of the world. We are a nation of immigrants. And to turn our backs on people who are fleeing from oppression, fleeing for their lives, and say to them 'we are going to dump them in the sea'—this to me is about as contrary to American tradition as anything that I ever heard of.

George Meany

❧484❧

Labor Solidarity Has No Borders

From a mural by Mike Alewitz, on Southern California Library for Social Studies and Research building, Los Angeles, 1990

❧485❧

The workers have nothing to lose in this but their chains. They have the world to gain. Workers of the world unite!

Karl Marx (1818-1883), German economist, political theorist, social philosopher, revolutionary, ushered modern communism

→486←

Workers of the World, Unite!

IWW slogan

→487←

By and large, we were decent men and women who fought the day-to-day battles, took the blows, and shed the blood that made today's labor movement possible, a movement that could profit from a fresh infusion of Wobbly commitment to social justice. We made mistakes, but were destroyed as an organization only because we were too successful. We made our mark.

Henry McGuckin, organizer, Industrial Workers of the World
(IWW or Wobblies), Memoirs of a Wobbly, 1987

→488←

The greatest enemy of the union-busting process is unity of solidarity and a strong commitment and belief in what the employees are doing.

Martin Jay Levitt

→489←

You can't have solidarity with sheep.

Anonymous

→490←

Solidarity is not a matter of sentiment, but of fact, cold and impassive as the granite foundations of a skyscraper. If the basic elements, identity of interest, clarity of vision, honesty of intent, and oneness of purpose, or any of these is lacking, all sentimental pleas for solidarity, and all other efforts to achieve it will be barren of results.

Eugene Debs

→491←

It is we who plowed the prairies,
    built the cities where they trade.
Dug the mines and built the workshops,
    endless miles where railroads laid;
Now we stand outcast and starving
    'mid the wonders we have made,
But the union makes us strong.

Ralph Chaplin lyrics from song, Solidarity Forever

⇨492⇦

An injury to one is the concern of all.

Terence Powderly

⇨493⇦

The lessons of all the ages upon this point is, that a wrong done to one man is a wrong done to all men. It may be ... delayed, but so sure as there is a moral government of the universe, so sure will the harvest of evil come.

Frederick Douglass

⇨494⇦

It says something about the labor movement in America when both pianists Van Cliburn and Jerry Lee Lewis are in the same union.

Mark Russell, political humorist and commentator, songwriter

⇨495⇦

You must either reach down and lift them up, or they will reach up and pull you down.

Joseph Ettor addressing skilled workers in support of
unity with unskilled workers

⇨496⇦

A union movement in America will always be a scandal. ... The subversive thing about labor is not the strike, but the idea of Solidarity.

Thomas Geoghegan, *Which Side Are You On?*, 1991

⇨497⇦

Reaffirming the importance of community is a way, both symbolically and politically, of challenging the dominance of corporation, market and job over everything else of value in society.

David O. Moberg, journalist

⇨498⇦

We must share in the problems of our city even if we have moved our families out to the suburbs. We owe something to the city where we make our bread. We must put something back.

Severino Biagioni, Boston Packinghouse local president, on Union
Community Involvement, in *Out of the Jungle*, 1968

Striking SEIU janitors thank tenants for their support, Los Angeles. Photograph courtesy Johnny A. Knox, staff photographer, SEIU Local 660, Los Angeles.

✢499✢

I know this is the culture of narcissism, and that community, solidarity, etc., are on the way out. But if labor laws changed, if we had laws like France or Poland, I think Americans would join unions like crazy, simply out of self-interest, raw, Reaganite self-interest.

Thomas Geoghegan, *Which Side Are You On?*, 1991

✢500✢

When the Union's inspiration through the workers' blood
     shall run
There can be no power greater anywhere beneath the sun.
Yet what force on earth is weaker than the feeble
     strength of one?
But the union makes us strong.

Ralph Chaplin song, *Solidarity Forever*

✢501✢

One element remains essential—true and lasting solidarity. Solidarity remains the indispensable key to the future.

Lane Kirkland

✦502✦

If the union doesn't exist with workplace, it doesn't exist.

Sam Gindin, official, Canadian Auto Workers

✦503✦

In light of this fundamental structure of all work ... in light of the fact that, labor and capital are indispensable components of the process of production in any social system ... it is clear that even if it is because of their work needs that people unite to secure their rights, their union remains a constructive factor of social order and solidarity, and it is impossible to ignore it.

Pope John Paul II

✦504✦

You are the ones who can say the word Solidarity. And call each other comrades. The oppressor can claim nothing—but his greed.

Mother Jones, *The Autobiography of Mother Jones*, 1925

✦505✦

We believe 'Solidarity' means sticking together, not getting stuck together.

John J. Sweeney

✦506✦

What is it that makes a union indestructible? It isn't wages and hours alone. It is that union men are free men. Union towns are free towns.

John Brophy, in *Labor Baron—A Portrait of John L. Lewis*, 1944

✦507✦

Men who will not fight together are traitors to each other. I am tolerant of difference of opinion. I am willing that everybody should have a hearing as any man should, but in the face of a battle no division can be tolerated.

Samuel Gompers

✦508✦

The strength of a labor group remains within its own hands. No sort of legislation will work for weak unions. 'Them as has gets.'

Heywood Broun, in *Men Who Lead Labor*, 1937

✦509✦

They can testify … the ones who drive the trucks. Because they were in a union, they couldn't be fired except for 'just cause.' They, unlike the supervisors, could stroll into court, testify, and just walk past the Boss and wave.

Thomas Geoghegan, *Which Side Are You On?*, 1991

✦510✦

When labor speaks of free medical care, it is saying we need it for blacks who do not have it and whites who are concerned that they will have to pay for giving it to them. When labor calls for full employment, it is talking about blacks who are without jobs and whites who want to protect the ones they have. When labor says we must build more homes, it is seeking to create a society where the black brother need not be enraged because he does not have a home and the white need not fear for the home he has.

Bayard Rustin (1910-1987), black social activist and a founding member of Congress of Racial Equality (CORE) and Southern Christian Leadership Conference (SCLC), civil rights organizer, Fellowship of Reconciliation, field and race relations secretary (1941-1953), in *Overcoming Middle Class Rage*, 1971

✦511✦

It would add infinitely to the significance and glory of Labor Day, if it should be, as it was designed to be, a day upon which all lines dividing labor, real or ideal, should be obscured and the supreme law of brother-hood have full sway.

Eugene Debs, 1895

✦512✦

Whatever their faults, unions have been the only powerful and effective voice working people have ever had in the history of this country, and this town knows that more than any other.

Bruce Springsteen, rock musician, songwriter, supporting Detroit newspaper strikers, 1996

✦513✦

The first thing I want to say to you as individuals and as a movement—if you're going to be something, if you're going to do something, you have to be proud of yourself. And you have to be proud of your heritage as a Labor Movement just as you are proud of your family, or your religion, or whatever else it might be.

Senator Hubert H. Humphrey (D-Minn., 1949-1964)

UE Local 201 members from Lynn GE join in support of striking Lowell GE picketers, 1/21/1946. Eventually, workers in 75 GE plants joined the strike, one of the largest labor actions of the postwar period. Courtesy Print Department, Boston Public Library.

❧514❧

The 14 million members of the unions of the AFL-CIO differ from other Americans only in one way—they carry a union card.

George Meany (In 1999, the AFL-CIO was comprised of 68 unions with approximately 13 million members.)

❧515❧

Today, workers in declining industries keep their unions as merged segments of larger organizations which are better able to serve them. Every merger broadens and strengthens the entire labor movement.

Lane Kirkland, 1980

❧516❧

There are those who say that the labor movement has lost its momentum. Let them recall the hundreds of thousands who marched on Solidarity Day.

Senator Edward Moore Kennedy (D-Mass., 1963-), 11/18/1981

→517←

In order to achieve social justice in the various parts of the world, in the various countries and in the relationships between them, there is a need for ever new movements of solidarity of the workers and with the workers.

Pope John Paul II, on *Human Work (Laborem Exercens)*

→518←

Often, when the younger generation in the union wants to learn about the 30s, they're always left with the impression that all the exciting and great battles are behind us. But it will be said of you that you performed an equally historic function, in helping the membership reclaim its great union.

Victor Reuther, labor leader, author, 1989

→519←

Unions will continue to be the social conscience. I believe our charge will carry us well into the 21st century, 'cause there's nobody around who can protect people and be the social conscience any better.

Paul Anderson, unionist, in *For Labor's Sake*, 1995

Chapter 6

The Law

❖520❖

In the year 1800 the United States government considered workers
organizing into unions a conspiracy, punishable by sentencing to jail.
Today the same government recognizes the worth of the American worker
and permits the organization of workers into unions and protects them
under the law.

> Massachusetts AFL-CIO, in *Learning About Labor*, early 1980s

❖521❖

The merchants may agree upon their prices; the lawyers upon their fees;
the physicians upon their charges; the manufacturers upon the wages
given to their operatives; but the *laborer* shall not consult his interest and
fix the price of his toil and skill. If this be the *law*, it is unjust, oppressive
and wicked.

> John Greenleaf Whittier (1807-1892), poet, abolitionist, editor,
> writer, in *A Pictorial History of American Labor*, 1972

❖522❖

When the laws undertake to make the rich richer and the potent more
powerful, the humble members of society—the farmers, mechanics and
laborers—have a right to complain of the injustice of their government.

> President Andrew Jackson (1829-1837)

❖523❖

Public officials have only words of warning to us—warning that we must
be intensely orderly and must be intensely peaceable, and they have the
workhouse just back of all their warnings. The strong hand of the law
beats us back when we rise into the conditions that make life bearable.

> Rose Schneiderman, 1911

❖524❖

Justice is incidental to law and order.

> John Edgar Hoover (1895-1972), criminologist,
> director (1924-1972), Federal Bureau of Investigation

❧525❧

[Trade unions are] a mouthpiece for the struggle for social justice.

Pope John Paul II

❧526❧

And who but an enemy of organized labor would advocate the enactment of a law that so much as squints at depriving organized labor of the only weapon it possesses of maintaining its rights against those whose policy is oppression?

Eugene Debs, commenting on the Espionage Act of 1917, curtailing free speech, which had the effect of ousting labor leaders through prosecution for voicing opposition to U.S. involvement in the World War, 1917

❧527❧

Without the right to freely organize and bargain collectively, workers have no say in their own destiny.

Stanley M. Smith, secretary-treasurer of San Francisco Building and Construction Trades Council

❧528❧

Employees shall have the right to organize and bargain collectively through representatives of their own choosing.

National Labor Relations Act (NLRA) of 1935, more popularly known as the Wagner Act after its author, Robert Ferdinand Wagner, Sr. (D-N.Y., 1927-1949)

❧529❧

The law is on our side!

John L. Lewis, on the right to organize and bargain collectively under the just enacted NLRA, 1935, in *High Treason*, 1950

❧530❧

Long ago we stated the reason for labor organizations. We said that union was essential to give laborers opportunity to deal on an equality with their employer.

U.S. Supreme Court, *NLRB v. Jones & Laughlin Steel Corp.*, *301 U.S. 1*, 1937

❧531❧

We'll bargain till hell freezes over, but they won't get a goddamn thing.

Harry Bennett, CEO of Ford Motor Company, on being ordered to bargain by NLRB, 1941

✣532✣

The unlawful refusal of an employer to bargain collectively with its employees' chosen representatives disrupts the employees' morale, deters their organizational activities and discourages their membership in unions.

Justice Hugo Lafayette Black (1886-1971), Senator (D-Ala., 1927-1937), appointed by Franklin D. Roosevelt (1937), *Frank Bros. v. NLRB, 321 U.S. 702, 704,* 1944

✣533✣

The Taft-Hartley statute [1947] is the first ugly, savage thrust of Fascism in America. It came into being through an alliance between industrialists and the Republican majority in Congress, aided and abetted by those Democratic legislators who still believe in the institution of human slavery.

John L. Lewis

✣534✣

Now comes the Taft-Hartley Act ... in America, where we always believed heretofore that we had a free labor movement.

John L. Lewis

✣535✣

If you would use the power of the state to restrain me, as an agent of labor, then, sir, I submit, that you should use the same power to restrain my adversary in this issue, who is an agent of capital.

John L. Lewis, to FDR, about a strike against U.S. Steel, when strikes were discouraged due to the war effort, 1941, in *Labor Baron—A Portrait of John L. Lewis,* 1944, and in *The World of the Worker,* 1980

✣536✣

It is a sad commentary upon our form of government when every decision of the Supreme Court seems designed to fatten Capital and destroy Labor.

John L. Lewis, in *Words for Workers in Changing Times,* 1993

✣537✣

The right to join a union of one's choice is unquestioned today and is sanctioned and protected by law.

President Harry S. Truman

❖538❖

Only a fool would try to deprive working men and women of the right to join the union of their choice.

President Dwight David Eisenhower (1953-1961), general and
Allied Supreme Commander in World War II

❖539❖

Why encourage collective bargaining? Simply stated, because there is an overriding national interest in assuring fair and decent labor standards and the collective bargaining system is the surest means to that end that does not require further government regulation.

Thomas Donahue

❖540❖

Grievance machinery under a collective bargaining agreement is at the very heart of the system of industrial self-government.

Justice William Orville Douglas (1898-1980), longest serving
justice (1939-1975), 1960

❖541❖

No issue is more important for the future than the procedures through which the legal framework of collective bargaining evolves.

John Thomas Dunlop, Secretary of Labor (1975-1976), Ford
Administration, educator, author, mediator, arbiter

❖542❖

Many long and expensive strikes have grown out of disagreements not primarily related to compensation but to the structure of bargaining.

John T. Dunlop

❖543❖

Laws that define workers' basic legal rights don't necessarily assure that workers can exercise these rights free of coercion. ... Collective bargaining is the only American institution that gives workers the ability to claim both kinds of protection—from outside and inside.

John Hoerr, labor-management journalist, 1991

❖544❖

The contract is written and then it gets interpreted.

Thomas C. Graham, chairman, CEO, USX Corporation/Clairton
Works, in *Words for Workers in Changing Times*, 1993

❧545❧

Some men rob you with a six-gun—others rob you with a fountain pen.

Woody Guthrie (1912-1967), folksinger, songwriter, social
activist, columnist, author

❧546❧

In the old days all you needed was a handshake. Nowadays you need forty lawyers.

Jimmy Hoffa, in *Hoffa: The Real Story*, 1975

❧547❧

Taft can dig it, and Hartley can haul it, but I'm gonna
leave it in the ground.

United Mine Workers of America slogan, after Taft-Hartley strike
injunction law was imposed, 1977, in *Overtime*, 1990

❧548❧

The labor laws of our country, of the United States, have been written to protect our nation and at the same time to protect the rights of the workers.

President James Earl "Jimmy" Carter (1977-1981), 3/6/1978

❧549❧

As president, I call on the mine workers, the coal-mine operators and all Americans to join in a common effort under the law to protect our country, to preserve the health and safety of our people, and to resolve fairly the differences which have already caused so much suffering and division in our land.

President Jimmy Carter, message in invoking the
Taft-Hartley Act, 3/6/1978

❧550❧

In hundreds of cities, on many occasions, local labor leaders and rank and filers have been confronted with injunctions. Their experiences, while diverse in details, have all had the same bottom line; that only by defying injunctions has the labor movement made any progress at all.

Peter Rachleff

✦551✦

First and foremost, it is important to recognize that employers turn to injunctions as a weapon of last resort. They would prefer to handle their labor conflicts more directly and out of the glare of the public eye. So when we see an employer seeking an injunction we should realize that this is a sign of the strength of the union involved. The employer is admitting that he cannot defeat the union in a head-to-head battle.

Peter Rachleff

✦552✦

American labor laws are not self-enforcing, so unions have an important role in helping government agencies monitor compliance.

[Frederick] Ray Marshall, labor scholar, author, Secretary of Labor
(1977-1981), Carter Administration

✦553✦

Laws tend to work best where unions are present to make sure the laws are enforced. The fact is, nonunion employees are at greater risk of suffering from employer abuses—no matter what the letter of the law may say. At the same time, a panoply of standardized government-imposed rules administered by government agencies is likely to be a greater obstacle to managerial flexibility than unions ever were.

John Hoerr, 1991

✦554✦

Breaking the law, i.e., firing people, is absurdly cheap. Like jaywalking. The best deal in America, in cold business terms.

Thomas Geoghegan, on employers defying the National Labor
Relations Board in organizing drives, *Which Side Are You On?*, 1991

✦555✦

Only in America does the law allow management free rein to terrorize workers who seek to stand up for themselves.

Thomas Donahue

✦556✦

[It was] the violation of the rights of workers ... that led to the fundamental crisis of systems claiming to express the rule and, indeed, the dictatorship of the working class.

Pope John Paul II, in *Centesimus Annus*, 1991

⇥557⇤

(Right-to-Work laws) are a virtual conspiracy of the crafty, the ignorant, or the misguided to subvert industrial peace, exploit men's need to work and deluge the community with industrial irresponsibility. 'Right-to-Work' laws do not create jobs; they only victimize the worker and make his organization ineffective.

> Reverend Dr. Walter George Muelder, educator, economist,
> ethicist, dean of Boston University School of Theology

⇥558⇤

The merchandisers of 'right-to-work' are fond of packaging their proposal in the name of individual liberty. What right-to-work has meant wherever it has appeared is lower wages and benefits, a diminished standard of living and substandard legal protection for workers and their families.

> Joseph Faherty, president, Mass. AFL-CIO

⇥559⇤

The fact is that when workers can see their one small piece of the American dream ripped out of their hands, all of us are threatened, every job is at risk, and every American has to know that they could be next.

> Richard Trumka, on the Striker Replacement Bill

⇥560⇤

The right to strike is the only legal means workers have of bringing economic pressure to bear on employers to protect their wages and working conditions. The right to permanently replace striking workers reduces the right to strike to the right to be fired.

> Congressman William Clay

⇥561⇤

The permanent replacement of striking workers is both bad economic policy and morally reprehensible. It is a policy that rewards employers for failing to settle labor disputes at the bargaining table and forces workers into the streets.

> Congressman William Clay

⇥562⇤

The thing about this practice of lining up permanent replacements is it nullifies the inherent obligation of an employer ... to bargain in good faith.

> Lane Kirkland, 1991

❧563❧

This country needs, and I support, Labor Law Reform.

President Jimmy Carter, 1980

❧564❧

When workers make concessions to keep companies afloat, it's wrong for companies to use bankruptcy laws to bust unions.

Vice President Walter Mondale

❧565❧

We need to make this economy more competitive. But we need more high wages; we don't need a low-wage strategy, we need a high-wage strategy. ... I'm not for repealing Davis-Bacon.

President William Jefferson "Bill" Clinton (1993-2001), supporting the prevailing-wage law, 4/1995

❧566❧

A local president, it seemed to me, had everybody after him, if he were doing his job: Inland, Pittsburgh, the Daley Machine, Vrdolyak, the Labor Department in Washington, the assholes in his own local. ... I wanted to spend my whole life representing these guys.

Thomas Geoghegan (labor lawyer), *Which Side Are You On?*, 1991

❧567❧

When people ask me, 'Why can't labor organize the way it did in the thirties?' the answer is simple: everything we did then is now illegal.

Thomas Geoghegan, *Which Side Are You On?*, 1991

Chapter 7

Civil Rights

❖568❖

Every advance in this half-century—Social Security, civil rights, Medicare, aid to education, one after another—came with the support and leadership of American Labor.

President Jimmy Carter, 1980

❖569❖

America did not invent human rights. In a very real sense, human rights invented America.

President Jimmy Carter

❖570❖

It was the tradesmen who came to the legislature to plead the cause of public education, for they realized that their sons and their daughters would forever remain slaves to an industrial machine unless given equal opportunity for education with the sons and daughters of the wealthy.

Horace Mann

❖571❖

When the rest of the nation accepted rank discrimination and prejudice as ordinary and usual—like the rain, to be deplored but accepted as part of nature—trade unions, particularly the CIO, leveled all barriers to equal membership.

Martin Luther King, Jr., *Where Do We Go From Here?:*
Chaos or Community, 1967

❖572❖

Black people, brown people, they're all part of the union. If you don't like it, then get out, but we're not going to change it.

Cesar Chavez, in *Cesar Chavez: Autobiography of La Causa*, 1975

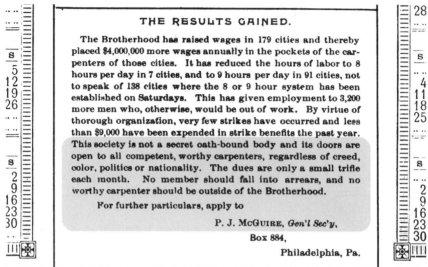

THE RESULTS GAINED.

The Brotherhood has raised wages in 179 cities and thereby placed $4,000,000 more wages annually in the pockets of the carpenters of those cities. It has reduced the hours of labor to 8 hours per day in 7 cities, and to 9 hours per day in 91 cities, not to speak of 138 cities where the 8 or 9 hour system has been established on Saturdays. This has given employment to 3,200 more men who, otherwise, would be out of work. By virtue of thorough organization, very few strikes have occurred and less than $9,000 have been expended in strike benefits the past year. This society is not a secret oath-bound body and its doors are open to all competent, worthy carpenters, regardless of creed, color, politics or nationality. The dues are only a small trifle each month. No member should fall into arrears, and no worthy carpenter should be outside of the Brotherhood.

For further particulars, apply to

P. J. McGuire, *Gen'l Sec'y*,
Box 884,
Philadelphia, Pa.

Detail from Brotherhood of Carpenters and Joiners of America 1888 calendar stating the union's "open to all" policy (*see* calendar page 11). Courtesy George Meany Memorial Archives.

⇥573⇤

Labor's commitment to human rights for all carries no ideological or doctrinaire label; it is a natural outgrowth of labor's day-to-day role in the world of work. Without freedom of speech, freedom of the press, freedom of assembly, the right to petition for the redress of grievances, unions could not function or even begin to organize. Workers would be, as they have been through most of history, at the mercy of those who would employ them.

Statement: *Human Rights Role in Organized Labor*, AFL-CIO

⇥574⇤

We need the force of law to carry out our own principles.

George Meany, on the prospective 1964 Civil Rights Act, 1963

⇥575⇤

The struggle for equal rights and opportunities has been a long one and American labor has always been in its forefront.

W. J. Usery, Jr., Secretary of Labor (1976-1977),
Ford Administration

⇥576⇤

The labor movement has led the fight for progressive social legislation from civil rights to Social Security and minimum wage laws.

Ray Marshall

⇥577⇤

Many of the values embedded in the labor movement's search for social justice reflect our own faith values.

Cardinal Roger M. Mahony, speaking as chairman of the U.S.
Catholic Conference's Domestic Policy Committee, 8/27/1999

At 1961 AFL-CIO convention, Martin Luther King, Jr. and A. Philip Randolph flank a Brotherhood poster on which George Meany is quoted, "What we want for ourselves, we want for all humanity." Courtesy Alexander Negative Collection, George Meany Memorial Archives.

❧578❧

Trade unionists, by their political action, abolished slavery in Hawaii, secured the lien laws, which guarantee a man his wages when he has worked; the breaker boys, who work in the mines of Pennsylvania, were liberated through the miners' strike.

Samuel Gompers, 1906, in *History of the Working Class*, 1927

❧579❧

Where trade unions are most firmly organized, there are the rights of the people most respected.

Samuel Gompers

❧580❧

If it is unfashionable for the men to bear oppression in silence, why should it not also become unfashionable with the women, or do they deem us more able to endure hardship than they themselves?

Sarah Monroe, United Tailoresses Society, 1831

❧581❧

American ladies will not be slaves.

Slogan, Woman Shoemakers, Lynn, Mass., 1833, repeated in Lynn Shoemaker's Strike, 1860 (*see* drawing page 63)

❧582❧

The physical organization, the natural responsibilities and the moral sensibility of women prove conclusively that her labors should be only of a domestic nature.

The Committee on Female Labor, 1836

❧583❧

For the last half a century, it has been deemed a violation of woman's sphere to appear before the public as a speaker, but when our rights are trampled upon and we appeal in vain to legislature, what shall we do but appeal to the workers?

Sarah G. Bagley, suffragette, labor organizer, 1845, in *Women and the American Labor Movement*, 1982

❧584❧

Those who have employment fit for women, to bestow, ought to give their preference, for there are fewer occupations of which they are capable, and they need help and encouragement more than men.

Proposal, Women's Rights Pioneers, 1846, in *Women and the American Labor Movement*, 1992

Elvira Hall, wife of a shoemaker and chair of this meeting, addresses hemmers and stitchers before they voted to support the shoeworkers in the Great Lynn Shoe Strike, 2/28/1860. Courtesy Lynn Historical Society.

✢585✢

They are going to make men of women, and when they do, that the correlative must take place that men must become women. So I suppose we are to have women for public officers, women to do military duty, women to work the roads, women to fight the battles of this country, and men to wash the dishes, men to nurse the children, men to stay at home, while the ladies go out and make stump speeches.

> Senator John Henninger Reagan (D-Texas, 1887-1891), opposing
> the admission of Wyoming to the Union in 1890 because it had
> allowed women to vote since 1869

✢586✢

It can readily be seen that women workers either must become organized and receive not only equal pay for equal work, but also equal opportunities for working, or they will, by degrees, naturally form an inferior class in every trading which they enter.

> Ida Van Etten, Working Women's Society, 1891, in *Women and the
> American Labor Movement*, 1992

✦587✦

Join the union, girls, and together say Equal pay for Equal work.

Susan Brownell Anthony (1820-1902), in suffrage newspaper,
The Revolution, 3/18/1869

✦588✦

Equal pay for equal work.

Popular contemporary slogan, generally used on the
issue of female and black workers performing equal work
at lower rates of pay

✦589✦

Women should have free access to every field of labor which they care to enter, and when their work is as valuable as that of a man, it should be paid as highly.

President Theodore Roosevelt, 1902

✦590✦

As labor continues to organize women, it will be forced to deal with new issues such as pay equity and comparable worth.

Glennis Ter Wisscha, 10/1985

✦591✦

Women do two-thirds of the world's work ... yet they earn only one-tenth of the world's income and own less than 1 percent of the world's property. They are among the poorest of the world's poor.

Barber B. Conable, Jr., president, World Bank, 1986

✦592✦

It is no wonder that those who vote no on the ERA are the same people who have strong Chamber of Commerce ratings and poor labor ratings on legislative issues.

Eleanor Smeal, on the *Equal Rights Amendment* (ERA)

✦593✦

Before feminism, work was largely defined as what men did or would do. Thus, *working woman* was someone who labored outside the home for money, masculine-style.

Gloria Steinem, feminist writer, a leader of
feminist movement since 1960s, a founder of *Ms.* magazine,
Outrageous Acts and Everyday Rebellions, 1983

❖594❖

The makeup issue is the last vestige of sexism in the airline industry. I've talked to women from other airlines who've had to change their hair color. It's ridiculous.

Teresa Fischette, airline ticket agent, victim of sexism, who was
fired for not wearing makeup and fought to get her job back

❖595❖

Women finally received the franchise (to vote) one hundred and fifty years after the Revolution. The right of freedom of speech was vastly extended. Workers finally won some rights in the 1930s ... after a very bloody struggle. They've been losing them ever since, but they won them to some extent.

Noam Chomsky

❖596❖

You can freely exercise all of your constitutional rights except one: the right of freedom of association when that association happens to be a union. It's one thing to join the Knights of Columbus. It's quite another to organize to protect your rights on the job.

Thomas Donahue

❖597❖

The right of workingmen to combine and to form trade unions is no less sacred than the right of the manufacturer to enter into associations and conferences with his fellows. ... My experience has been that trade unions upon the whole are beneficial both to labor and to capital.

Andrew Carnegie, president of Carnegie Steel, in *Toil and Trouble*,
1964 (*see* Homestead text page 136)

❖598❖

The rights of employees freely to organize for the purpose of collective bargaining should be fully protected.

President Franklin D. Roosevelt, message to Congress, 2/2/1935

❖599❖

I am glad to see that a system of labor prevails under which laborers can strike when they want to. ... I like the system which lets a man quit when he wants to and wish it might prevail everywhere.

Abraham Lincoln, 1860

✦600✦

Often those who seek only license for their plundering, cry 'liberty.' In the guise of this old American ideal, men of vast economic domain would destroy what little liberty remains to those who toil.

John L. Lewis, CIO convention, 1938

✦601✦

I tell you, gentlemen ... there is no man strong enough to entirely subvert the manhood of the workers of the United States; and if the time shall come when there is a man so strong, then American liberty is dead.

Clarence Darrow, 1898, in *Attorney for the Damned*, 1957

✦602✦

You can only protect your liberties in this world by protecting the other man's freedom. You can only be free if I am free.

Clarence Darrow

✦603✦

In Germany they came first for the Communists, and I didn't speak up because I wasn't a Communist. Then they came for the Jews, and I didn't speak up because I wasn't a Jew. Then they came for the trade unionists, and I didn't speak up because I wasn't a trade unionist. Then they came for the Catholics, and I didn't speak up because I was a Protestant. Then they came for me, and by that time, no one was left to speak up.

Martin Niemöeller (1892-1984), German Lutheran Pastor, attributed in congressional record, 10/14/1968

✦604✦

Take sides. Neutrality helps the oppressor, never the victim. Silence encourages the tormentor, never the tormented.

Elie Wiesel, Romanian concentration camp survivor, author, 1986 Nobel Peace Prize

✦605✦

The hottest places in hell are reserved for those who, in a period of moral crisis, maintain their neutrality.

Dante Alighieri (1265-1321), poet, linguist, politician

✦606✦

On spaceship Earth, there are no passengers. Only crew.

Teresa Fischette

❧607❧

The most persistent threat to freedom, to the rights of Americans, is fear.

George Meany

❧608❧

We're here to protest the burning of the American flag. We say to George Bush: the American flag is burned every day at plant gates; a flag gets burned every time workers' rights are taken from them on the job.

Jack Sheinkman, former president, Amalgamated Clothing and Textile Workers Union (ACTWU)

❧609❧

To me there is only one standard—free trade unions for working people everywhere!

President Jimmy Carter, 1980

❧610❧

My proposal is very simple. Amend the Civil Rights Act of 1991, and add, as a civil right, the right to join a union without being fired.

Thomas Geoghegan

❧611❧

Canada ... is the free world.

Thomas Geoghegan, on the accessibility of organized labor in Canada and its 32% of unionized workers

❧612❧

It is now beyond partisan controversy that it is a fundamental individual right of a worker to associate himself with other workers and to bargain collectively with his employer.

President Franklin D. Roosevelt, address in San Diego, 10/2/1935

❧613❧

We have no wish to impose a single trade union model on the workers of other lands. We insist only that the workers of any country have the right to choose and run the affairs of their own unions without interference from the state or the employer. The refusal to grant that right as in Poland today tells us all we need to know about the character of a government and its attitude toward human rights.

Lane Kirkland, speech to graduating union trainees

❖614❖

We were lucky we had no rights when we started. (We couldn't just rally around some hero and vote for him.) We had to work in the grass roots and build a movement. We had to be honest to the best principles of unionism.

Ken Paff, ex-director, TDU

❖615❖

The First Amendment does not say, "No <u>American</u> shall *abridge the freedom of speech."* The Amendment restrains <u>governmental</u> actions only. It has no application to the conduct of private individuals, including those who own businesses. Consequently, the First Amendment does not give workers in the private sector constitutional rights on their jobs.

Robert M. Schwartz, attorney, *Your Rights on the Job,* 1983

❖616❖

Greed to make the last dollar of profit led those employers to use violence, the courts and blacklists as weapons against unionism. They sought to deny workers their First Amendment rights—to act together and speak freely to encourage others to join their cause. Those rights endangered their profits, and they felt—and some still feel—money to be more important than rights.

George Meany

❖617❖

It is a constitutional right for a man to be able to vote, but the human right to a decent house is as categorically imperative and morally absolute as was that constitutional right. It is not a constitutional right that men have jobs, but it is a human right.

Martin Luther King, Jr., 1965

❖618❖

What more sacred property rights are there than the right of a man to his job?

Upton Sinclair, 1937

❖619❖

The American trade union movement—unlike any other labor movement in the world—is committed to working within the American political and economic system in order to achieve the social and economic justice promised by the Declaration of Independence and the Constitution.

George Meany, AFL-CIO Labor Day message, 1978

⇾620⇽

The state must in some way come to the aid of the workingman if democratization is to be secured.

Justice Louis Brandeis, in *Brandeis, A Free Man's Life*, 1946

⇾621⇽

Democracy is not the icing on our cake. It is our bread and butter. ... We cannot survive as a trade union movement except where there is democracy. Human rights are the very lifeblood of our movement.

George Meany

⇾622⇽

In every single democracy in the world you will find a vibrant, vital labor movement. The reason is that in a democratic society, where you have a system of checks and balances, a labor movement is absolutely indispensable. ... There will always be unions as long as there are bosses.

Douglas Fraser, in *Robust Unionism*, 1991

⇾623⇽

No society that scorns human rights generally will make an exception on trade union rights. And so, ever since Samuel Gompers, American labor has vigorously urged the promotion of democracy and human rights as the heart of U.S. foreign policy.

George Meany, in *George Meany and His Times*, 1982

⇾624⇽

When employers have rights and employees don't, democracy itself is at risk. It isn't easy to spend the day in a state of servile subjugation and then emerge, at 5:00 p.m., as Mr. or Ms. Citizen-Activist. Unfreedom undermines the critical spirit, and suck-ups make lousy citizens.

Barbara Ehrenreich, commenting on the lack of free speech for private sector employees

⇾625⇽

We do not boycott to put anyone out of business. We are boycotting to put justice into business.

Martin Luther King, Jr.

⇾626⇽

No system has ever as yet existed which did not in some form involve the exploitation of some human beings for the advantage of others.

NAACP, 1963

❧627❧

No man can put a chain about the ankle of his fellowman, without at last finding the other end of it about his own neck.

Frederick Douglass, 1895,
The Life and Times of Frederick Douglass, 1991 edition

❧628❧

Of course, slavery was abolished in this country many years ago, so we must apply these principles to the way Americans work today, to employees and employers. Christians have a responsibility to submit to the authority of their employers since they are designated as part of God's plan for the exercise of authority in the earth by man.

Passage from *Christian Coalition Leadership Manual*

❧629❧

The rights and interests of the laboring man will be protected and cared for—not by the labor agitators, but by the Christian men to whom God in His infinite wisdom has given the control of the property interests of the country.

George F. Baer, in letter to a clergyman, 7/17/1902, which, when made public, led to government intervention in UMW strike and settlement with Reading Railroad system through arbitration

❧630❧

Human freedom is a worldwide struggle.

Samuel Gompers

❧631❧

People may remember that when Chinese students sat down in the streets of Beijing, coal miners sat down on a road in Virginia. The U.S. Government reacted quite differently to the two events. It hailed the students' action as a victory for democracy and an exercise of basic human rights. But the miners were promptly hauled off to jail by the hundreds.

John David, labor historian

❧632❧

There is no halfway house to human freedom.

Walter Reuther, 1963

❧633❧

Let my people go!

Protest sign at New England Provision Company (NEPCO) on refusal of company to let workers freely use restrooms

❧634❧

If it was just a question of winning six cents an hour, I wouldn't be interested. ... I will be dissatisfied as long as one American child is denied the right to education. As long as one American is denied his rights, I will do all I can to dispel the corruption of complacency in America and seek a greater sense of national purpose.

Walter Reuther, on the union and its role in the community

❧635❧

We believe all housing built with the aid of federal funds or credit, or any other form of financial assistance, should be made available to minority families on an equal basis with all other families.

Resolution of the first AFL-CIO convention in 1955

❧636❧

Organized labor's mission is to ensure that working men and women are treated in a manner commensurate with their inherent human dignity. And, of course, that end can only be achieved in a nation truly dedicated to maximizing personal freedom.

George Meany

❧637❧

The AFL-CIO has been one of the benchmarks of the Leadership Conference on Civil Rights, which has been responsible for so much of the national legislation under which we now make progress.

NAACP, 1963

❧638❧

When it comes to discrimination, I put my leadership on the line, and if they don't like it, then they have to get rid of me. I would go gladly on an issue like that. I'm not going to buy leadership at that expense.

Cesar Chavez, in *Cesar Chavez, Autobiography of La Causa*, 1975

❧639❧

The fight for equality must be fought on many fronts—in the urban slums, in the sweatshops of the factories and fields. Our separate struggles are really one—a struggle for freedom, for dignity, and for humanity. You and your valiant fellow workers have demonstrated your commitment to righting grievous wrongs forced upon exploited people.

Martin Luther King, Jr., to Cesar Chavez, in *Cesar Chavez: Autobiography of La Causa*, 1975

Mrs. Coretta Scott King presents the Martin Luther King, Jr. Peace Prize of the Southern Christian Leadership Conference to Cesar Chavez, 1974. Courtesy George Meany Memorial Archives.

⇥640⇤

The fight is never about grapes or lettuce. It is always about people.

Cesar Chavez

⇥641⇤

The AFL-CIO continues to believe that human rights must be the heart of American foreign policy.

AFL-CIO convention resolution, 1979

⇥642⇤

I am for civil rights and equal opportunity because freedom is an indivisible value, and so long as any person is denied his freedom, my freedom is in jeopardy.

Walter Reuther, 1963

→643←

We in the labor movement know that you don't have to be a union member to support the doctrine of human rights, but we also know that without human rights there can be no free labor movement.

George Meany

→644←

Prejudice is cultivated.

A. Philip Randolph

→645←

No Irish Need Apply

Frequent notices in 1870s concerning municipal employment

→646←

Latino power through the union card and the ballot box.

Slogan—Labor Council for Latin American Advancement
(LCLAA)

→647←

Kodak's only contribution to race relations was the invention of color film.

Saul Alinsky, in *Let Them Call Me Rebel*, 1989

→648←

We're no longer arguing about riding on the back of the bus, but being the bus driver or the president of the bus company. We're not pushing for the right to buy the hot dog, but selling the hot dog and the right to own the hot dog franchise.

Benjamin Hooks

→649←

We are not going back to the good old days. We have been back there, and there is no power between heaven and hell that can send us back there.

Benjamin Hooks

→650←

Why should a Negro worker be penalized for being black? Why should anybody be penalized for something over which he has no control?

A. Philip Randolph, 1935, in *Men Who Lead Labor*, 1937

⁘651⁘

The Negro should organize himself, because with organization he will be better able to break down the barriers and prejudices of white workers against him than he will without it.

A. Philip Randolph, in *Men Who Lead Labor*, 1937

⁘652⁘

Most unions have mutual interests with us; both can profit in the relationship.

Martin Luther King, Jr., on unions and the black community

⁘653⁘

The two most dynamic and cohesive liberal forces in the country are the labor movement and the Negro freedom movement.

Martin Luther King, Jr., 1961

⁘654⁘

As I have said many times, and believe with all my heart, the coalition that can have the greatest impact in the struggle for human dignity here in America is that of the blacks and forces of labor, because their fortunes are so closely intertwined.

Martin Luther King, Jr.

Martin Luther King, Jr. speaks at AFL-CIO convention, 1961. George Meany is seated at far left. Courtesy Alexander Negative Collection, George Meany Memorial Archives.

✦655✦

The voice of black labor is not going to be consonant with those [voices] that come from non-Negro sources, or from Negroes themselves that are nonlabor.

A. Philip Randolph

✦656✦

Agitate.

Frederick Douglass, in response to a question of how young blacks
can assure equity for existing conditions in their lives

✦657✦

Black and white workers did not fight each other because they hated each other, but they hated each other because they fought each other. They fought each other because they did not know each other. They did not know each other because they had no control or communication with each other because they were afraid of each other.

A. Philip Randolph, 1961

✦658✦

One of the great ironies of U.S. history is that the white poor and working people have been the most racist sectors in the U.S. populace. Major energy must be devoted to educating and organizing these sectors.

Ron Daniels, community labor organizer

✦659✦

I bet that if you brought some people joining the KKK [Ku Klux Klan] and some followers of Louis Farrakhan into a room together, they'd probably agree on 85 percent of things. They want decent homes, good health care, safe streets, and good paying jobs.

Thomas Martinez, confessed former racist

✦660✦

As the white civil rights movement blowtorches affirmative action, it cannot scorch a resistant truth: African-Americans are the last hired and first fired.

Derrick Z. Jackson, writer, speaker, columnist, *Boston Globe*

✦661✦

Take a look where affirmative action lands: school systems, trade unions, police departments, fire departments, sanitation and urban mass transportation systems. ... Affirmative action, banged through as law, does not hit the media, the big banks or the U.S. Congress. It doesn't affect judges, lawyers or professors.

Mike Barnicle, columnist, commentator

✦662✦

That's the big problem with issues like affirmative action, busing and quotas. One class of people—largely white, largely well-off, largely going unhungry—tells other classes of people—largely breaking even and of all color—to bear the burden, pay the price and maintain the standard of social goals set by those who go absolutely untouched by public actions.

Mike Barnicle

✦663✦

I would rather a thousand times be a free soul in jail than a sycophant and a coward in the streets. If it had not been for men and women in the past who have had the moral courage to go to jail, we would still be in the jungles.

Eugene Debs, who opposed World War I and four days later was
indicted for violation of the 1917 Espionage Act, 6/16/1918

✦664✦

The essence of trade unionism is social uplift. The labor movement has been the haven for the dispossessed, the despised, the neglected, the downtrodden, the poor.

A. Philip Randolph

✦665✦

The seeds of a new labor movement lie in the assertions of workers' rights by rank-and-file groups throughout the country. The civil rights movement, the women's movement, the health and safety struggle, the campaigns to defend the democratic rights of union members, have all vastly expanded our notion of what the labor movement could be.

James R. Green, labor historian, educator, author,
The World of the Worker, 1980

Chapter 8

The Economics

⇥666⇤

All riches come from inequity, and unless one has lost, another cannot gain. Hence, that common opinion seems to be very true, 'the rich man is unjust, or the heir to an unjust one.' Opulence is always the result of theft, if not committed by the actual possessor, then by his predecessor.

> Saint Jerome (c. 347-420), Catholic scholar, theologian

⇥667⇤

The basic law of capitalism is you or I, not both you and I.

> Karl Liebknecht (1871-1919), German socialist leader, a founder of Spartacist League (renamed Communist Party), 1907

⇥668⇤

Capitalism is the extraordinary belief that the nastiest of men, for the nastiest of reasons, will somehow work for the benefit of us all.

> John Maynard Keynes (1883-1946), English economist, author, government official, editor, businessman

⇥669⇤

When morality comes up against profit, it is seldom that profit loses.

> Congresswoman Shirley Anita Chisholm (D-N.Y., 1969-1983)

⇥670⇤

A foolish American myth has it that the rich and super-rich are entrepreneurial Daniel Boones who decry the restraints of government and, as rugged individualists, fare forth to wrest fame and fortune from other like-minded souls. With some notable exceptions, nothing could be farther from the truth. In the main, the rich are the clever and adroit who understand the purposes and functions of government and bend it to their purposes. Government becomes a device, which they use to expand their fortunes, then hide behind to make certain their gains remain intact.

> Harry M. Caudill (1922-1990), lawyer, historian, activist, legislator, 1976

⇻671⇺

Religion teaches those who toil in poverty all their lives to be resigned and patient in this world, and consoles them with the hope of reward in heaven. As for those who live upon the labor of others, religion teaches them to be charitable in earthly life, thus providing a cheap justification for their whole exploiting existence and selling them, at a reasonable price, tickets to heavenly bliss.

> Thomas Jefferson to John Adams, 5/5/1817,
> in *The Great Quotations*, 1961

⇻672⇺

Time has been kind to these men who have been variously called, according to taste, giants of industry, the Potentates, and the Robber Barons. Carnegie is remembered for his libraries and philanthropies, Huntington for a great library, Frick for his lovely French house on New York's Fifth Avenue and its collection of exquisite paintings. Even their own offspring were hardly aware that the fortunes that could commission those palaces were built on the open shop, the seventy-hour week, and immigrant labor.

> Alistair Cooke, journalist, broadcaster, author,
> *Alister Cooke's America*, 1973

→ The 1892 Homestead strike against Carnegie Steel began after Carnegie's partner and the manager of the plant, Henry Frick, declared that he would not bargain with the union. Workers were essentially fired and could be rehired at less pay only as individuals with no collective rights. When union members struck, Frick incited workers throughout the country by forcibly evicting strikers' families from company housing and by publicly declaring that he would rather see the workers dead than to bargain with their union.

Frick enlisted, with Carnegie's consent, about 300 Pinkerton guards to run the mill. A week later, barges loaded with heavily armed Pinkerton guards arrived via the river by the plant and engaged in a brutal gun and cannon battle that left more than a dozen workers and guards dead. After the guards surrendered and pled for mercy, outraged strikers beat them, despite promises of protection by strike leaders. Thereafter, state militia occupied the mill and protected nonunion laborers who worked the steel mills for four months until the strike collapsed. Unionization of the steel industry would not be successful until the 1930s.

Carnegie had carefully orchestrated his reputation to portray himself as a benevolent employer, progressive business/labor reformer, and philanthropist. In his published essays he proclaimed his support for the right of workers to form unions (*see* quotation 597) and, that he believed workers should not take each other's jobs (they should not be replacement workers or scabs). His complicity in the Homestead tragedy exposed him to ridicule as a hypocrite and coward. The *St. Louis Post Dispatch* editorialized, "10,000 Carnegie public libraries would not compensate the country for the direct and indirect evils resulting from the Homestead lockout." ⇺

The Great Battle of Homestead. Drawing by Kurz & Allison – Art Studio, Chicago. Courtesy George Meany Memorial Archives. Contrary to the text on the illustration, the Pinkerton captives were not "on their way to prison" as the strikers believed. They were never prosecuted.

❧673❧

I am absolutely convinced that no wealth in the world can help humanity forward, even in the hands of the most devoted worker in this cause. The example of great and pure individuals is the only thing that can lead us to noble thoughts and deeds. Money only appeals to selfishness and irresistibly invites abuse. Can anyone imagine Moses, Jesus or Gandhi armed with the moneybags of Carnegie?

> Albert Einstein (1879-1955), physicist, pacifist, 1921 Nobel
> Prize for physics, *Ideas & Opinions*, 1934

❧674❧

The labor movement was the principal force that transformed misery and despair into hope and progress. Out of its bold struggles, economic and social reform gave birth to unemployment insurance, old age pensions, government relief for the destitute, and above all new wage levels that meant not mere survival but a tolerable life. The captains of industry did not lead this transformation.

> Martin Luther King, Jr.

❧675❧

The working class, the dirty, uneducated, uncouth class, is actually responsible for every gain that the world has. Responsible yes, but you don't get the credit for it. The bosses, the professionals, the moneymen, they get the credit. They're considered to be real world shakers; dynamos. But they know without you, they would have nothing.

> Ron Hively, steelworker, in *Overtime*, 1990

❧676❧

Melancholy is the condition of that people whose government can be sustained only by a system which periodically transfers large amounts from the labor of the many to the coffers of the few.

> President James Knox Polk (1845-1849), 1845

❧677❧

There are two classes in society, one incessantly striving to obtain the labor of the other class for as little as possible.

> Samuel Gompers

⇥678↤

What is wanted is for every union to help inculcate the grand ennobling idea that the interests of labor are one; that there should be no distinction of race or nationality; no classification of Jew or Gentile, Christian or infidel, that there is one dividing line, that which separates mankind into two great classes, the class that labors and the class that lives by others' labor.

National Labor Union NLU) address, 1868

⇥679↤

Capital should be at the service of labor and not labor at the service of capital.

Pope John Paul II

⇥680↤

Labor is prior to, and independent of, capital. Capital is only the fruit of labor and could never have existed if labor had not first existed. Labor is the superior of capital and deserves much the higher consideration

President Abraham Lincoln, message to Congress, 12/3/1861

⇥681↤

We affirm, as a fundamental principle, that labor, the creator of wealth, is entitled to all it creates.

Wendell Phillips, in resolution at the Labor-Reform Convention,
Boston, 9/1870

⇥682↤

The annual labor of every nation is the fund which originally supplies it with all the necessaries and conveniences of life.

Adam Smith (1723-1790), Scottish laissez-faire economist,
sociologist, philosopher, An Inquiry into the Nature and Causes of the
Wealth of Nations, 1776

⇥683↤

You cannot weigh a human soul on the same scale as a piece of pork. You cannot weigh the heart and soul of a child with the same scales upon which you weigh a commodity.

Samuel Gompers

❧684❧

The labor of a human being is not a commodity or [an] article of commerce.

United States Congress, clause in the Clayton Antitrust Act,
Sec. 6, 1914, which forbade anti-trust laws from stopping union
activities, in *Survey of Labor Relations*, 1987

❧685❧

It is not the employer who pays the wages—he only handles the money. It is the product that pays the wages.

Henry Ford

❧686❧

Wages, instead of being drawn from capital, are in reality drawn from the product of the labor for which they are paid.

Henry George, in *Critics & Crusaders*, 1948

❧687❧

Of course, capital can do nothing without the assistance of labor. All there is of value in the world is the product of labor. The laboring man pays all the expenses. No matter whether taxes are laid on luxuries or on the necessities, labor pays every cent.

Robert G. Ingersoll

❧688❧

Labor and capital are not enemies in the production process—without machines there are no workers. There are no wages. Without workers there are no profits. Machines and labor are complements, not substitutes. Anyone who confuses capital and labor as being enemies has got his proverbial economics head wedged.

Arthur B. Laffer, economist, speaker, Economic Policy Board,
Policy Committee, Reagan Administration, 1982

❧689❧

The facts of life in the mining homes of America cannot be pushed aside by the flamboyant theories of an idealistic economic philosophy.

John L. Lewis

❧690❧

Capital is but the accumulated result of the work of our hands. Yet the sword of capital is forever directed against the throat of labor.

Peter McGuire, c. 1880s

→691←

I can hire one-half the working class to kill the other half.

> Jay Gould (1836-1892), financier, railroad businessman,
> on not worrying about an impending strike at
> Southwestern rail system, 1886

→692←

This railroad president shed tears because the United Mine Workers were spoiling the souls of these poor children, and yet he was willing to take the earnings of these poor children that he and his family might be richer because of their toil.

> Clarence Darrow, defending UMWA,
> in *Attorney for the Damned*, 1957

→693←

Labor has been willing to fight long and hard even when its own narrow, institutional interests were not involved. Can anyone recall the last crusade for economic justice waged by the Gucci-shod Wall Street crowd so dedicated to cutting their own capital gains taxes?

> Mark Shields, columnist, political analyst, commentator for
> *The NewsHour with Jim Lehrer,* Public Broadcasting System (PBS)

→694←

I won't take my religion from any man who never works except with his mouth and never cherishes any memory except the face of the woman on the American silver dollar.

> Carl Sandburg

→695←

There is no political democracy without economic democracy.

> Popular banner

→696←

Trying to have economic democracy without unions is like trying to have political democracy without political parties.

> Ray Marshall

→697←

Slaves had jobs. Is that what we're talking about now?

> Leo Purcell, labor leader, president, Massachusetts Building Trades
> Council, condemning Massachusetts Governor William Weld
> (R-Mass., 1990-1997) on proposed use of convict labor at $2 an
> hour, replacing union jobs, 1/7/1991

✢698✢

We used to own our slaves. Now we just rent them.

> Edward R. Murrow (1908-1965), radio and television journalist,
> news broadcaster, quoting a farmer describing migrant workers,
> *Harvest of Shame*, CBS, 1960

✢699✢

Ours is an economic struggle, a genuine struggle, and people don't give up on those very easily—any more than on religion. If we had any other kind of struggle, we'd be dead.

> Cesar Chavez, in *Cesar Chavez, Autobiography of La Causa*, 1975

✢700✢

A just wage for the worker is the ultimate test of whether any economic system is functioning justly.

> Pope John Paul II

✢701✢

Where would the United States and its market economy be if not for the decent wages and benefits achieved through collective bargaining?

> Monsignor George G. Higgins, *Organized Labor and the Church*, 1993

✢702✢

The message ... is that unions need to stop seeing labor struggles as power struggles or contests played between groups of men for individual workers' rights. The issues of labor are the issues of community and survival of economics and democracy. ... Labor will not achieve its goals without understanding the connection between wages and the deep structures of political and social life.

> Neala Schleuning

✢703✢

A society that gives to one class all the opportunities for leisure, and to another all the burdens of work, dooms both classes to spiritual sterility.

> Lewis Mumford (1895-1990), sociologist, American rural
> architect, urban planner, critic, author, historian, 1940,
> in *Survey of Labor Relations*, 1987

☆704☆

Some have gone so far as to say that there is a natural, a necessary conflict between labor and capital. These are very shallow thinkers, or else very great demagogues. Argument is of no use against these people; either they cannot or will not see the falsity of their statement.

Eugene Debs, in *The Bending Cross*, 1949

☆705☆

There can be no such quarrel (between capital and labor) unless it is caused by deliberate piracy on one side and unreasonable demands on the other.

Eugene Debs, 1886 speech

☆706☆

Well, labor and capital may be partners in theory, but they are enemies in fact.

John L. Lewis

☆707☆

How can anyone with a straight face propose a capital gains tax cut when owners of capital are running off with these gains from workers?

Robert Reich, political and economic theorist, author, Secretary of Labor (1993-1997), Clinton Administration, on legislation to cut capital gains taxes, 1995

☆708☆

From 1935 until 1980, America produced more wealth for a greater number of people than any society in history. Collective bargaining and the labor movement were crucial to that process.

Congressman William Clay

☆709☆

There are many people who now take the position that the 'damned unions' are to blame for declining living standards of the American worker. In fact, the period in our nation's economic history when the middle class prospered is also the time when unions represented the greatest number of workers. The glory days, roughly from 1946 to 1973, witnessed unprecedented economic growth.

Russell Eckel, labor management consultant, 1994

❧710❧

It is no coincidence that when our nation's standard of living was at its height, the incidence of unionization was also at its height. For three decades after World War II, our standard of living and our workers' wages were the highest in the world; and the percentage of the work force in unions was the highest in our history.

James A. Cavanaugh, AFL-CIO

❧711❧

The labor problem ... calls for active involvement on the part of those who believe in social justice. While organized labor is undoubtedly far from perfect ... I even have intimations at times that my own church is far from perfect ... no other movement in sight would enable American workers to protect their legitimate economic interests. No other movement would enable American workers to play an effective and responsible role in helping to promote the general economic welfare both at home and abroad.

Monsignor George G. Higgins

❧712❧

On the economic side, the working class serves as a model. They have succeeded, at least to some extent, in protecting their economic interest. We can learn from them too, how this problem can be solved by the method of organization.

Albert Einstein, 1944

❧713❧

It is defense spending, not the workers, which is responsible for fueling the fires of inflation.

Leonard Woodcock, 1970

❧714❧

You can't have guns and butter at the same time.

Albert Fitzgerald, president, UE, 1972,
in What's Happening To Labor, 1976

❧715❧

Every gun that is made, every warship launched, every rocket fired— signifies, in the final sense, a theft from those who are cold and not clothed. This world, in arms, is not spending the sweat of its laborers, the genius of its scientists, the hopes of its children. This is not a way of life at all, in any true sense. It is humanity hanging on a cross of iron.

President Dwight D. Eisenhower, 1953

✦716✦

An economic conversion—I would hastily add—is not a religion. It's a rational, intelligent and absolutely essential way to get a grip on our current military madness—to promote full employment, reduce inflation, and make the commitment necessary to rejuvenate our industrial base and spur productivity.

William Winpisinger, 1981

✦717✦

The engine of the inflation that we've experienced for some time now has four fundamental factors; (most of the economy has behaved at modest inflationary levels)—four things have driven it into double-digits—Food, Housing, Energy and Health Care—and none of those are highly union-ized sectors of the economy, none of those have a wage-drain effect on the economy, but they are the result of avarice on the part of the owners of the product or the service in raw materials.

William Winpisinger, on inflation causes

✦718✦

Every time the cost of labor goes up $1 an hour, 1,000 more robots become economical.

Roger B. Smith, chairman, GM, *New York Times*

✦719✦

The real enemy isn't Roger Smith. It's the whole economic system. It's not fair, it's not just, and most of all, it's not democratic. I'd like to see it change in my lifetime.

Michael Moore, documentary film maker, director, print journalist,
National Public Radio commentator, producer and protagonist in
his film *Roger and Me*

✦720✦

Organized labor has produced skilled craftsmen through apprentice training programs. It has improved the efficiency of the work force and has provided the American economy with the highest gross national product of any nation in the world.

Massachusetts AFL-CIO, Dept. of Education

✦721✦

It's a mystery to me ... why so many conservative American businessmen complain about American unions. ... What do they [workers] buy? They buy what conservative American businessmen are selling.

George Will

✦722✦

The principal effect of American unions has been to increase the purchasing power of American men and women. ... Now, thanks to the unions, they have the money to buy a home in the suburbs, maybe a cottage by the lake, a camper to drive to and from their home and their cottage.

George Will

✦723✦

The chief problem of lower-income farmers is poverty.

Governor Nelson Aldrich Rockefeller
(R-N.Y., 1959-1973), attributed

✦724✦

The working classes didn't bring this one. It was the big boys that thought the financial drunk was going to last forever and over-bought, over-merged and over-capitalized.

Will Rogers, on the Great Depression, 10/25/1931

✦725✦

We charged everything and made nothing. Not ideas. Not jobs. Not new factories. Not individual accomplishment. The only thing we built was debt. The only legacy created was the weight of it all, a burden that will be carried down through the decades as our survivors labor to pay off our bills.

Mike Barnicle, describing the 1980s decade

✦726✦

My generation did something to yours that was never done to us or to any other generation of Americans. We stiffed you, I'm sorry to say. We didn't pay our bills.

Lee A. Iaccoca, CEO Chrysler Corp., in speech to students, 1992

✦727✦

There's no such thing as a free lunch.

Milton Friedman, economist, 1976 Nobel Prize for economics,
widely attributed

✦728✦

Whether you work by the piece,
    Or work by the day—
Decreasing the hours,
    Increases the pay.

Anonymous: AFL song

✦729✦

Labour, like all other things which are purchased and sold ... has its natural and its market price.

David Ricardo (1772-1823), British economist

✦730✦

If workers in Mexico earn only a fraction of the wages of Ford workers in Detroit, but produce as many engines as Detroiters, then potentially we have a problem that Henry Ford would understand: too many Fords, not enough customers.

Walter Russell Mead, author, political economist, explaining how undercutting wages can cut the U.S. standard of living

✦731✦

Collective bargaining is not a gravy train for trade unions, it is not a candy tree. Collective bargaining is a problem-solving process and when there are real problems it is a way to address them naturally, where each side can make appropriate contributions to the resolution of those problems. It does not always yield great increases or continual improvements for workers. It frequently has to address the problem of what we have to do to save this place of employment and to save these jobs.

Lane Kirkland

✦732✦

Why subsidize an American high-tech company that's going to do much of its development work abroad? Far better to subsidize any global company, headquartered anywhere—but only on condition that it use the government support to do research, development, and related engineering here in the United States, utilizing American workers.

Robert Reich

✦733✦

The test for whether foreign investment is good for America should be whether it is likely to improve the skills and productivity of Americans.

Robert Reich

✦734✦

The widespread, deeply rooted Negro poverty in the South weakens the wage scale for the white as well as the Negro. Beyond that, a low wage structure in the South becomes a heavy pressure on higher wages in the North.

Martin Luther King, Jr., 1965

✦735✦

I am prepared to say to the poor: You have to learn new habits. The habits to being poor don't work.

Congressman Newt Gingrich, Speaker of the House of
Representatives (1995-1999), on the failure of poor blacks to
achieve in society, 1995

✦736✦

Nurses do not ... want to be physicians. What they want is to be able to provide increased access to high-quality, cost-effective and efficient health care for the citizens of Massachusetts.

Barbara M. Roderick, Mass. Nurses Association

✦737✦

In the 30s, a benign crackpot named Francis Townsend contended that if the government would only pension off old folks—'Sixty dollars a month at Sixty' was the slogan—jobs would open up for unemployed young people, and the economy would recover. This idea, slightly sanitized, became Social Security.

Robert Louis Kuttner, economic writer, editor, columnist, *Boston
Globe* and *Washington Post Syndicate*

✦738✦

So far as power is concerned, does anybody believe the premiums of insurance companies are almost all uniform by accident? It is an accident that if the price of gasoline goes up in one company, all the other prices go up the same rate in a matter of weeks?

Jimmy Hoffa

✦739✦

I've heard all that stuff like GE is moving out because of me. And the company is going to get back at us because of our militancy. But I don't buy into that premise at all for the following reason: Welch is a business-man. The minute he starts making economic decisions based on pure emotions is the day he's done.

Kevin Mahar, president, IUE local, Lynn, Mass, answering charges
that the GE plant may move based on the local's militancy

✦740✦

I am here today to speak for the middle class. They have no more to give. ... They are either tuition-poor or they are mortgage-poor; or they are poor because they do not have a long-term care policy and they are taking care of their mothers and fathers. They have no more to give because they pay high property taxes, they pay high health insurance, and they pay for their car insurance.

> Senator Barbara Ann Mikulski (D-Md., 1987-), first women to
> serve in both houses of congress, novelist, 1991

✦741✦

As a general rule, when something gets elevated to apple-pie status in the hierarchy of American values, you have to suspect that its actual *monetary* value is skidding toward zero. ... Would we be so reverent about the 'work ethic' if it wasn't for the fact that the average working stiff's hourly pay is shrinking, year by year, toward the price of a local phone call?

> Barbara Ehrenreich

✦742✦

The counter argument (equally silly) is that if raising the minimum wage increases joblessness, why don't we *lower* it a dollar or two and then dream of full employment? ... To those who oppose both, I say: If permitting people to *work* their way out of poverty amounts to unwarranted tampering with the economy, what escape would you recommend?

> William Raspberry, author, columnist, *Washington Post*, 1994
> Pulitzer Prize for commentary, on the minimum wage debate

✦743✦

The economy needs ... the added purchasing power those increases will have.

> Andrew John Biemiller (1906-1982), former Congressman
> (D-Wis. 1945-1947, 1949-1951), AFL-CIO lobbyist,
> testifying for minimum wage

✦744✦

We don't bat an eye at CEOs and Hollywood producers making millions of dollars. At the same time, public officials, acting as corporate shills, run around the country denouncing proposals to raise the minimum wage. We live in a nation where it's routine to deny countless Americans what they need so that we can continue to give a few what they merely want.

> Bill Doyle, pipefitter, *Newsweek*

↦745↤

Republicans believe in the minimum wage—as minimum as possible!

President Harry S. Truman

↦746↤

Over the long term, we need periodically to raise the minimum wage in line with increases in the cost of living or continually face the need to increase the value of the earned-income credit to keep more families from falling into poverty. ... The moral: Maintain a reasonable minimum wage or face an increasing public subsidy.

Barry Bluestone, economist

↦747↤

The demise of Communism has left the free enterprise system triumphant—and a good thing, too. But ... unchecked and uncontrolled, it will attempt to live up to its Marxist caricature. In a way, this is what certain American companies have been doing. To fire workers when you don't absolutely need to—to treat people as if they were tantamount to machinery—all but vindicates Marx. At the very least—theory aside—it stinks.

Richard Cohen, columnist, *Washington Post*

Labor leaders and striking steelworkers: Mother Jones is flanked (*left*) by James H. Maurer, socialist and president of Pennsylvania State Department of Labor; (*far left*) by Philip Murray; and (*right and behind*) by William Z. Foster, three-time Communist Party presidential candidate, 1919. In the first half of the twentieth century, many of the most effective organizers and supporters of the labor movement were American socialists and communists. Courtesy Charles H. Kerr Co., Chicago.

→748←

The labor union and cooperative are foremost among new forms of association that have served to keep alive the symbols of economic freedom. ... They have been the first objects of economic destruction in totalitarian countries.

Robert A. Nisbet, *The Quest for Community*, 1958

→749←

Workers normally do not make long-range investments in stocks, bonds or developments, but they spend weekly. Therefore, their paychecks turn over several times within the community.

Stanley M. Smith

→750←

It is cheaper from a business standpoint today to risk a $1000 workman's compensation payment to a disabled or dead worker than to invest in better equipment and better workplace ventilation.

Frank Wallick, author

→751←

My own strongly held views that givebacks undercut everyone's wage and salary standards and do not result in saving jobs differ from the views of many traditional labor leaders.

Marvin Miller, attorney, author, baseball labor leader,
executive director, Player's Association (1966-1992) in
A Whole Different Ball Game, 1991

→752←

The givebacks in the automobile industry didn't save jobs; they were instead followed by layoffs, plant closings, and record-high bonuses, salaries, stock options, and pensions for the top and middle executives of the auto companies. I was never a givebacker; management doesn't volunteer to share its prosperity with labor when profits roll in.

Marvin Miller, *A Whole Different Ball Game*, 1991

→753←

The establishment people tell us that if the workers wanted to share the profits, it was called communism. When management wants to share profits, it's called a bonus.

Phil [Philip John] Donahue, syndicated television talk show host,
father of audience participation talk shows

✦754✦

Knowing what we now know, to continue with the extreme forms of slash-and-burn downsizing and the macho restructuring that follows from it, is really tantamount to management malpractice.

Peter Scott-Morgan, educator, analyst for Arthur D. Little

✦755✦

Our merchants and master-manufacturers complain much of the bad effects of high wages in raising the price and thereby lessening the sale of their goods both at home and abroad. They say nothing concerning the bad effects of high profits.

Adam Smith

✦756✦

The main effect of classical wage theories has been to justify an existing situation by explaining an imaginary one.

Barbara Wootton, writer

✦757✦

If the federal government can pay farmers for not raising food, they can subsidize honest jobs for people.

Coleman Alexander Young, labor leader, civil rights activist,
Detroit Mayor (1974-1994), in *My Soul Looks Black,
Less I Forget*, 1993

✦758✦

Our country would go bankrupt in a day if the Supreme Court suddenly ordained the powers that be to pay back wages to children of slaves and to women who have worked all their lives for half-pay or no pay.

Delegate Eleanor Holmes Norton (D-D.C., 1990-), lawyer,
educator, in *My Soul Looks Black, Less I Forget*, 1993

✦759✦

DEREGULATION: Removing regulations and restrictions from existing legislation, thus giving free enterprise the green light. Where the interests of Capital and Labor collide, deregulation gives relief to the greedy and places restrictions on the needy.

Ernest DeMaio, labor writer,
Words For Workers In Changing Times, 1993

❖760❖

Through collective bargaining, the 'bad, low paying' jobs of a prior generation—factory jobs, construction jobs, railroad jobs and the like—became the 'good, decent paying' jobs that enabled hard working Americans to buy a home, to raise a family, and send their kids to college. ... and through collective bargaining, a myriad of other labor standards were established that we take for granted today.

Thomas Donahue, 9/8/1994

❖761❖

Don't shop where you can't work. Buy where you can work.

Slogan, Chicago Whip, 1930

❖762❖

We have numerous economic problems, almost all of which can only be solved by cooperation between government, labor, and the private sector. This triumvirate is unbeatable.

Robert Anderson, former CEO, Atlantic Richfield Company
(ARCO), in *Unheard Voices* (book jacket), 1987

❖763❖

The safety nets ... that allowed greater worker participation in policy making and in the fruits of the economy were not just to catch those who were falling out of the market system, but also to sustain that system itself.

Ray Marshall, *Unheard Voices*, 1987

❖764❖

My conclusion is that unions are integral and necessary institutions in a democratic market economy. A union-free environment would jeopardize a free enterprise system. Unions will survive because this principle is well established in the democracies.

Ray Marshall, *Unheard Voices*, 1987

❖765❖

Trade unionism is a phenomenon of capitalism quite similar to the corporation. One is essentially a pooling of labor for purposes of common action in production and in sales. The other is a pooling of capital for exactly the same purposes. The economic aims of both are identical gain.

John L. Lewis, 1927, in *Labor Baron—
A Portrait of John L. Lewis*, 1944

→766←

The outstanding characteristic of American trade unionism, and the one that distinguishes it from trade-union movements just about everywhere else in the world, is its devotion to the principles of capitalism.

Robert Hargreaves, *Superpower*, 1973

→767←

The Winner-Take-All Society—How more and more Americans compete for ever fewer and bigger prizes, encouraging economic waste, income inequality and an impoverished cultural life.

Book title, Robert H. Frank & Philip J. Cook, 1995

→768←

The workers desire to get as much as possible, the masters to give as little as possible. It is not, however, difficult to foresee which of the two parties must, upon all ordinary occasions, have the advantage in the dispute.

Adam Smith

→769←

Sooner or later, gross inequality and unfair working conditions have an impact on all of society. ... In other words, no one benefits when a six-buck-an-hour security guard heads for the emergency room with pneumonia because he lacked the health insurance needed to get treatment earlier, or when a single mom working second shift at the neighborhood 7-Eleven needs food stamps to support her kids.

Sean Reilly, journalist

→770←

To curb the old-style excesses and myopia, a little comeuppance for unions was certainly in order. But since the seventies, comeuppance for unions has given way to gross injustice for workers. As productivity increases and executive compensation rises to even more exorbitant heights, it's only fair that workers share in the wealth. We need unions to make sure they do.

Sean Reilly

→771←

If wages fall for the millions, an economy that depends on consumer purchasing power will be a society where inequality spreads, growth barely totters forward, and resentment and bitterness poison our social and political relations. ... They will not pay for prosperity, either. Without prosperity, true growth, democracy, like the workers' family, is imperiled.

Bill Moyers, network television journalist, 1992

✦772✦

By miraculously creating a prosperous American middle class more concerned with property tax rates than minimum wage laws, the New Deal of Franklin Roosevelt and Harry Truman politically sowed the seeds of its downfall. Forgetfulness about both the humbleness of our origins and most especially all of the help we received along the way is sadly a common human failing.

Mark Shields

✦773✦

I don't see why there should be any controversial reaction to the simple factual statement that the free enterprise economy, perceived as a system, not only has no conscience, but does not even see a need for one. It is up to individuals functioning within that system to demonstrate that they personally, at least, would never dream of underpaying their employees, overcharging their customers, or selling inferior or dangerous merchandise.

Steve Allen

✦774✦

Companies that use low wages as a basis for doing business cannot be profitable. Someone, somewhere, can offer lower wages.

Robert Reich

✦775✦

The good thing about a strike is it displaces economic activity. It doesn't destroy it.

Diane Swonk, economist, on the effects of a major strike on the
U.S. economy, 1996

✦776✦

Time is money.

Benjamin Franklin

✦777✦

The American worker is not lazy. Workers are prepared and, indeed, are doing more than their share in the fight against inflation already. They are driving less; their houses are colder; chicken has replaced beef on the table.

Lane Kirkland

⇢778↞

America needs a raise.

> John J. Sweeney, making the case for decade-long loss
> of worker income, 1995

⇢779↞

Never, ever underestimate the political potency of a declining paycheck.

> Robert Reich

Chapter 9

Politics

✦780✦

Politics is the science of who gets what, when and why.

Sidney Hillman

✦781✦

(The purpose of government is) to counteract the moneyed interests.

Thomas Jefferson, attributed

✦782✦

Pure capitalism is a system of extremes. It is capable of marvelous innovation and stunning brutality. Only political democracy can temper those excesses, diffuse the benefits and allow the nonrich to fight back.

Robert Kuttner

✦783✦

We have only one political party in the country—the Money Party. And it has two branches—the Republican branch and the Democratic branch.

Arnold Miller, president, UMW, president
Technology Strategy Group, vice president Xerox Corp.,
in *What's Happening To Labor*, 1976

✦784✦

It is quite evident to me that the present Tweedledee and Tweedledum two-party system and its virtues have been greatly overrated.

George Meany, 1949

✦785✦

Labor is going to have to fight that battle by itself; America is now the only Western country that does not have a party representing workers. We have two flavors of party representing capital, period.

Thomas Geoghegan, advocating a national wage policy

→786←

No men living are more worthy to be trusted than those who toil up from poverty, none less inclined to take or touch ought which they have not honestly earned. Let them beware of surrendering a political power which they already possess, and which, if surrendered, will surely be used to close the door of advancement against such as they, and to fix new disabilities and burdens upon them, till all of liberty shall be lost.

President Abraham Lincoln, message to Congress, 12/3/1861

→787←

Unions can no more live without democracy than a fish without water.

Lane Kirkland, 1980

→788←

It is one of the characteristics of a free and democratic modern nation that it has free and independent labor unions.

President Franklin D. Roosevelt, speech before Teamster's union,
Washington, D.C., 9/11/1940

→789←

Under democracy, one party always devotes its chief energies to trying to prove that the other party is unfit to rule—and both commonly succeed and are right.

H.L. Mencken

→790←

The first thing a dictator does is abolish the free press. Next he abolishes the right of labor to go on strike. Strikes have been labor's weapon of progress in the century of our industrial civilization. Where the strike has been abolished ... labor is reduced to a state of medieval peonage, the standard of living is lowered, the nation falls to a subsistence level.

George Seldes, *Freedom of the Press*, 1935

→791←

When the rich concern themself with the poor, that's called charity. When the poor concern themself with the rich, that's called revolution.

William Winpisinger, 1981

→792←

We must respect those above us. It pays. Be loyal to your employer. Don't be fooled by wrong talk. Speak well of your bosses to other workmen.

U.S. Dept. of Labor: Federal Citizenship textbook, 1925

❧793❧

... all job holders from corporation presidents to ragpickers.

James D. Hodgson, Secretary of Labor (1970-1973),
Nixon Administration, on the role of Dept. of Labor and
its role of representation

❧794❧

[Low wages are] one of the greatest evils of political communities.

Benjamin Franklin

❧795❧

Time has arrived when working people should decide on the necessity of united action as citizens at the ballot box.

Resolution of the American Federation of Labor, 1886

❧796❧

It is ridiculous to imagine that the wageworkers can be slaves in employment and yet achieve control at the polls.

Samuel Gompers, AFL convention, 1894,
in *History of the American Working Class*, 1927

❧797❧

To wield the ballot intelligently and heroically is the workingmen's last resort; in fact, it is the remedy which contends itself to all right thinking men.

Eugene Debs, 1888, in *The Bending Cross*, 1949

❧798❧

We reward our friends and punish our enemies.

Samuel Gompers to union voters

❧799❧

You have got to unite in the same labor union and in the same political party and strike and vote together, and the hour you do that, the world is yours.

Eugene Debs, 1914

❧800❧

There's a direct relationship between the ballot box and the bread box, and what the union fights for and wins at the bargaining table can be taken away in the legislative halls.

Walter Reuther

→801←

Increased interest and participation by labor in the affairs of government should make for economic and political stability in the future. Labor has a constitutional and statutory right to participate.

John L. Lewis

→802←

The labor movement's political activity is aimed at encouraging the greatest possible participation in elections. Democracy cannot succeed if only the rich and powerful have and use the votes.

George Meany, 1978

→803←

We in labor don't control how our members vote. I don't even control my wife's vote.

George Meany

→804←

The union bosses will have their troops out on election day digging up derelicts, vagrants, and anyone else who will take a dollar to cast a vote. ... We must stop these villains from seizing total control of our elections.

Congressman John Edward Cunningham, III (R-Wash., 1977-1979), in a constituent letter as cited in the *Federationist*, an AFL-CIO publication, 8/1978

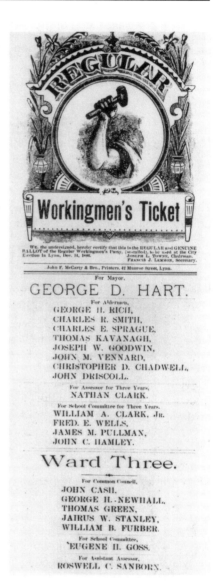

Poster, "Workingman's Ticket," Lynn, Massachusetts, 12/14/1886. Courtesy Lynn Historical Society.

❖805❖

We got you in—We'll get you out.

Protest placard by public workers aimed at incumbent politicians,
New York, 1991

❖806❖

(Business agents and shop stewards are ...) the unacknowledged legislators of the world.

Thomas Geoghegan

❖807❖

Today in America, unions have a secure place in our industrial life. Only a handful of reactionaries harbor the ugly thought of breaking unions and depriving working men and women of the right to join the union of their choice. I have no use for those—regardless of their political party—who hold some vain and foolish dream of spinning the clock back to the days when organized labor was huddled, almost, as a helpless mass.

President Dwight D. Eisenhower

❖808❖

And, it seems to me just as proper to ask some questions about the role of the captains of American industry—those who pretend to be defenders of free enterprise—in seeking to destroy a labor movement that has always supported and promoted free enterprise.

George Meany

❖809❖

Working and used-to-be-working people no longer matter in a politics where the scapegoat category rises higher and higher on the social scale. Blame used to be the exclusive property of welfare mothers; and now we have passed it upward to stubbornly lazy American industrial workers. In due course approved wisdom will settle the blame on everyone else except the CEOs and the very rich, who are forever invulnerable to censure because every statesman, whatever his party, is their slavish dependent for campaign contributions.

Murray Kempton (1917-1997), newspaper journalist,
columnist, author

❖810❖

When I want to buy up any politician, I always find the anti-monopolists the most purchasable. They don't come so high.

William H. Vanderbilt (1821-1885),
railroad industrialist, attributed

⇥811⇤

In politics, as in other things, there is no such thing as one getting something for nothing. The payoff may involve compromises that may strike at the ideals and principles one has held dear all his life.

A. Philip Randolph

⇥812⇤

The blue-collar worker will continue to be a progressive so long as it is progress for everyone but himself.

Senator Fred Roy Harris (D-Okla., 1964-1973)

⇥813⇤

A liberal is a man who leaves the room when the fighting begins.

Heywood Broun

⇥814⇤

A red is any son-of-a-bitch who wants thirty cents when we're paying twenty-five.

John Steinbeck (1902-1968), 1940 Pulitzer Prize for fiction,
1962 Nobel Prize for literature, *Grapes of Wrath*, 1939

⇥815⇤

The two agitators in this strike are Goodyear hours and wages. They are native products. They were not imported from Moscow.

Attributed to a leader of the Rubber Workers' strike on a radio
program, Akron, Ohio, 1936, in *Labor's New Millions*, 1938

⇥816⇤

Unions tend to Sovietism.

President William Howard Taft (1909-1913)

⇥817⇤

As long as redbaiting is tolerated, the trade union movement will diminish, civil liberties and rights will be vulnerable, and peace will be threatened, but crime, corruption, decline and decay, will flourish.

Ernest DeMaio, *Words For Workers In Changing Times*, 1993

⇥818⇤

Many of us have questions about the purging of progressive thinkers by unions and universities during the McCarthy era, which effectively destroyed the 1930s alliance of intellectuals and labor. However, more damaging is the perception that labor is not progressive.

Kim Fellner, educator, director, National Writers Union (NWU)

✦819✦

Republicans can hear the whispers of business, but not the yells and screams of working people.

President Harry S. Truman

✦820✦

The rising tide must lift all boats, not just the yachts. That is our duty as progressives. That is the defining mission of the Democratic Party.

Senator Edward M. Kennedy

✦821✦

Organizations of workers, wisely led, temperate in their demands and conciliatory in their attitude, make not for industrial strife, but for industrial peace.

Governor Franklin D. Roosevelt, in address before the New York
Women's Trade Union League, 6/8/1929

✦822✦

President Roosevelt wants you to join the union.

CIO leaflet during New Deal drive in late 1930s

✦823✦

Mr. Roosevelt is the only man we ever had in the White House who would understand that my boss is a son of a bitch.

North Carolina mill worker, reported in the *Boston Globe*, 1934

✦824✦

For a labor movement that believes the country should constantly be taking steps forward, holding our own is not good enough.

Andrew J. Biemiller in *Labor Looks at Congress—1978*

✦825✦

Labor's job and Labor's obligation are perfectly plain no matter who sits in the White House.

Heywood Broun, in *Men Who Lead Labor*, 1937

✦826✦

Every president of the United States in this generation has been faced by the fact that when labor relations are strained to the breaking point there remains but one high court of conciliation—the government of the United States.

President Franklin D. Roosevelt, 10/2/1935

❧827❧

A president does not have to agree with everything labor says, but who-ever wants to lead this nation, if he really wants to be the president of this country, must respect and involve and listen to the workers of America as expressed through their leadership.

Vice President Walter Mondale

❧828❧

The government's position has long been known to be that sooner or later there would have to be a showdown in the minefields. Its attitude is that if a strike must be, it must be, and the sooner the issue is disposed of the better.

Herbert C. Hoover, Secretary of Commerce (1921-1928),
Harding and Coolidge Administrations, 1922

❧829❧

The only time that the president and the congress step in is when the unions have a chance of winning a strike.

Andrew Moneypenny, president, Transport Workers Union, after
back-to-work order

❧830❧

I am an American, free born, with all the pride of my heritage. I love my country with its institutions and traditions. With Abraham Lincoln, I thank God that we have a country where men may strike. May the power of my *government* never be used to throttle or crush the efforts of the toilers to improve their material welfare and elevate the standard of their citizen-ship.

John L. Lewis, answering President Woodrow Wilson's
charges of being a labor dictator, 1919, in *John L. Lewis:
An Unauthorized Biography*, 1949

❧831❧

It ill-behooves one who has supped at labor's table and who has been sheltered in labor's house to curse with equal fervor and fine impartiality both labor and its adversaries when they become locked in deadly em-brace.

John L. Lewis, response to President Franklin D. Roosevelt
in national dispute, 1937

→832←

You shall not press down upon the brow of labor this crown of thorns. You shall not crucify mankind upon a cross of gold.

William Jennings Bryan,
Democratic Presidential Convention, 1896

→833←

The true right to a country—as to anything else—springs not from political or court authority, but from work.

David Ben-Gurion (born David Green, 1886-1973), Zionist
politician, first prime minister of Israel (1948-1953 and 1955-
1963), *Earning A Homeland*, 1915

→834←

This nation, this generation, in this hour, has man's first chance to build a Great Society, a place where the meaning of man's life matches the marvels of man's labor.

President Lyndon Baines Johnson (1963-1969)

→835←

We must be partisan for a principle and not for a party.

Samuel Gompers

→836←

No party politics ... shall have place in the Federation.

Samuel Gompers, in *Open Shop* editorials, AFL Bureau of
Literature, Washington, D.C., 1908

→837←

I am willing to step aside if that will promote our cause, but I cannot and will not prove false to my convictions that the trade unions pure and simple are the natural organizations of the wage-workers to secure their present material and practical improvement and to achieve their final emancipation.

Samuel Gompers, railing against his union joining a political party,
1890, in *History of the American Working Class*, 1927

→838←

Both personally and officially, I disavow the sit-down strike as a part of the economic and organizational policy of the AFL.

William Green

✦839✦

We disaffiliate.

> John L. Lewis to William Green, on the official split
> of UMWA from AFL, 12/12/1947

✦840✦

The test of a politician's worth to the labor movement was where he stood on the 'slave labor law.'

> John Kenneth Galbraith, *A Life in our Times*, 1981

✦841✦

So the elderly, the labor movement, and some of us in Congress raised our voices and marshaled our votes. We took our message to the people. We said that Social Security was a right that Americans have earned and paid for. ... We organized on that issue—we fought and won.

> Senator Edward M. Kennedy, 1981

✦842✦

Those members of Congress who want labor's support in November will have to support labor in April.

> Robert A. Georgine, president,
> Building & Construction Trades, AFL-CIO, 1982

✦843✦

The conservative tide will probably be turned back because the labor movement's idea of simple justice for working people and the poor, at home and abroad, represent the ideals of equity and a decent break for people who, unorganized, would have a hard time getting a decent break.

> Steven Kelman, labor writer and instructor

✦844✦

As long as I have a voice, the rank and file will vote on these contracts. And if Congress tries to enforce any idea of stopping the rank and file from voting on contracts, the UAW will march on Washington and do a most effective job of stopping them.

> Walter Reuther, 1970

✦845✦

Not until Congress takes action to cut down on the powers, the liberties, the immunities and the privileges of our large labor unions, will we make the kind of progress which is needed.

> Senator Barry Morris Goldwater (R-Ariz., 1953-1965 and 1969-
> 1987), 1964 presidential candidate, air force general, 1/13/1970

❧846❧

We're going to have massive unemployment if this inflation doesn't stop. I was the happiest man in the world back in the 30s when Congress passed the Wagner Act. Labor was weak then. Now labor sits on the other side of the table with all the muscle. I don't know what changes there should be and I don't want to see labor's right to strike ever denied, or compulsory arbitration. But we are at the point where we must level their power to that equation.

Senator Barry Goldwater, 1/27/1970

❧847❧

I believe the biggest threat is big government, but it is supported by and feeds on big labor, and I fear that there are those in business who see a chance at monopoly, whether they use the word or not, if they go along with big government. I'm afraid the fight is never-ending, but we must continue.

Ronald Reagan

❧848❧

Nobody has a right to stop the processes of labor until all the methods of conciliation and settlement have been exhausted.

President Woodrow Wilson, in *Toil and Trouble*, 1964

❧849❧

I can think of nothing, no law, no civil rights act, that would radicalize this country more, democratize it more, and also revive the Democratic Party, than to make this one tiny change in the law: to let people join unions if they like, freely and without coercion, without threat of being fired, just as people are permitted to do in Europe and Canada.

Thomas Geoghegan, *Which Side Are You On?*, 1991

❧850❧

While strikes sometimes cause public inconvenience, they are an inherent part of the liberties we all enjoy—free speech, freedom of association, the right of contract. The exercise of liberties in a democratic society is not only healthy; it is vital.

George Meany

✦851✦

Throughout the 1980s, too much time and energy was devoted to making the rich even richer. Tax laws, always an inequitable gimmick, were rigged to help the wealthy owe less. Government, presided over by an old man whose hair was brown only because his head was filled with B. S., became a pimp for the elite.

Mike Barnicle, on the policies of President Reagan

✦852✦

Despite a fraudulent tax cut which favors the very rich, we continue to believe in real tax justice for workers and the middle class. And on this issue, we have only just begun to fight.

Senator Edward M. Kennedy, 1981

✦853✦

That is known as the carrot-and -stick policy: for the rich, the carrot; for the poor, the stick.

Lane Kirkland, on President Reagan's economics

✦854✦

President Reagan is asking for sacrifice from all of you. All of you does not include the oil companies, other big industries and wealthy folks. It does, however, include workers and the needy.

Stephen Lukosus, Boston area president, APWU, 1982

✦855✦

Where are all those leaders and people who remember or helped build schools, libraries, fire stations during the depression—not close them down? Shall we call this decade the 'Silence of the Donkeys?'

James Bollen, labor writer, editor, educator, on Congress cutting
funds and closing public facilities, 1991

✦856✦

It's like getting in an elevator and punching the up and down buttons at the same time.

Congresswoman Shirley Chisholm on Reaganomics

✦857✦

Maybe, just maybe, the effects of the tremendous cutbacks of this administration will be a realization of the part of millions of workers that they cannot be taken for granted; and they, too, belong in the union movement.

Albert Shanker, on Reagan cutbacks

Secretary of Labor Frances Perkins inspects Golden Gate Bridge construction in San Francisco, a Depression-era project that put people back to work, 1935. Courtesy George Meany Memorial Archives.

→858←

Ronald Reagan is going to force a renaissance in the labor movement.

Domenic Bozzotto

→859←

The president says we should give his program more time. ... If you see a house burning, if you see a ship sinking, if you see a man drowning, do you give it more time?

Lane Kirkland, reacting to President Reagan's economics

→860←

There have been all sorts of presidents in our history—conservative and liberal. However, this president and this Administration has pushed through Congress what is clearly the most anti-union program in recent memory—what must we do? We must fight back! We will fight back from the union halls to the halls of Congress. We will use our numbers. We will use our votes. We will use our money.

Moe Biller, on President Reagan and his policies

❧861❧

Those who would destroy or further limit the rights of organized labor—those who cripple collective bargaining or prevent organization of the unorganized—do a disservice to the cause of democracy.

President d John F. Kennedy

❧862❧

In 1963, President Kennedy spoke for the last time to a labor organization. He spoke of his dream for a decade that then seemed far distant—the dream that Americans in the 1980s could continue to live in prosperity—in a growing and progressive economy. Now the 1980s have come, and you and I are keepers of that dream—it is a dream that gives hope to life—a better future for our children—a better, stronger, greater America for all our people. It is the living dream that is the source of our solidarity. And today I am more certain than I have ever been before that this truly is a dream that shall never die.

Senator Edward M. Kennedy, 1981

❧863❧

In the pious name of a 'balanced budget'—that last refuge of those who care nothing about the poor, the young, the old, the weak and the helpless, or indeed, about workers—these programs are being dismantled. ... We object, and strenuously, to having, not the general welfare, but the scale on which we weigh the decision to wipe out a half-century of progress.

Thomas Donahue, 1981

❧864❧

The attack on OSHA is the wrong war, against the wrong foe, at the wrong time.

Harold Buoy, on the Occupational Safety & Health Act

❧865❧

He is a madman or fool who believes that this river of human sentiment, flowing as it does from the hearts of these thirty millions, who with their dependents constitute two-thirds of the population of the United States of America, can be dammed or impounded by the erection of arbitrary barriers of restraint.

John L. Lewis, in speech condemning the division of AFL and CIO, 7/16/1936, in *Labor's Untold Story*, 1955

✦866✦

If my political philosophy were at the negotiating table, we couldn't win. Because it's the mainstream that wins, and my membership is mainstream.

Domenic Bozzotto

✦867✦

This bill will not encourage strikes. In fact, it may prevent them because it will ensure that workers and employers can meet face-to-face across the bargaining table—without the fear that their rights will be violated.

Congressman David Edward Bonior (D-Mich., 1977-), on
favoring the Workplace Fairness Act, a proposed striker
replacement bill that failed in the Senate

✦868✦

Prosperity is just around the corner.

President Herbert C. Hoover, one of a series of noted pontifical
declarations during the stock market crash era, 1929

✦869✦

I'm not worried so much about the shoes in Mulroney's closet—I'm more worried about the loafers in his Cabinet.

General John Cabot Trail, Canadian humorist, on Prime Minister
Brian Mulroney's penchant for purchasing shoes

✦870✦

Politics is not going to replace what the labor movement lacks.

Robert Schrank, consultant

✦871✦

Even the most ardently anti-minimum wage-law, union-busting, capital-gains-tax-abolishing conservative candidate wants to be seen by voters in shirt sleeves, not in the company of a think tank full of supply-side economists or some covey of wet-haired investment bankers, each with his own Adam Smith suspenders.

Mark Shields

→872←

The Democrats have learned so well that organized labor's support isn't enough to carry an election as to have forgotten how seldom they have won without it. Neglectful as they have too often been, the unions happen to be among the few institutions left to defend what meager degree of equity survives these things.

Murray Kempton, 1992

→873←

Whenever a bold elected official defends the progressive income tax and the minimum wage, or resists further tax breaks for the well-to-do, or seeks to advance social insurance, or urges that big corporations be held accountable, some conservative editorialist or congressman can be counted on to sneer.

Robert Kuttner

→874←

(The) spirit of Charles Dickens is alive and well in the Labor Department.

Lane Kirkland, responding to a government proposal to allow letting teenagers work longer hours in certain jobs, 1982

→875←

Clear it with Sidney.

President Franklin D. Roosevelt, attributed, responding to CIO President Sidney Hillman's veto power over selection of FDR's running mate

→876←

Both parties cry out that the poor must work for their welfare, but neither could dream of providing the public revenues necessary to capitalize enough public sector jobs for the poor to take. Benefits under the Aid to Families with Dependent Children program were slashed 42% between 1970 and 1991, yet Congress is still slashing them and seeks to end them as a federal entitlement.

Ronnie Dugger, journalist

→877←

I want to correct some misinformation that went out. The governor in his message last week said 36% of city [Chicago] employees were patronage, and that is inaccurate, untrue, and false. There is less than 8%.

Chicago Mayor Richard Daley

→878←

I might have been a senator and sat on my ass all day long.

John L. Lewis, in *Labor Baron—A Portrait of John L. Lewis*, 1944

→879←

Think of me as a coal miner, and you won't make any mistakes.

John L. Lewis, when being asked of his partisan affiliation, in *Labor Baron—A Portrait of John L. Lewis*, 1944

→880←

If the political mainstream doesn't address the issue of economic insecurity, the political fringe surely will—by scapegoating immigrants, minorities, foreigners and by stoking people's fears.

Robert Kuttner

→881←

One of the oldest truths in American politics is that people vote their pocketbooks. When their pocketbooks runneth over, they hail the president's vision, wisdom, statesmanship and erect posture. But if they look in the pocketbook and see only lint and Kleenex, they ask how a boob like that ever stumbled into public office.

Mike Royko, Chicago newspapers columnist, author, biographer, 1972 Pulitzer Prize for commentary

→882←

As far as Vietnam is concerned, we in the AFL-CIO are neither 'hawk' nor 'dove' nor 'chicken.'

George Meany, in *George Meany and his Times*, 1982

→883←

The working class who make the sacrifices, who shed the blood, have never yet had a voice in declaring war. The ruling class has always made the war and made the peace.

Eugene Debs, 1918

→884←

I myself have had sympathy with the fears of the workers of the United States; for the tendency of war is toward reaction, and too often military necessities have been made an excuse for the destruction of laboriously erected industrial and social standards.

President Woodrow Wilson, in *History of the American Working Class*, 1927

⇥885⇤

If workers don't believe that change is possible because of their experience in the union day to day, forget about politics.

Sam Gindin, 1989

⇥886⇤

The most powerful opposition I have ever seen comes not from Jimmy Hoffa's Teamsters or from Big Steel or from Republican job-seekers, but from big commercial farm groups every time legislation is introduced that would stop the importation of migrant farm workers from foreign countries.

James P. Mitchell, Secretary of Labor (1953-1961), Eisenhower
Administration, in *Organized Labor and the Church*, 1993

⇥887⇤

We depend on misfortune to build up our force of migratory workers, and when the supply is low because there are not enough unfortunates at home, we rely on misfortune abroad to replenish the supply.

From *Report of the Commission on Migratory Labor* (no date)

⇥888⇤

We can close the loophole in our immigration laws that permits U.S. firms to replace their permanent employees with temporary foreign 'guest workers' at lower wages. The Republicans portray steps like these as unacceptable meddling in the workings of the free market; I believe they are inescapable responsibilities in the interests of national community.

Governor Mario Matthew Cuomo (D-N.Y., 1983-1995),
Reason to Believe, 1995

⇥889⇤

Immigrants built this country, and immigrants built our labor movement. When times are good, immigrant workers are eagerly recruited. But when the economy begins to sour, immigrants who have slaved to create the nation's wealth are told that they are stealing jobs from those of us whose parents immigrated a generation ago.

Paul Bigiman, labor activist

⇥890⇤

Democrats think low wages are a problem. Republicans think low wages are the solution.

Congressman Richard Andrew Gephardt (D-Mo., 1977-)

✣891✣

The Republicans traditionally worry about costs, incentives, and productivity—often to the exclusion of such concerns as pollution, work safety, and workers' rights. The Democrats traditionally worry about pollution, work safety, and workers' rights—often to the exclusion of costs, incentives, and productivity.

Senator Paul Efthemios Tsongas (D-Mass., 1979-1985),
The Road From Here, 1981

✣892✣

Never forget that men who labor cast the votes, set up and pull down governments.

Senator Elihu Root (R-N.Y., 1909-1915) diplomat, Secretary of
State (1905-1909), Theodore Roosevelt Administration,
1912 Nobel Peace Prize

✣893✣

Things always get better at election time.

Senator Fred Harris

✣894✣

The issues before the country now involve the ideals that keep the labor movement young—and make it, at the dawn of its second century, the surest guardian of progress and the most powerful force for change in America.

Senator Edward M. Kennedy, 11/18/1981

✣895✣

Every piece of progressive social legislation passed by Congress in the 20th century bears a union label.

George Meany

Chapter 10

Public Employment

⁌896⁌

Employees of the government have exactly the same desires and aspirations as do employees in the private sector.

George Meany, *New York Times*, 4/17/1970

⁌897⁌

The ability of federal workers to participate in the political life of their communities is severely limited through the Hatch Act [1940]. Federal employees are the only group in the nation's workforce whose salaries are under wage controls.

W. Howard McLennan, 1979

⁌898⁌

Few politicians can resist the temptation of kicking the hell out of federal employees.

Congressman William David Ford (D-Mich., 1965-1995),
chairman of Committee on Post Office and Civil Service,
97th through 101st congress

⁌899⁌

If you ever saw a cat and a dog eating out of the same plate, you can bet your ass it was the cat's food.

Congressman William Clay, chairman, Committee on Post Office
and Civil Service, 102nd and 103rd congresses, commenting on the
suggestion that public employee unions form a coalition with
President Jimmy Carter, 1980

⇥900⇤

Why are we the pigs? The public employees I know are social workers who care for abused and neglected children. Or they work with mentally ill and mentally retarded adults and adolescents. They find homes for the homeless. They keep the roads repaired and clean. They open and close the bridges. They run the 911 emergency system. They keep the city and state hospital systems working. They run the state prisons. Public employees are police officers and firefighters. Public employees help keep you healthy and safe.

Sandy Felder, local resident, protesting editorial cartoon against
public employees in a letter, *Boston Globe*

⇥901⇤

And I would remind those in national leadership today that it is hypocrisy to praise the free union movement in Poland and then turn around and ignore it and try to undermine it in the United States of America.

Vice President Walter Mondale, 1981

⇥902⇤

The Polish Workers have won rights in a communist nation. Why must there continue to be economic capital punishment and lifelong blacklisting for American postal workers?

Moe Biller

⇥903⇤

A postal worker voting Republican is like a chicken voting for Frank Perdue.

Bob Riordan, retired postal worker

⇥904⇤

Don't Hesitate! Negotiate!

Postal workers' slogan used by APWU, 1981

⇥905⇤

Chump change.

Moe Biller, terming bonuses in lieu of raises

⇥906⇤

Fool's gold.

Billy Quinn, president, Mailhandlers Union, terming the
acceptance of bonuses in lieu of raises

Firemen make their appeal for a basic $7,000 annual wage for New York's 6,000 firefighters to Mayor Robert F. Wagner, Jr. (1954-1965), the son of Robert F. Wagner, Sr., author of 1935 Wagner Act, 4/21/1956. A few days earlier, six members of Fire Fighters Local 94 were killed when a burning Bronx movie house wall collapsed. Courtesy George Meany Memorial Archives.

❧907❧

PRIVATIZATION: The practice of transferring government property, enterprises and services to private ownership. ... Legalized looting of public assets. The spoils that go to the winners of elections. The final step in the rip-off of the public purse.

Ernest DeMaio, Words For Workers In Changing Times, 1993

❧908❧

Privatization is not about saving money but only shifting income to a few already wealthy business owners who are usually contributors to the campaigns of the current administration. This, you see, is a new form of patronage.

Paul Jodoin, businessman

❧909❧

Public employees are being made scapegoats for the current problems of state and local governments, and some of the leaders of the anti-public chorus are businessmen who are trying to get their hands on more government dollars through lucrative contracts.

John D. Hanrahan, Government For Sale, 1977

❧910❧

Government is most often called upon to provide services that private-sector companies find unprofitable. Contracting-out often means lower wages and benefits for workers, reduced services to citizens, and the possibility that vendors will deal only with profitable, easy-to-serve clients and abandon the needy.

Joseph Faherty, commenting on the perils of privatization

❧911❧

Privatization—that market-driven idea about how to get the old machinery cranked up again while destroying all sense of collective responsibility—will drive all who believe they have some responsibility of their own for the way we live back into the shadows of the rocks from which we came.

Robin W. Winks, Yale history professor

❧912❧

You can't privatize the concerns and needs of educating the people in the city.

Boston Mayor Ray Flynn

Reprinted with permission ©Huck/Konopacki, courtesy Mike Konopacki.

❧913❧

The end result of privatization is not cost-saving but cost-shifting: from workers' wages into contractors' profits.

> Debbie Goldman, Public Employees Department

❧914❧

The mails must go through!

> President Grover Cleveland's (1885-1889 and 1893-1897) cry to
> send federal troops to break the Pullman Strike of 1894

❧915❧

There is no right to strike against the public safety by anybody, anywhere, any time.

> Governor Calvin Coolidge (R-Mass., 1919-1921) in telegram to
> Samuel Gompers, AFL president, during Boston policemen's
> strike, 9/14/1919

❧916❧

In government, we cannot shut down the assembly line.

> Governor Ronald Reagan (R-Calif., 1967-1975), 1970

❧917❧

You can rest assured that if I am elected president, I will take whatever steps are necessary to provide our air-traffic controllers with the most modern equipment available and to adjust staff levels and work days so that they are commensurate with achieving a maximum degree of public safety.

> Ronald Reagan, Republican presidential candidate, in a letter to
> Professional Air-Traffic Controllers Union (PATCO) president,
> Robert Poli, 10/20/1980

❧918❧

I pledge to you that my administration will work very closely with you to bring about a spirit of cooperation between the president and the air-traffic controllers. Such harmony can and must exist if we are to restore the people's confidence in their government.

> Ronald Reagan, presidential candidate, in a letter to Robert Poli

❧919❧

Government workers have proved that when they are not dealt with justly, they will defy the law. And they have proved that, in such situations, government is powerless.

> Jerry Wurf (1919-1981), president of AFSCME, 1970

→920←

Don't we all admire the Solidarity trade-union movement in Poland for essentially doing the same thing as the air-traffic controllers—striking against their own government?

Moe Biller

→921←

If the name of the union had been Solidarity instead of PATCO, the strikers would have been hailed as standing up for what they believed in. Instead, they were fired, and the air-traffic control system in America would pay for it for years.

Roger Simon, columnist

→922←

They are in violation of the law, and if they do not report for work within 48 hours, they have forfeited their jobs and will be terminated.

President Ronald Reagan, on striking PATCO workers, 8/1981

→923←

Of course, the easiest advice anyone can give public employees dissatisfied with working conditions is to quit their jobs. If all of us took that advice, we'd still be working 12-hour days a week. Paid vacations, paid sick leave, health insurance, seniority rights and pensions were won by workers who refused to quit their jobs.

Michael Grace, director of public relations, Public Employee Department, AFL-CIO

→924←

By striking, they've quit their jobs.

President Ronald Reagan on PATCO strikers, 8/1981

→925←

The most blatant form of union busting I have ever seen. It will not end the strike.

Robert Poli, PATCO president, responding to President Reagan

→926←

If they (the administration) ever went after organized crime the way they went after our members, the country would be a safe place to live in.

Robert Poli, former PATCO president, 8/16/1981

✦927✦

The irony is that were I ever faced with the same set of circumstances, with just a few exceptions, I would do it again.

Robert Poli, after leading national air-controllers' strike against the government

✦928✦

It is one thing to use the full force of government to break a small union of hard-pressed public employees. That, I suppose, does express the harshest construction of the law and is, perhaps, popular, but is it then just and fitting to go out upon the field and shoot its wounded?

Lane Kirkland, commenting on President Reagan's firing of the PATCO workers, 1981

✦929✦

Ours is the only democracy in the world that sentences its government workers to 'economic capital punishment'—that takes their jobs away because they chose to strike. That's something which should be re-examined.

Moe Biller, on PATCO firings by President Reagan

✦930✦

Many statements were made here, about the 1920s and the 1930s and the struggles that many of you had. Brothers and sisters, the 1920s and the 1930s are here now.

Robert Poli, at AFL-CIO convention, 1981, on the fired air-traffic controllers of 1980 and 1981

✦931✦

I assure you that every one of our members are proud, will walk with their heads up and never, never be ashamed to be called trade unionists.

Robert Poli, at AFL-CIO convention, 1981, on the air-traffic controllers' strike of 1980

✦932✦

As children, we're taught to despise bullies, yet we watch our country pulling on its boots, winking and smiling in open acknowledgement that it's ok to have a double standard for Poland and PATCO; that it's ok, to have two Americas, one impoverished and below the water line, struggling for the breath of life, and the other waxing fat and gluttonous.

Ed Asner, actor, former president of Screen Actors Guild (SAG), in speech at AFSCME convention, San Francisco, 1984

✦933✦

Like other minority groups, government workers realize nothing will be conceded until it is demanded—and won, with the historic methods used by other trade unions.

Michael Grace

✦934✦

You don't solve a problem by passing a law that says it's illegal.

Lane Kirkland, on laws making strikes by public employees illegal

✦935✦

There has not, never has been, never will be any substitute for the right of employees to withhold their labor as a method of advancing their interests.

Sidney A. Goodman, former president, National Postal Union,
in *Labor Struggle in the Post Office*, 1992

National presidents Moe Biller of APWU and Vince Sombrotto of National Association of Letter Carriers (NALC) led thousands of postal unionists in a call for a fair and decent contract on Postal Solidarity Day, 1/13/1990, in front of U. S. Postal Service headquarters, Washington, D.C. Courtesy American Postal Workers Union, AFL-CIO.

➷936➶

Some of our members can master mathematical equations with the best of them. Some among us speak four and five languages; some have traveled every continent; and some have read great literature. So, who are they trying to scare—those who would have us reassigned to the unsightliness of poverty by belching their threats whenever we are ready to sit down and find a way not to diminish, but to improve, our piece of the action, our place in the sun?

Ben Zemsky, on impending postal negotiations, 1981

➷937➶

I've always maintained that if government workers had the legal right to strike, you would see fewer strikes. I am convinced that there would be a greater feeling of responsibility all around and more sophistication—less need for people to show how macho they are.

Moe Biller

➷938➶

There was a time when our thinking, and I think the general thinking, was that, of course, public sector employees could not strike. Obviously, that was a given. ... We were wrong.

Ida Klaus, national arbitrator, *Between Labor and Management*, 1995

➷939➶

There are many postal union officials who are calling for Congress to give us the right to strike. ... In fact, I think it would be sheer hypocrisy for Congress to deny us this right. Didn't Congress just shut down the government including services that are vital to a whole lot of people—to try to get the budget they want? How can they say it is wrong for us to shut down the mail service for a while to fight for a decent wage?

Paul Felton, postal steward, editor, 1996

Chapter 11

The Media

✦940✦

Newspapers are really great—they assign the labor beat, if they have one—to the *business* department. That's like having Republicans cover Democrats.

Editorial, *South Carolina Postal Workers News*

✦941✦

It seems to me that the press continually reports the negatives of American organized labor but are strangely silent on the positives of unionism in America. ... The truth is there are more crimes reported within management and within politics than in labor.

Thomas Scarnato, postal worker

✦942✦

Notice something about the media? They always refer to labor as a special interest. When you fight for the needs of 90% of the population, you're a special interest. Damn right. Unions, minorities, women are special interests groups. Of course, corporations are not special interests.

Victor Reuther, in *The Great Divide*, 1988

✦943✦

The trade union movement does not object to being called an interest group. We object only to being called a 'narrow' interest group.

Lane Kirkland

✦944✦

When the newspapers start to say good things about me, that's the time to get the recall machinery in motion.

Harry Bridges, in *Harry Bridges—The Rise and Fall of Radical Labor in the U.S.*, 1972

⇥945↤

At the management level, the press has clear economic interests, and people often forget that. And politicians—from both parties—are supported by these interests. They frame the debate in the same way as the press, and no one talks about reducing military spending. They talk as if military contracts were the only sources of jobs, when they know full well that the human-service sector creates far more.

Eleanor Smeal

⇥946↤

You cannot get the media to buy good news about federal civil servants. That is a basic fact.

Donald J. Devine, director, U.S. Office of Personnel Management, columnist, writer, educator, treasurer, American Conservative Union (ACU)

⇥947↤

If you want to win a strike, get backing from members of Congress and plenty of sympathetic play in the press, but do it in Eastern Europe or the Soviet Union, where the price of freedom isn't going to come out of an American capitalist's pocket.

Alexander Cockburn, commenting on the lack of media coverage of labor in America

⇥948↤

Who Is This Nut?

Featured headline of the *New York Post*, criticizing its new owner, Abe Hirschfeld, after firing 70 workers, then rehiring 69 of the 70, 3/16/1993

⇥949↤

The bitter antagonism of labor's unfair foes—the open threats and covert plans of our opponents to crush our organized labor—have quickened the pulse beats of our brave labor editors and aroused them to protect and defend the rights of toilers in our country.

It should be the aim of every union member, as well as every sympathizer with our great cause, to be helpful in every way, to extend the beneficent influence of the labor press.

Samuel Gompers, 1904

→950←

Freelance writers are the cowboys of the 20th century: People think we lead romantic lives, while in fact we're underpaid and overworked, and we have to deal with tons of bull.

Charles Thiesen, writer

→951←

Unlike other tradesmen, we do not write to eat; we eat to write. Our purpose is the transformation of society.

Murray E. Denofsky, a union writer arguing against his local affiliating with a national union and losing individuality of purpose

→952←

Good writing must be organized.

Slogan on National Writers Union T-shirt

→953←

I aimed at the public's heart, and by accident I hit it in the stomach.

Upton Sinclair, on the public furor caused by his novel, *The Jungle*, an exposé of the meat industry and its conditions, 1906

→954←

Our members are less concerned by fears of corruption or mob influence within organized labor. The problems have been the dominance by white males and support for issues such as the Vietnam War. A vision of a just society is often not put forward by the labor movement.

Kim Fellner

→955←

We have the potential to create a strong voice that explains clearly why so many decent jobs went elsewhere, why so much of corporate America seemingly cares not a whit about the dignity of work. ... There should not be a major issue discussed in public in this country that workers do not know our position on.

Thomas Deary, labor journalist, on creating a labor media

→956←

When we ran our last series of minimum-wage ads, two days later a group of Republicans introduced a bill to increase the minimum wage. We think we did our job.

Richard Trumka, on radio ads targeting congressional races, 1996

✦957✦

There is nothing that travels faster than the news of an important gain won by workers elsewhere.

Anonymous labor leader

✦958✦

(TV rarely shows) the positive contributions that labor has made to this country.

Ed Asner, president, SAG

✦959✦

Throughout the year (union) locals perform wonderful deeds donating time and money to charitable causes. Very rarely do these deeds make the press. Strikers, violence and indictments seem to receive the only coverage.

Joe Kirylo, shop steward

✦960✦

TV continues to ignore labor's contributions to the community and the nation. TV, the most powerful persuader and educator in the country, is guilty of presenting negative messages about workers and their union, undermining our efforts to reverse America's growing concentration of wealth and power in the hands of the few.

J.C. Turner, president, International Union of Operating Engineers (IUOE)

✦961✦

We haven't explained ourselves well enough to the American people.

Thomas Donahue, on public perception of labor unions, 1995

✦962✦

The success of a strike—if it becomes necessary to strike—will, in large part, depend upon public opinion.

Walter Reuther, in Walter Reuther: Labor's Rugged Individualist, 1972

✦963✦

No battle is remembered after a time unless there is a play, a film, a song, a television program, a sculpture or a picture that tells of the event. We are the actors, but know what ails working people because we share in what ails them.

Theodore Bikel, president, Associated Actors and Artists of America, Lifetime Achievement Award in the Arts

AFL Printing Pressmen, Local 86, fill sandbags at water's edge. Organized labor brought 10,000 volunteers to Des Moines, Iowa to help with flood control, 6/25/1954. Courtesy George Meany Memorial Archives.

Chapter 11: The Media

Chapter 12

Voices for Labor

→964←

The labor movement means just this: It is the last noble protest of the American people against the power of incorporated wealth.

Wendell Phillips, 1871

→965←

I would, without fear of being challenged, say that the trade union movement is the only institution America has ever created to deal meaningfully with injustice.

William Winpisinger

→966←

The plain truth is that labor is the chief representative force that keeps the real special interests from dominating American political life.

Lane Kirkland

→967←

In its contribution to the well-being of real people in the real world, that union [custodians' union] surpasses any achievement of any of the celebrities on any of the walls of any of your restaurants.

Jack Beatty, editor, *Atlantic Monthly*, on refusing to have his caricature on the walls of Palm chain restaurants because of the chain's non-union labor policy

⇥968⇤

The trade unions are the legitimate outgrowth of modern society and industrial conditions. ... They were born of the necessity of workers to protect and defend themselves from encroachment, injustice and wrong. ... To protect the workers in their inalienable rights to a higher and better life; to protect them, not only as equals before the law, but also in their health, their homes, their firesides, their liberties as men, as workers, and as citizens; to overcome and conquer prejudices and antagonism; to secure to them the right to life; the right to be full sharers in the abundance which is the result of their brain and brawn, and the civilization of which they are the founders and the mainstay; to this the workers are entitled. ... The attainment of these is the glorious mission of the trade unions.

Samuel Gompers, speech, 1898

⇥969⇤

What does labor want? We want more schoolhouses and less jails, more books and less arsenals, more learning and less vice, more constant work and less crime, more leisure and less greed, more justice and less revenge.

Samuel Gompers, known as the More! More! More! speech,
repeated many times, Chicago, 8/28/1893

⇥970⇤

What do we want? Food on the table, a rug on the floor, a picture on the wall, music in the home.

Philip Murray (1886-1952), co-founder and president of CIO
(1940-1952), UMWA officer, USWA officer (1942-1952)
(*see* photograph p. 195)

⇥971⇤

I have been a daughter; I have been a wife; I have been a mother; I have been a grandmother; but I never truly was a woman until I became a sister when I joined the union.

Lucille Dickess, president, Clerical and Technical Workers,
Yale University

Secretary of Labor Frances Perkins, flanked by Philip Murray (*left*), Sidney Hillman (*behind Philip Murray*), and John L. Lewis (*far right*) leave the White House after AFL mediation, 3/13/1939. Courtesy George Meany Memorial Archives.

✦972✦

The union is not for yourself but for your children. It does not arise to avenge the past but to claim the future. ... It is an expression not of the dignity of its leaders but the dignity of all. It was called into being to celebrate the majesty of one person. ... It is not property but mission. ... Anyone can belong to a union; but a union belongs to no one and least of all to anyone who is ashamed of where he or she came from and indifferent to those he/she left behind. The union leader is not the owner of an institution; he/she is the caretaker of a tradition.

Murray Kempton

✦973✦

Unions are not economic institutions competing for market shares. They have no independent life of their own apart from their members, as corporations have. They are not instruments of industry but of people, to be made, unmade or changed as the interests of those people may dictate.

Lane Kirkland

❧974❧

The labor movement is organized upon a principle that the strong shall help the weak. That principle of the organizations of America is American, that the strong shall help the weak.

John L. Lewis, in *John L. Lewis: An Unauthorized Biography*, 1949

❧975❧

Fighting for social justice, it seems to me, is one of the profoundest ways in which man can say yes to man's dignity, and that really means sacrifices. There is no way on this earth in which you can say yes to man's dignity and know that you're going to be spared some sacrifice.

Cesar Chavez, 1975

❧976❧

As long as there are such trade unionists, labor will be opposed by those who seek to portray workers and their unions as separate entities— referring to unions as an unneeded 'third force,' just as the diehard segregationists falsely labeled civil rights organizations as 'outside agitators.'

George Meany, 1979

❧977❧

Our labor unions are not narrow, self-seeking groups. They have raised wages, shortened hours, and provided supplemental benefits. Through collective bargaining and grievance procedures, they have brought justice and democracy to the shop floor.

President John F. Kennedy, 1962

❧978❧

We in the trade union movement do not object to being called an interest group, but we strongly object to being called a 'narrow' interest group. The interests we represent are those of Americans in their roles of workers—and they are not narrow. With their skills, their industry and their productivity, they are the backbone of our economic society.

Lane Kirkland

❧979❧

The AFL-CIO has done more good for more people than any [other] group in America in its legislative efforts. It doesn't just try to do something about wages and hours for its own people. No group in the country works harder in the interests of everyone.

President Lyndon Johnson, 1965

⇸980↚

We have the most wealth of any nation because our workers have the skill to create it. We have the best products because they know how to make them. We have the most democratic system because of the values our trade unions have to sustain it.

Vice President Walter Mondale, 1981

⇸981↚

We never forget that all of our victories are temporary and provisional and that what we have gained at the bargaining table and in legislatures can be swept away. ... The labor movement was built for the long haul.

Lane Kirkland

⇸982↚

I believe in building a better world—not just a better house or more material things for myself—but to better people's lives. And I believe trade unions are necessary to preserve the American way of life. I don't think we can have a free democratic society without a free democratic labor movement.

Murray Finley, president, ACTWU, 1976

⇸983↚

The American Labor Movement has consistently demonstrated its devotion to the public interest. It is, and has been, good for all America.

President John F. Kennedy

⇸984↚

Our children must be made to realize that their forefathers labored under pitiful and dangerous conditions and finally raised up to shed oppression and gain their dignity. These children are the beneficiaries of these struggles.

Fred Kaltenstein

⇸985↚

I ask you leaders of labor; I ask you union members; I ask you young people who have yet to be tested: Why are you so weak? Why are you so self-serving? Why are you not outraged? Will all have to be lost before you awaken? How much is enough?

Ron Benevento, shop steward, IUE, commenting on the
apparent lack of action protesting a Supreme Court ruling
giving rights to strikebreakers

⇢986⇠

I did it my way, and I would freely admit to any shortcomings you want to attribute. But, I would suggest to you that the great problem of the American trade union movement is not leadership, it is followership.

Lane Kirkland, AFL-CIO farewell speech, 8/1/1995

⇢987⇠

At the collective bargaining table, in the community, in the exercise of the rights and responsibilities of citizenship, we shall represent the interests of all the American people.

We pledge ourselves to the more effective organization of working men and women; to the securing to them of full recognition and enjoyment of the rights to which they are justly entitled; to the achievement of ever higher standards of living and working conditions; to the attainment of security for all the people sufficient to enable workers and their families to live in dignity; to the enjoyment of the leisure which their skills make possible; and to the strengthening and extension of our way of life and the fundamental freedoms which are the basis of our democratic society.

From the preamble of the constitution of the AFL-CIO

⇢988⇠

I don't want you to follow me or anyone else. If you are looking for a Moses to lead you out of the capitalist wilderness, you will stay right where you are. I would not lead you into this Promised Land, if I could, because if I could lead you in, someone else could lead you out.

Eugene Debs

⇢989⇠

As long as there is a bottom class, I am of it.

Epitaph, Eugene Debs

⇢990⇠

We have no classes in this country. We are all workers here.

Philip Murray

⇢991⇠

All labor asks is 25 lousy cents an hour. The genesis of the campaign against labor is a labor-baiting, poker-playing, whiskey-drinking, evil old man whose name is Garner. Garner's knife is searching for the quivering, pulsating heart of labor. I am against him officially, individually and personally, concretely and in the abstract.

John L. Lewis, reacting to the opposition to his demands by Vice President John Nance Garner (1933-1941), Franklin D. Roosevelt Administration, in *The Glory and the Dream*, 1974

✦992✦

You should never have an ideology more specific than that of the founding fathers; 'For the general welfare.'

Saul Alinsky

✦993✦

Prosperity makes cowards of us all.

Saul Alinsky

✦994✦

Once you get fat and comfortable and reach the top, you want to stay there. You're imprisoned by your own so-called freedoms. I've seen too many lean and hungry labor leaders of the '30s grow fat-bellied and fatheaded. So I turned down the job and devoted myself to full-time activity in the radical movement.

Saul Alinsky, in turning down a management job

✦995✦

Next time I'm in jail, Tom, I hope you'll come and visit me.

John J. Sweeney, to Thomas Donahue in debate over AFL-CIO presidency, New York, 1995

✦996✦

I resent the fact that you are more hated in Rochester than I was.

John L. Lewis to Saul Alinsky

✦997✦

Don't worry boys; we'll weather this storm of approval and come out as hated as ever.

Saul Alinsky, to his staff, on the favorable reception of his book, *Rules for Radicals*, 1972

✦998✦

On the whole I have felt that his career was a great American tragedy in terms of what might have been.

Saul Alinsky, a friend and biographer of John L. Lewis, in *John L. Lewis: An Unauthorized Biography*, 1949

+999+

He was a visionary and a man of courage who fought for the dignity of all workers.

Alexis M. Herman, Secretary of Labor (1997-), Clinton
Administration, on the induction of Cesar Chavez into the U.S.
Department of Labor's Hall of Fame, 3/1999

+1000+

It might sound self-serving, but *dedicated* union men didn't dwell on maximizing their income; their aim was to protect the workers' rights, perhaps even to correct some of society's ills. Working for a not-for-profit organization always has seemed to me to be in a different category than employment in a profit-making enterprise.

Marvin Miller, *A Whole Different Ball Game*, 1991

+1001+

Labor is like motherhood to most of our political leaders—a calling so fine and noble that it would be sullied by talk of vulgar, mundane things like pay.

Barbara Ehrenreich

+1002+

I can, with perfect propriety, point out that those who seek perfection in an imperfect world are doomed to disappointment. But he who follows the pathway of logic and reason, looking beyond the inconsequential faults of a small minority, will realize that we are making a fine record in a most imperfect world.

William Green

+1003+

The American Federation of Labor is an open forum. We speak with frankness; we act the same way; we face all issues. We proclaim our virtues, and we admit our faults.

William Green

+1004+

We're there to build this labor movement in Canada stronger than it has ever been, with numbers larger than we've ever had, and we will prove to all [that] they can challenge us, they can try to wipe the floor with us, they can kill people on the job, they can do all these things, but they're no longer going to get away with it.

Shirley Carr, president of the Canadian Labour Congress, 1986

✢1005✢

During the savage 1960s, there were race riots, campus riots, political riots, youth riots, even musical riots, but there were no labor riots.

Gus Tyler, labor journalist, historian

✢1006✢

The role of the labor movement, through the institution of collective bargaining, is to bring democracy to the workplace.

George Meany

✢1007✢

We know it remains the policy of our nation to encourage collective bargaining. It states over and over ... but a large segment of the business community devotes a great deal of the money that they should be paying to taxes thwarting that policy.

Lloyd McBride (1916-1983), president (1977-1983), USWA

✢1008✢

Don't let any man into your cab, your home, or your heart, unless he's a friend of labor.

Attributed to Jimmy Hoffa, in the film, *Hoffa*

✢1009✢

We're not labor statesmen here. We're not humanitarians or longhairs. Look, what do you hire us for? Is it to throw a picnic for you? Is it to study the European situation? Or is it to sell your labor at top dollar!

Jimmy Hoffa

✢1010✢

If he stole $2.00, he gave $1.00 back to the men.

Teamster veteran fondly recalling the late Jimmy Hoffa

✢1011✢

We have an age-old mandate to educate and agitate.

Lane Kirkland

✢1012✢

Sit down and read. Educate yourself for the coming conflicts.

Mother Jones

Mother Jones marching with striking miners' children in Trinidad, Colorado, 1914. Courtesy Charles H. Kerr Co., Chicago.

✣1013✣

I have always advised men to read. All my life I have told them to study the works of those great authors who have been interested in making this world a happier place for those who do its drudgery.

Mother Jones, *The Autobiography of Mother Jones*, 1925

✣1014✣

You look at any mill towns in the history of this country and you won't find, to this day, flower beds or tree-lined streets. You won't find music halls unless the guy himself brings a guitar or harmonica. If the boss had his way, you'd never find libraries and books. They're dangerous. Shouldn't there be parks and theaters and libraries in my community?

Ed Sadlowski, Chicago director, USA, in
American Dreams: Lost and Found, 1980

✣1015✣

We hire people who have no education and little direction. They are the kind of people who look at their shoes when they apply for a job.

Harry Quadracci, company owner, on hiring methods to stifle
union-minded employees

✦1016✦

The labor movement is, on the one hand, an act of faith, and on the other, a thousand small movements rowing vigorously in their own directions.

Wilfrid Sheed, author

✦1017✦

Ten thousand times has the labor movement stumbled and fallen and bruised itself and risen again; been seized by the throat and choked into insensibility; enjoined by the courts, assaulted by thugs, charged by the militia, shot down by regulars, frowned upon by public opinion, deceived by politicians, threatened by priests, repudiated by renegades, preyed upon by grafters, infested by spies, deserted by cowards, betrayed by traitors, bled by leeches, and sold out by leaders. But not withstanding all this, and all these, it is today the most vital and potential power this planet has ever known.

Eugene Debs, in *Them and Us*, 1974

✦1018✦

Where you find a weak trade union official who has been corrupted, you will also find an employer who has been a party to corrupting him; and if you are going to send a weak trade union leader to prison for malpractices, then reserve the adjacent cells for the insurance agent and the personnel director.

Walter Reuther, in *The Brothers Reuther*, 1976

✦1019✦

One of the chief arguments used to support the policy of an open shop is that every man has an inalienable and constitutional right to work. I never found that in the constitution. If a man has a constitutional right to work, he ought to have the constitutional right to a job.

Clarence Darrow, *The Railroad Trainman*, 1909

✦1020✦

I have heard this open-shop talk before. The open shop is a harlot with a wig and artificial limbs, and her bones rattle. But how much production will she give us?

John L. Lewis, in *Labor Baron—A Portrait of John L. Lewis*, 1944

✦1021✦

'But,' said Mr. Hennessy, *'those open shop men you mention say they are for unions if properly administered.' 'Sure,'* said Mr. Dooley, *'if properly conducted. And there we are; and how would they have them conducted? No strikes, no rules, no contracts, hardly any wages and damn few members.'*

Finley Peter Dunne (1867-1936), columnist, editor, in his
writings through his creation, *Mr. Dooley*

✦1022✦

The American Federation of Labor proposes that every workingman shall do his thinking for himself and not go down on his knees to any man, no matter who he is or what position he holds.

Samuel Gompers, 1886

✦1023✦

Any song that points out something that is wrong, needs fixing, and shows you how to fix it—is the undying song of the working people. If it is made a little jazzy or sexy that ain't wrong—what book could you read to a crowd that would make them dance?

Woody Guthrie, in *Woody Sez*, 1975

✦1024✦

Miners and mill workers have had a long, fierce, and often tragic struggle to build a union. This combination of isolation, singing tradition, and bitter struggle has provided what might be called the perfect climate for the production of protest songs.

Edith Fowke and Joe Glazer,
folk historians, *Songs of Work
and Protest*, 1973

✦1025✦

A pamphlet, no matter how good, is never read more than once, but a song is learned by heart and repeated over and over.

Joe Hill

Joe Hill (*see* quotation 175). Courtesy George Meany Memorial Archives.

✣1026✣

We stand together to defend our belief that it is the registered nurse who bears the responsibility for the delivery of nursing care. That responsibility cannot be delegated; it must not be fragmented or compartmentalized, however cost-effective it might appear.

Barbara M. Roderick

✣1027✣

If Smith truly wants to keep hospitals alive, he should advise his management clients on how to trim their own waistlines, rather than feeding the rest of us red herring.

Nancy Mills, responding to a letter on how to
organize hospital workers

✣1028✣

The fight of General Motors workers is a fight to save truly free enterprise from death at the hand of its self-appointed champions.

Walter Reuther

✣1029✣

Our union is at a low ebb. Its very life may be uncertain. If it is destined that I be its undertaker, well, I am and always have been a good soldier—I shall not try to duck my fate.

David Dubinsky

✣1030✣

Labor needs to be strong in numbers, in effective organization, in the justice of its cause, and in the reasonableness of its methods. It relies on moral suasion.

Samuel Gompers

✣1031✣

If companies have a moral responsibility not to fill the movie theater and airwaves with violence and moral degradation, do they not also have a responsibility to keep workers employed when profits are rising? A moral responsibility to upgrade worker skills, an obligation to fully fund pension plans to provide health care?

Robert Reich

→1032←

The employer needs the unions 'to stay him from the fall to vanity;' the employees need them for their own protection; the community needs them to raise the level of the citizen. Strong, stable trade unions can best serve those ends.

Justice Louis Brandeis, attributed

→1033←

I've often said that if you could awaken all the martyrs in history and ask them if they wanted to be martyrs again, my belief is that they would say not. But if you asked them would they do it all over again, they would say yes.

Moe Biller, reflecting on labor strife

→1034←

Labor Day differs in every essential from the other holidays of the year in any [other] country. All other holidays are in a more or less degree connected with conflicts and battles of man's prowess over man, of strife and discord for greed and power, of glories achieved by one nation over another. Labor Day ... is devoted to no man, living or dead, to no sect, race, or nation.

Samuel Gompers

→1035←

The prophets of doom have badly misread both the present strength and the future prospects of trade unionism in America, and I think my view is shared by America's union-busting business leaders. If unions were dead or dying, they would save their energy and money.

Lane Kirkland, 1980

→1036←

I don't give a hang what happened yesterday; I live for today and tomorrow.

John L. Lewis, in *Men Who Lead Labor*, 1937

→1037←

The future of labor is the future of America.

John L. Lewis

Chapter 13

Unemployment

→1038←

Perhaps more than any other people, Americans define themselves by their work. Many of our most important values, such as competition and self-reliance, are forged through the discipline of the labor market. Employment, with a steady paycheck and a chance to move up, fulfills the promise of opportunity in America.

Paul E. Harrington, educator, author

→1039←

Losing your job is like being shipwrecked: a great experience if you survive it. Get through this and, in a way, nothing and nobody will ever really frighten you again.

Jack [John Russiano] Miles, journalist, literary critic, editor,
author, 1996 Pulitzer Prize for biography

→1040←

In the first horror of unemployment, your dignity, your future and your identity may all seem to be slipping from your grasp. No one but you knows quite how that feels.

Jack Miles

→1041←

Losing your job in America means you risk losing your place in society. You don't count for as much. ... The forces that count in our needy, greedy materialistic world no longer want or need you the way they did before. No one wants your grief.

David Nyhan, columnist, *Boston Globe*

→1042←

What you have to realize is that being employed to a lot of people defines who they are. If they're not employed, it's a matter of going around saying, 'Who am I?'

Susan Hache, unemployed worker

❖1043❖

Men may suffer terribly from the death of a loved one, the breakup of a marriage, or some other personal tragedy. But what brings them to a point of immobilization most often is the loss of their job.

Myron Brenton

❖1044❖

You take my life
When you do take the means whereby I live.

William Shakespeare (1564-1616), English dramatist, poet, *The Merchant of Venice*, published 1600

❖1045❖

An "unemployed" existence is a worse negation of life than death itself.

José Ortega Y Gassett, essayist, philosopher, *The Revolt of the Masses*, 1932

❖1046❖

'You're fired!' No other words can so easily and succinctly reduce a confident, self-assured executive to an insecure, groveling shred of his former self.

Frank P. Loucchen, CEO

❖1047❖

The rhetoric of America and American Manhood stresses the work role, the importance of self-sufficiency. ... but lack of self-esteem is more painful. Being unemployed, I feel unwanted, useless, failed. Depression and desperation fill my weeks. I feel powerless, and the fundamental tenets of manhood and society tell me I should have power. Is it me?

Steve Rayshich, unemployed steelworker, in *Overtime*, 1990

❖1048❖

If you are not a success (or worse, not working), you are at fault, are inferior, are a failure. We base our standards of acceptance on Job Title, Accomplishment, Size of Paycheck. We glorify the rich and famous, justify corruption and crass commercialism with phrases like 'He's laughing all the way to the bank.' We look down on the poor as dangerous, inherently bad 'moochers.'

Steve Rayshich, in *Overtime*, 1990

❖1049❖

It seems clear to me that the governor has never been in a situation where he has been unemployed. I have, and I know that that check is what keeps families together.

Leo Purcell, on projected cuts in unemployment benefits by
Governor William F. Weld (R-Mass., 1990-1997)

❖1050❖

If work supports families, instills pride and creates communities, what does the lack of work do? Look around you. If men don't have decent jobs, they are unable to support their children. They don't marry. They commit crimes. They go to prison. America may be suffering from a lack of values, but it is also suffering from a lack of blue-collar jobs.

Cynthia Tucker, columnist, *Atlanta Constitution*

❖1051❖

The truth about layoffs is that they're killers. In addition to mounting evidence they are inefficient and costly, layoffs cripple communities. If you doubt it, visit the community surrounding a closing or closed military base.

Anne Laurent, *Federal Times Weekly*

❖1052❖

It is a public outrage that there are men out of work when there is plenty of work that needs to be done. It is a scandal that there are short work-weeks and idle plant capacity when legitimate needs for goods and housing go unsatisfied. ... Telling a man that work is the only way to achieve dignity, and then denying him that chance for dignity, is indefensible.

Fred Harris, former Senator

❖1053❖

We seem to be able to mobilize the resources of our country for Desert Storm and bailing out the savings and loans, but we haven't been doing it for our unemployed workers.

John Nathan Sturdivant, president, American Federation of
Government Employees (AFGE)

❖1054❖

Work gives many people the indispensable leverage they need to contain self-destructive habits and behaviors.

Arthur B. Shostak, educator, editor, author, in the study,
The Human Cost of Plant Closings, Federationist, AFL-CIO, 1980

✦1055✦

The greatest danger to America is not the red menace, but the pink slip.

Ray Flynn, 1991

✦1056✦

A lot of fellows nowadays have a B.A., M.D., or Ph.D. Unfortunately, they don't have a J.O.B.

Antoine "Fats" Domino, singer, songwriter, musician,
a rock n' roll forefather

✦1057✦

We learned that we were expendable.

Dr. Janice Nelson, on why she joined the Union of American
Physicians and Dentists, after layoffs by the Los Angeles County
Health Dept., 3/2/1999, *Los Angeles Times*

✦1058✦

Doctors are being fired; they're being cut back; they're being told what to do or how much to make. ... We have no power.

Dr. Lawrence Koning, on why doctors are joining unions,
3/2/1999, *Los Angeles Times*

✦1059✦

When you're 48 years old and the economy's in the mess it is, there's no chance to get a job—except some kind of Republican job at Hardee's or McDonald's frying hamburgers.

Roger Suddith, unemployed striker

✦1060✦

I keep having to mark 'Other' on my forms under 'Reason for leaving.' Did not quit, was not fired—wouldn't you think they'd have a category in the form by now for 'Employer went belly up?'

Molly Ivins, columnist, *Fort Worth Star-Telegram*

✦1061✦

People get little part-time jobs with no benefits, and they are listed as consultants. So they don't get listed as unemployed.

Ed Rinzler, unemployed worker

Reprinted with permission ©Huck/Konopacki, courtesy Gary Huck.

✦1062✦

This is not a layoff; this is operations improvement.

Peggy Slasman, spokeswoman for Massachusetts General Hospital,
on decision to eliminate over 400 jobs

✦1063✦

Fifty percent more people are affected by layoffs every year than are victims of crime in this country.

New York Times, 1996

✦1064✦

There is no need for anybody to be frustrated in getting a job in Chicago.

Chicago Mayor Richard Daley, 9/28/1968

✦1065✦

Americans have a right to work and a right to a job!

John L. Lewis

❖1066❖

A man's right to his job transcends the right of private property. We are the workers—they are the enemy.

John L. Lewis, in *The Radical Vision of Saul Alinsky*, 1984

❖1067❖

The expectation of decent job opportunities at a living wage is a moral right of individual citizens and, until that goal is reached, the American economic system is in some way deficient.

Father Edward F. Boyle

❖1068❖

I believe in the dignity of labor, whether with head or hand; that the world owes every man an opportunity to make a living.

John Davison Rockefeller, Jr. (1874-1960),
businessman, philanthropist

❖1069❖

America works best when all Americans are working.

Lane Kirkland

❖1070❖

We build roads for high-tech companies. Offer tax breaks to big industries. Cut electric bills for employers. So what can be done for ... towns where people live every day at the edge of a very violent margin? More than likely, government can do very little; and where it has tried, the failure rate has been phenomenal, because so many in power forget the basic rule that the best social program of all is spelled J-O-B. There isn't a welfare check invented that allows a recipient to purchase dignity.

Mike Barnicle

❖1071❖

Our test of a healthy economy is a job for every American who wants to work.

President Gerald Ford (1974-1977), 1976

❖1072❖

About half our problems would go away overnight if everybody in this country who wanted to work had a job.

President Bill Clinton, 1993

❧1073❧

All told, I personally fired hundreds of employees and planned for the batch firings of thousands more. ... Slowly, I began to see what *really* happens after a layoff. Morale hits rock bottom. Lines of communication within the company shatter. Productivity ebbs while high-priced consultants try to patch the business back together.

> Alan Downs, 'Corporate Hit-Man,' American Telephone &
> Telegraph Company, Inc. (AT&T), 1996

❧1074❧

One of the great principles for which labor in America must stand in the future is the right of every man and woman to have a job. ... If the corporations which control American industry fail to provide them with that job, then there must be some power somewhere in this land of ours that will go over and above and beyond those corporations, with all their influence and power, and provide a job and insure the right to live for that American.

> John L. Lewis, 1937, in *Labor Baron—
> A Portrait of John L. Lewis*, 1944

❧1075❧

The Republicans have always felt that the best way to control inflation was to have a certain portion of the American people out of work, to hold down the money we have to spend, to make the demand for goods not so great.

> President Jimmy Carter

❧1076❧

When a great many people are unable to work, unemployment results.

> President Calvin Coolidge

❧1077❧

The minimum wage should be repealed—it has caused more misery and unemployment than anything since the Great Depression.

> Ronald Reagan

❧1078❧

An increase in the number of people seeking work who did not find it.

> Larry Speakes, President Reagan's press secretary, on the
> cause of unemployment, 1983

Dilbert© by Scott Adams. Reprinted by permission of United Feature Syndicate, Inc.

⇥1079⇤

Take unemployment ... there is a kind of easy assumption by some afflu-ent Americans that people can find work if they wish. It is just not that simple or easy.

Hubert H. Humphrey, *The Education of a Public Man*, 1976

⇥1080⇤

There are also a lot of jobs available that some people call menial. Maybe we need to get back the Depression mentality, where there were no menial jobs. A job was a job, and anyone who got one felt lucky.

Presidential candidate Ronald Reagan, 1976

⇥1081⇤

If any man is out of a job, it's his own fault. ... The State is not warranted in furnishing employment for anybody so that person may work.

President Calvin Coolidge, in *High Treason*, 1950

⇥1082⇤

I don't think people ought to be paid for doing nothing.

Arthur Burns (1904-1987), educator, former chairman,
Federal Reserve, 1976

⇥1083⇤

Unemployment insurance is a prepaid vacation for freeloaders.

Candidate for governor, Ronald Reagan, 4/28/1966

⇥1084⇤

The fact is, unemployment is a full-time job. And as many of you are finding out, it's a tough job not working.

Tom Loftus, unemployed worker, 1990

✦1085✦

Continued dependence upon relief induces a spiritual and moral disintegration fundamentally destructive to the national fiber.

President Franklin D. Roosevelt, 1/4/1935, in *Regulating the Poor:*
The Functions of Public Welfare, 1971

✦1086✦

We don't need worker assistance programs; we need jobs.

Robert Wages

✦1087✦

The key issue is jobs. You can't get away from it: jobs. Having a buck or two in your pocket and feeling like somebody.

Studs Terkel

✦1088✦

Bush writes off loans of $260 million for Nicaragua and $430 million for Honduras. Forget about it; slate clean. But he won't put money in the hands of jobless Americans. This is the act of a man too powerful and too popular for too long.

David Nyhan, on President George Walker Bush's
(1989-1993) priorities

✦1089✦

We just forgave Egypt $7 billion in debts—half the sum I'm asking to put every blessed unemployed American back to work. ... But if you're an unemployed American? Scram. No handouts at home. Unless you've been running a bank or an S & L that went south. Then, my friend, you are entitled to special treatment.

David Nyhan, 1991

✦1090✦

Jonestown economics ... a budget program that administers economic Kool-Aid to the poor and the deprived and the unemployed of the country.

Lane Kirkland, on President Reagan's economics, 1982

✦1091✦

Job training and income maintenance and unemployment compensation are all well and good, but there must be a job at the end of the line.

Walter W. Heller (1915-1987), economist, teacher, economic
advisor, Kennedy and Johnson administrations, 3/10/1970

Reprinted with permission ©Huck/Konopacki Labor Cartoons, courtesy Mike Konopacki.

☞1092☜

The best form of welfare is a high-paying job.

President John F. Kennedy

☞1093☜

I'd say, by God, while the private sector is to be preferred, the overriding importance to society is to create jobs.

Congressman Morris King "Mo" Udall (D-Ariz., 1961-1991)

☞1094☜

I think we have to find a way to match people with work. There's no doubt in my mind we've got the work out there, and if we can't get people together with the work that society needs, then I am somewhat pessimistic about the future of the institutions we have.

Governor Edmund Gerald "Jerry" Brown, Jr.
(D-Calif. 1975-1983), 1976

→1095←

Economists tell us that high interest rates are supposed to cool an over-heated economy by raising unemployment.

Lane Kirkland, 1980

→1096←

Inflation is often described as America's number one economic problem. But rising unemployment, increasing poverty, and a worsening of the income distribution should be the real economic concerns today.

Rudy Oswald, former president, Industrial Relations Research Association, 1982

→1097←

Ten million unemployed is un-American, inhumane and contrary to every known economic law as an acceptable or tolerable alternative to inflation.

Leon Hirsch Keyserling (1908-1987), economist, economic advisor, 1976

→1098←

It just doesn't take much magic to exchange double-digit inflation for double-digit unemployment.

William Winpisinger

→1099←

There's no assurance against inflation like a pool of genuine unemployment. That's a blunt, hardheaded statement, but a fact.

Business Week, 5/19/1957

→1100←

Most Americans, whether employed or not, expect both a job and stable prices. While the relative importance of inflation increases when prices rise rapidly, providing jobs continued to be top priority.

Ray Marshall, 1978

→1101←

The supply-siders, as well as traditional conservatives, give inadequate attention to the human and material costs of unemployment. ... that the unemployment figures are overstated anyway, that workers are unemployed because their wages are too high, or that high unemployment is 'worth it' to reduce inflationary pressures. These attitudes ignore the real losses from unemployment, which are truly staggering.

Ray Marshall, *Unheard Voices,* 1987

→1102←

People who cannot count on secure employment cannot easily offer security to a family; they're likely to put off getting married, having children, and buying homes. One of the great paradoxes of contemporary politics is that the celebrants of traditional 'family values' also have such enthusiasm for unrestrained markets that jeopardize stable family and community life. An honest conservatism would confront the tensions.

Paul Elliot Starr, journalist, historian, author, editor,
1984 Pulitzer Prize for nonfiction

→1103←

Very few politicians seem concerned about addressing the problems of hundreds of thousands of people who have been laid off. There's all this discussion of technology. That's part of the problem of making conversion happen in this country. There's not an emphasis on putting people back to work. That's a big mistake.

Don Nakamoto

→1104←

It's no coincidence that in the last decade private business has taken an increasing share of the revenues for itself and distributed less to the employees. It's no coincidence that real wages for millions have stagnated. Massive layoffs ... increase the value of a company's stock. When government declares air controllers essential but shuts down unemployment offices, it furthers the same upside-down logic. Those who have will get to wherever they want. Those in need will get shafted.

David Broder, author, syndicated columnist,
1975 Pulitzer Prize, 1996

→1105←

The worst effects of the (1929 stock market) crash upon unemployment will be passed during the next 60 days.

President Herbert Hoover, 1929

→1106←

It's a recession when your neighbor loses his job; it's a depression when you lose yours.

President Harry S. Truman

→1107←

When blacks are unemployed, they are considered lazy and apathetic. When whites are unemployed, it's considered a depression.

Jesse Jackson, *Time* magazine, 4/6/1970

→1108←

I don't blame that white trade unionist for not wanting a black man to get his job, and I don't blame the black man for wanting to get that job; I want to see a policy under which they can both have jobs!

Jesse Jackson

→1109←

In America men often work long hours even when they are already well off; such men, naturally, are indignant at the idea of leisure for wage earners, except as the grim punishment of unemployment; in fact, they dislike leisure even for their sons. Oddly enough, while they wish their sons to work so hard as to have no time to be civilized, they do not mind their wives and daughters having no work at all.

[Earl] Bertrand Arthur William Russell (1872-1970), prolific
writer, educator, pacifist, 1950 Nobel Prize for literature, 1935,
In Praise of Idleness, 1970 edition

→1110←

I'm all for women's lib, but does the price of freedom have to be unemployment?

Fay Dunaway, actress

→1111←

There is no such thing as steady employment in the building trades. There never was and never will be, until the skies stop leading [leaking] snow and rain.

Arthur Huddell, tradesman and official to the Boston Building
Trades Council, commenting on the boom and bust cycles in the
building trade, 1921, in *With Our Hands*, 1986

→1112←

When a convict takes a free worker's job, the free worker has to pay a very big price for society's failures, and it's not fair.

John J. Zalusky, AFL-CIO economist

→1113←

The only way to get a job is to commit a crime.

Joseph Faherty, on legislation dealing with prison labor and wages

❧1114❧

Willie Horton was on a furlough.

> Message on a picket sign from a furloughed state worker from
> Massachusetts depicting the famous felon who committed a
> murder while on a furlough

❧1115❧

Increased military spending is costing this country jobs, pure and simple. It's undermining absolutely the full-employment goal. It's perverting the work ethic. And it's absolutely a drag on productivity.

> William Winpisinger, 1981

❧1116❧

If stranded investments in older power plants will be protected, so should the sweat investment of a lifelong utility worker. The legislature must act to take the profit motive out of job loss. Otherwise, we create the neutron bomb of utility competition: It destroys people but leaves buildings standing.

> Paul Loughran, International Brotherhood of Electrical Workers
> (IBEW), on deregulation plans of Massachusetts Department of
> Public Utilities (DPU), 1996

❧1117❧

In our most vital industrial sectors, it isn't our members who are disappearing, it is their jobs. Those who talk about the decline in America's economic standing as a decline in the work ethic ought to take a look and take note that it is not labor, but capital that seems to hold work in such low regard.

> Thomas Donahue

❧1118❧

Who among us can expect the homeless to remain forever, the unemployed to accept their lot quietly forever, the despairing to control their anger forever?

> John Jacobs, 1988

❧1119❧

It's really simple. I never turned down a job, not one ... ever.

> Lyle Talbot, co-founder of Screen Actors Guild, who appeared in
> over 150 films and was downgraded because of union activities

❧1120❧

Unemployment sucks.

> Vicki Lawrence, television personality

Chapter 14

The Corporate World

✦1121✦

The depravity of the business classes of our country is not less than has been supposed, but infinitely greater. ... In business (this all-devouring modern word, business), the one sole object is pecuniary gain. The magician's serpent in the fable ate up all the other serpents; and moneymaking is our magician's serpent, remaining today sole master of the field.

> Walt Whitman (1819-1892), editor, poet, journalist, fisherman,
> carpenter, *Democratic Vistas*, 1871

✦1122✦

The Corporation is a creature of the state. It is presumed to be incorporated for the benefit of the public.

> U. S. Supreme Court, 1906

✦1123✦

Corporation: an ingenious device for obtaining individual profit without individual responsibility.

> Ambrose Bierce, *The Devil's Dictionary*, 1906

✦1124✦

I am responsible for my actions, but who is responsible for General Motors?

> Ralph Nader, lawyer, consumer advocate, civic activist and
> organizer, 1996 Green Party presidential candidate

✦1125✦

Whatever is not nailed down is mine. Whatever I can pry up is not nailed down.

> Collis Potter Huntington (1821-1900), railroad tycoon,
> builder, attributed

❧1126❧

We accept and welcome ... the concentration of business in the hands of the few.

Andrew Carnegie

❧1127❧

No one ever considers the Carnegie libraries steeped in the blood of underpaid labor Homestead steelworkers, but they are. ... We do not remember that the Rockefeller Foundation is founded on the dead miners of the Colorado Fuel Company and a dozen other performances.

President Harry S. Truman

❧1128❧

We can have democracy in this country or we can have great wealth in the hands of a few, but we can't have both.

Justice Louis Brandeis

❧1129❧

United States Steel is not in the business to make steel; it is in the business to make profits.

David M. Roderick, chairman and CEO, USX Corp.
(formerly U.S. Steel)

❧1130❧

The public be damned! I work for my stockholders.

William H. Vanderbilt

❧1131❧

Any man who pays men more than the lowest he can get men for is robbing his stockholders. If he can get men for $6 and pays more, he is stealing from his stockholders.

Stockholder of American Woolen Company,
Lawrence, Mass., 1911

❧1132❧

The business of America is business.

President Calvin Coolidge

❧1133❧

What is good for the country is good for General Motors, and vice versa.

Charles Erwin Wilson (1890-1961), president GM, 1953

❖1134❖

What is good for General Motors may not necessarily be good for the country, but what is good for American workers and their families is almost certainly good for the country.

Ray Marshall, *Unheard Voices*, 1987

❖1135❖

Not often has the power of one man over another been used more callously than in the American labor market after the rise of the large corporation.

John Kenneth Galbraith

❖1136❖

As a general, though not invariable, rule, one finds the strongest unions in the United States where markets are served by strong corporations.

John Kenneth Galbraith

❖1137❖

We are unalterably opposed to any extension of union labor.

U.S. Steel Corporation, 1901

❖1138❖

Hell, everyone says unions like the Teamsters are too powerful. Well, you show me a union that's more powerful than GM or Standard Oil.

Al Barkett, Teamster union steward and truck driver, in
The Teamsters, 1978

❖1139❖

Unions are big business.

Dave Beck (1894-1993), former president (1952-1957), IBT

❖1140❖

This is the trouble with the American Labor Movement. It is becoming a part of the 'Establishment!'

Walter Reuther, 1966, in *The Most Dangerous Man in Detroit*, 1995

❖1141❖

I'm no different than the banks, no different than insurance companies, no different than the politicians. You're a damned fool not to be informed what makes a city run when you're trying to do business in the city.

Jimmy Hoffa

✦1142✦

I spent 33 years in the marines being a high-class muscleman for big business, for Wall Street and the bankers. On shore, I was a racketeer for capitalism. I helped purify Nicaragua for the international banking house of *Brown Brothers*. I helped make Mexico safe for American sugar interests. I helped make Haiti and Cuba decent places for *National City Bank* boys to collect revenue. I helped in the rape of half a dozen Central American republics for the benefit of Wall Street. I might have given Al Capone a few hints.

General Smedley Darlington "Old Gimlet Eye" Butler
(1881-1940), Commandant, U.S. Marines, in
Words for Workers in Changing Times, 1993

✦1143✦

Corporations know the price of judges, legislators, and public officials as certainly as an American knows the price of pork and mutton.

Eugene Debs

✦1144✦

I went through Macys' warehouse and couldn't find any products manufactured here [in America]. Corporate America made the decisions ... which products they will sell.

Ron Carey

✦1145✦

Is it not required that a corporate balance sheet give at least as much attention to the number and quality of jobs it has provided during the year as it does to profits?

Thomas Donahue

✦1146✦

We don't care if you build bombs in our town; just don't bring a union.

Alf Barnette, American promoter, luring Canadian businesses to
Jackson, Tenn., 1992

✦1147✦

The problem with American competitiveness has nothing to do with the work ethic of American workers. The problem has to do with chief executives who earn 100 to 150 times as much as their workers, multinationals that export jobs somewhere else, and a government that encourages it.

Jeff Crosby

❧1148❧

The U.S. car industry is the only one where the top executives freeze the salaries at the bottom and reward themselves for failure.

Ralph Nader

❧1149❧

I love these guys. We can't pay you more than $4.25 an hour because it's not fair to the other poor people, but we can pay CEO's $4 million and $6 million and $10 million bonuses, and apparently, it doesn't hurt nobody! Including grammar teachers. I don't get this.

Phil Donahue

❧1150❧

The ancient Christian concept of the 'occasion of sin' can be applied to the entire capitalist system. The worker is probably not much more tempted in the context of the system than he would be under socialism or communism, but the employer, the businessman, by the very nature of his function, is under constant temptation. Indeed, there can be no question that he frequently succumbs to it. The question worth serious consideration is: Does he ever overcome it?

Steve Allen, *Reflections*, 1994

❧1151❧

We are without doubt the biggest whores in the business. We constantly sell our talent just as a prostitute sells her body. Only we sell to the lowest bidder. And, as we do so we sacrifice our futures. We act out R&D [research & development]. We neglect education. We change our corporate culture. We change from entrepreneurial to one of avoiding risk—at all costs. And if we contractors and engineers are the biggest prostitutes, you owners are the pimps and procurers.

Ted C. Kennedy, CEO,
BE&K Construction Company, Inc. (BE&K)

❧1152❧

Over the years, corporations have endowed colleges and universities with millions of dollars. Yet, many of those same corporations are not willing to spend one cent on apprenticeship.

William Winpisinger

+1153+

At no time has there been a discernible outcry from the great corporate owners of America against the principle of organization. Far from it. They have run that principle as far into the ground as they can, beginning with the early monopolies and extending right up to the most modern conglomerate. ... Yet, let anyone *else* organize and the screams may be heard from here to there.

Karl Hess (1923-1994), *Dear America*, 1975

+1154+

Concerned about family values? Then it's time to reign in corporations that impose disruptive work schedules and slash wages, not because their survival is at stake, but simply because they can get away with it. Union leaders could have argued that what America really needed—instead of middle-class tax cuts—was an end to middle-class pay cuts.

David Moberg, 1995

+1155+

GAINSHARING: Corporate concept of linking productivity improvements with profit sharing for hourly paid workers. The emphasis is on increasing production by shrinking crews, combining jobs and speedup. The gain is mainly in production and profits, with very little beef in the sharing.

Ernest DeMaio, *Words For Workers In Changing Times*, 1993

+1156+

Downsize is a new corporate word to describe dumping American workers for higher profits.

Leo Persails, APWU official

+1157+

No company ever shrank to greatness.

Dwight L. Gertz, management consultant, reacting to his
corporate studies showing how Wall St. historically does not
reward downsizing

+1158+

Why shouldn't we require corporations to include in their annual reports an assessment of the impact of layoffs on their workers and communities? That might focus attention on the true social costs of downsizing?

Governor Mario Cuomo

Reprinted with permission, courtesy ©Patrick Hardin.

→1159←

American corporations have discarded the social compact of the '50s and '60s (when we all shared the gains of a growing economy) in favor of a 'winner take all' system. Our economy has grown by a third since the 1980s, but all the new income has gone to the wealthiest 20 percent in our society. The remaining 80 percent has seen real incomes stagnate or decline.

John J. Sweeney, 1996

→1160←

By no small coincidence, the 20-year decline in real wages in this country parallels a 20-year decline in the power of American unions. At a time when unions now represent only one in six American workers, it's no wonder that corporations are free to downsize for no other reason than to lower wages and make a quick profit.

John J. Sweeney, 1996

→1161←

They downsize. Wall Street approves. Corporate stocks rise. And workers go home, sick to their stomach with fear, to try to explain or to understand why they are now unemployed.

Mike Barnicle

"The Board has chosen you to handle the downsizing because you have no heart."

Reprinted with permission, courtesy ©Patrick Hardin.

→1162←

The triumph of profits over people.

Peter Laarman, minister, on corporate downsizing

→1163←

To get there—we did a lot of violence to the expectations of the American workforce. We downsized. We delayered. And we outsourced.

Frank P. Doyle, former GE vice president, explaining
GE's success in tripling their business since 1980
with half the workforce, 1995

→1164←

Over the past decade, corporate downsizing cost five million Americans their jobs, as business giants slashed payrolls, hoping to boost productivity and profits. ... But now, after a decade of downsizing, there's more and more evidence that the flood of pink slips simply did not work.

CBS News, *Eye on America* segment, on corporate downsizing

→1165←

If the *Item* really wants to show its patriotism during this week when we celebrate our independence from foreign domination, then they should level their criticism at GE Chairman, Jack Welch, and his decisions to rob American workers of their jobs by exporting them to a foreign market during a time that GE stockholders are earning record profits on what is being made in the United States.

Kevin Mahar, IUE official, criticizing anti-union editorial by local newspaper, *Lynn* (Mass.) *Item*

→1166←

80 percent of Americans will remain hostage to the AT&T's and the GM's—and their cheering stockholders who bid the price up when the pink slips are distributed.

Editorial, *Tyranny of the Market*, *The Progressive*

→1167←

Employees of giant corporations often are propagandized to believe they belong to some kind of company family. This suits the business purpose of the company. When business turns bad, however, the family idea is dropped. Loyalty goes out the window and dismissal notices go out in the mail.

[Andrew Aitken] Andy Rooney, columnist, television commentator, *60 Minutes*, CBS

→1168←

In corporate America, a business answers to its shareholders and no one else. Workers' interests do not factor into the equation. The directors of a company have a fiduciary responsibility that obliges them to place the owner interests first; if that means going to part-time help, layoffs, cutting benefits and pay, that is what will happen.

Steve Delaney, letter to the editor, *Boston Globe*

→1169←

Caught between the lawmakers in Washington and the dealmakers on Wall Street have been millions of American workers forced to move from jobs that now pay $7. If, that is, they aren't already the victims of mass layoffs, production halts, shuttered factories and owners who enrich themselves by doing the damage and then walking away.

Donald L. Bartlett and James B. Steele,
America: What Went Wrong?, 1992

⇥1170⇤

The corporations prefer cheap foreign labor without workers' compensation, maternity leaves, health insurance and other benefits.

Ralph Nader

⇥1171⇤

Businessmen who tip big in nightclubs are odds-on to be stingy with their employees.

Jimmy Cannon, syndicated columnist

⇥1172⇤

Aptitude tests show that you will succeed in a business where your father is the boss.

Lawrence J. Peter (1919-1990), author, educator,
management theorist

⇥1173⇤

Can anyone stop the corporate whining about 'mandates?' These same multinationals pay some form of national health insurance costs in every other industrialized country in the world. But not for American workers.

Jeff Crosby

⇥1174⇤

U.S. corporations are the most pampered in the world. Under NAFTA [North American Free Trade Agreement], they have been encouraged to scour the world at taxpayer expense, to search for the poorest and most repressed workers on the planet. They are the only corporations that can bring in scabs to permanently replace workers who go on a legal strike in their home country. They are the only corporations who do not have to help fund a national health plan in their home country.

Jeff Crosby

⇥1175⇤

As a management person, if I don't have a union, I don't want one. But ... look at this more broadly. Free societies are missing something important if they do not have an organization in the private sector, such as a trade union movement (that gives workers the clout labor has exerted to help pass safety and pension laws).

George P. Shultz, former Secretary of Labor (1969-1970),
Nixon Administration

✦1176✦

Greedy corporations not only want to escape fair wages and benefits by going to Mexico, they want to escape health and safety regulations and environmental regulations. Any trade agreement with Mexico or any other country should have a workers' humane and environmental rights clause.

Phil Mamber, UE local president, on proposed legislation that
would loosen legislation on exporting jobs

✦1177✦

Greed is all right, by the way ... I think greed is healthy. You can be greedy and still feel good about yourself.

Ivan F. Boesky, financier, securities analyst, investment banker,
commencement address at School of Business, U.C. Berkeley,
5/18/1986 (Boesky was later convicted of filing false documents
and insider trading violations and was fined $100 million.)

✦1178✦

I don't believe we should have the corporations ruining the world. We work so hard to get environmental laws, labor laws, human rights laws. I just don't believe corporations should rise above government rules.

Jean Rosner, protester, commenting to a *Los Angeles Times* reporter
during the massive protests of the World Trade Organization
(WTO) summit, Seattle, Wash., 11/30/1999

✦1179✦

There cannot be much health left in a social order where corporations can clamorously proclaim a failure on Friday with entire assurance that, therefore, their stock will go up on Monday.

Murray Kempton, 1995

✦1180✦

In the last generation, families became less permanent and neighborhoods less stable. Our companies became our communities, our co-workers became our extended family. Now, gradually, we are losing that neighborhood, too, as we are turned into competitive, transient and temporary workers. It's another kind of isolation.

Ellen Goodman, syndicated columnist, *Boston Globe*,
Washington Post Writers Group

✦1181✦

Labor unions will not flourish, and workers will not be able to successfully deal with their employers at work and in the political system, until the unions become a way for workers to directly confront corporate power.

David Cormier, educator

→1182←

Management is the art of getting other people to do all the work.

Anonymous

→1183←

Management is right ... in miraculously few cases.

Ed Asner, 1982

→1184←

Corporations are people too.

William Edward Simon, Secretary of the Treasury (1974-1977),
Nixon and Ford Administrations, on proposed
tax breaks for corporations.

"Aside from being a Jackass, is there anything
else that would qualify you for a position
in Management?"

Reprinted with permission, courtesy ©Patrick Hardin.

✦1185✦

I could get rid of all the workers who earn their laborers $15 an hour and bring in a contract house that will pay their laborers $7 an hour. But that breaks the spirit and trust of the employees. If you close a factory because you can get work done for $2 an hour elsewhere, you break the American Dream.

Aaron Feuerstein, CEO, Malden Mills, Inc., 9/1986

✦1186✦

Take care of those who work for you, and you'll float to greatness on their achievements.

H.S.M. Burns, president, Shell Oil Company

✦1187✦

I don't see any way you can justify somebody making $1 million or more a year when the low-level workers aren't making enough money to afford a house.

Ben Cohen, CEO, Ben & Jerry's Homemade, Inc.

✦1188✦

The fundamental difference is that I consider our workers an asset, not an expense.

Aaron Feuerstein, on why his Malden Mills' employees consider
him a hero after his factory burned down and he promised to
rebuild in Malden, Mass., 1986

Chapter 15

Brave New World

✦1189✦

Firing is a necessity when companies merge or restructure in response to free trade and global economic pressures.

Statement on advertising copy for a corporate seminar
for a Canadian brewer

✦1190✦

Use free trade as a catalyst to mobilize employees to cut costs. ... Nothing clears the mind so much as the specter of being hung in the morning.

Ray Verndon, president, Nabisco Inc., urging employers to use free
trade as a club in negotiations

✦1191✦

When Reagan and Bush were running in 1980, they said, 'We're going to get American industry moving again.' And they did—to Taiwan, Mexico, Saudi Arabia—everywhere except here.

Jim Hightower

✦1192✦

For workers—do you think you should be loyal to your company—and your company loyal to you? Forget it. Welcome to the '90s.

Ted Koppel, television journalist, ABC *Nightline*

✦1193✦

History is a frustrating thing because it is never clear and clean. There's never two steps forward without at least one step back. History moves in better and worse directions at the same time. Many of the people I know who are disillusioned these days belong to a generation that believed everything would come to them in their time.

Si Kahn, union organizer, singer, folk musician

✦1194✦

Downsizing. Streamlining. Making a company leaner, more efficient, better able to compete globally; these are the cold phrases today's titans employ to describe how thousands are screwed out of hope and security.

Mike Barnicle

✦1195✦

These new takeover business leaders are going to eliminate unnecessary jobs and increase the profit. ... It matters not to the businessmen that they often are firing loyal employees who made the business worth acquiring in the first place.

Andy Rooney

✦1196✦

The average working guy has been told over and over again that he's the cause of the problem, but that guy doesn't agree with givebacks. He's willing to take a wage freeze, but not the rollbacks. Because where do you stop once you start that?

C. Sam Theodus, president, Teamsters Local 407, Cleveland, on Teamster contracts, 1982

✦1197✦

You can't eat a leveraged buyout. You can't drive a junk bond. And flipping burgers doesn't put a permanent roof over a worker's head. We need to keep our industrial base. We need to strengthen it. We need to expand it. The Japanese know that. The Germans know that. The newly industrialized countries are learning it, and it would be foolish for this country to forget it.

Governor Mario Cuomo

✦1198✦

Across the country, employers are waking up. For 20 years [employers] have been told, 'If you want to compete, break the unions, slash benefits and wages.' Yet our competitors in Germany and Japan have maintained a competitive edge by investing in their work force.

Senator Edward M. Kennedy, commending the opening of a union-run apprentice training center, 1991

✦1199✦

Whenever employees give back, they are now investors. They own whatever percentage is given back.

Robert Schrank

IUE Local 201 officials, Fuzzy Herrick and Jeff Crosby, led a coalition of unions and community groups protesting NAFTA. Courtesy Lynn Historical Society.

✦1200✦

This generation has no right to give away, or sell for money, conditions that were handed on to us by a previous generation.

> Eric Hoffer, in *Harry Bridges—*
> *The Rise and Fall of Radical Labor in the U.S.*, 1972

✦1201✦

Bring Back The 8 Hour Day

> Bumper sticker

✦1202✦

By working faithfully eight hours a day, you may eventually get to be a boss and work twelve hours a day.

> Robert Lee Frost (1874-1963), poet, teacher, farmer, awarded four
> Pulitzer Prizes for poetry: 1924, 1931, 1937, and 1943, in
> *The Portable Curmudgeon*, 1992

→1203←

It is a fundamental contradiction in our society today to call for democracy in the society and attempt to institute a dictatorship in the workplace.

Juan Gonzalez, columnist

→1204←

The danger of the past was that men became slaves. The danger of the future is that men may become robots.

Sigmund Freud

→1205←

If a machine can do a job, a man shouldn't.

Personnel manager interviewed on a PBS documentary

"Of course things change: Our fathers were replaced by machines — We'll be replaced with new software."

Reprinted with permission, courtesy ©Patrick Hardin.

✦1206✦

We believe that if men have the talent to invent new machines that put men out of work, they have the talent to put those men back to work.

President John F. Kennedy, 9/27/1962

✦1207✦

Automation is imperceptibly but inexorably producing dislocations, skimming off unskilled labor from the industrial force.

Martin Luther King, Jr.

✦1208✦

The society that performs miracles with machinery has the capacity to make some miracles for men—if it values men as highly as it values machines.

Martin Luther King, Jr.

✦1209✦

There isn't any employer we do business with that will tell you we've ever stopped automation. We simply get for the workers their share of the savings of automation.

Jimmy Hoffa, in *Toil and Trouble*, 1964

✦1210✦

The robot is going to lose. Not by much. But when the final score is tallied, flesh and blood is going to beat the damn monster.

Adam Smith [George Jerome Waldo Goodman], journalist, financial writer, novelist

✦1211✦

The unions' continued reluctance to grapple with a technology revolution that might eliminate mass labor could spell their own elimination from American life over the next three or four decades.

Jeremy Rifkin, futurist, author, president, Foundation on Economic Trends, 1995

✦1212✦

Employers must be made to understand that when they make technological changes, they must bring us along. To live in yesterday's world will only prove to be disastrous.

James Spinoza, vice president, ILWU, 5/15/1999

→1213←

If you are a secretary, if you are a bank teller or sales clerk, if you are a machinist, librarian, telephone operator, wholesaler or middle manager, your job is headed for extinction.

Jeremy Rifkin, 1995

→1214←

Don't be attractive. Don't be too smart. Don't be assertive. Pretend you're not a woman. Don't be single. Don't be a mom. Don't be a divorcee.

Respondent to a *Catalyst* survey of senior women executives on how best to succeed, *Washington Post*, 1996

→1215←

The goal is to exaggerate to the brink without lying. You can give yourself a new title. ... If you're a salesman, you can call yourself can 'account executive.' A janitor becomes a 'maintenance engineer'—if you don't have a job at all—*voila!*—you're an instant 'consultant.' Jobs themselves are no longer jobs, but 'job opportunities!'

Bella English, explaining job hunting in the 1990s

→1216←

The payoff in motivation is to get what everybody is looking for—not more money—to get a maximum job, not a minimum one.

Employer interviewed on PBS

→1217←

When I was Secretary of Labor, I used to hear the same cynical refrain: 'Sure, there are plenty of jobs to be retrained for. I should know. I've got three of them.'

Robert Reich, 6/18/1999

→1218←

You can be fired because somebody else is willing to do the job for less, or because the company is moving to Singapore, or because the boss had a bad breakfast. If anything, the new economy makes individuals more vulnerable. Only one mechanism institutionalizes fair play and the opportunity to voice workplace grievances without fear of retaliation—a union.

Robert Kuttner

✦1219✦

I feel the employer-employee market is a naturally exploitative environment. A company will take an employee as far as he or she will allow
them to be taken.

David Roper, career-development specialist, describing "Survivor's
Syndrome" during the Massachusetts recession of 1991

✦1220✦

In a hierarchy, every employee tends to rise to his level of incompetence.

Lawrence J. Peter and Raymond Hull, *The Peter Principle*, 1969

✦1221✦

If I were an organizer [today], I'd let the workers know about the companies who are taking our wealth and shipping it around the world to get
the work done for next to nothing. It's not un-American to unionize; it's
un-American to send our jobs overseas.

Ralph Fasanella

✦1222✦

We shift the cost of benefits to our employees. We eliminate any wage
increases. We retire the older, more expensive talent. We reclassify people
as probationary to avoid paying benefits and we abandon any meaningful
retirement plan except Social Security. We do it all in the name of competitiveness and a free market.

Ted C. Kennedy

✦1223✦

We still have the audacity to believe in the American dream: a job, a
chance to improve things for your family and your town through hard
work. It simply shouldn't be that your employer makes extraordinary
profit, your productivity increases every year, you work harder every year
and you lose your job while your boss takes his tax breaks and skips to
North Carolina or Mexico with the catch-all cover, 'I have to be competitive.'

Jeff Crosby

✦1224✦

In general, the effect of the free-trade agreements will be to move to the
lowest common denominator with regard to wages and environmental
protection.

Noam Chomsky, on the North American Free Trade Agreement
(NAFTA), *Keeping the Rabble in Line*, 1994

Reprinted with permission ©Huck/Konopacki Teacher Cartoons, courtesy Mike Konopacki.

→1225←

The logic of global competition is like a limbo contest, how low can you go. ... lower wages ... lower environmental protections. What will be dealt away next in order to increase the profit margin?

Sam Kirkland, auto worker

→1226←

The selfish spirit of commerce, which knows no country, and feels no passion or principle but that of gain.

Thomas Jefferson, 5/15/1809

→1227←

Since 1990, our company alone has eliminated 33,000 jobs in the United States, about one in three. During that same period, we have added 15,000 jobs outside the United States. We have no reason to believe this trend for corporate America will change soon. If anything, it will accelerate.

George David, chairman, CEO,
United Technologies Corporation, 1995

→1228←

As U.S. capital moves to seize on opportunities for investment in Eastern Europe, how are U.S. workers to obtain protection against a new epidemic of international runaway jobs? Are our members to be sacrificed on the altar of reactionary stupidity and political backwardness?

Michael Eisenscher, *Organizing in the '90's*

→1229←

Management's social contract with workers and the community has been broken as managers have turned to making money by means other than production. ... Top managers in central offices leave entire communities and regions economically stranded. Imported goods replace American goods. Jobs in producing occupations are severely reduced, hardly affected by the trickle of work in high-tech industries.

Seymour Melman, professor of industrial engineering, Columbia University, 1983, in *Unheard Voices*, 1987

→1230←

Emancipation of human labor from economic servitude and exploitation, i.e., from organizations in which the conditions of work are determined by a master class who owns the means of production, and in which the fruits of work are alienated from the workers to the benefit of the masters.

Mortimer Jerome Adler, author, critic, philosopher, educator, editor, encyclopedist

→1231←

I say that if two products are of equal value, you should buy the American-made one. But I don't say you should buy American no matter what, because that encourages manufacturers to make junk.

Paul Tsongas, Democratic presidential hopeful, 1992

→1232←

The problem with protectionism, the problem with 'Buying American,' is that it doesn't address who the enemies are. It's not the workers in Mexico who decide to move these plants down there.

David Johnson, writer

→1233←

We must understand that limits on wages and working conditions in southern Illinois can be determined by a company based in Houston with interests in South America.

Richard Trumka

→1234←

Workers are falling into paycheck poverty—by the millions we are becoming expendable hired hands, interchangeable units of work, governed in what counts by entities that have abandoned the traditional quest for a loyal work force, much less a happy one. Corporations are extracting cuts in wages and benefits from their experienced workers, low-balling new workers in two-tier wage systems requiring mandatory overtime and hiring temps to reduce the fringe benefits they have to pay, and letting hundreds of thousands of workers go while exporting their jobs to low-wage areas around the world.

Ronnie Dugger

→1235←

Although we claim to be a society where everyone is equal, in reality we are not. ... There are many who want to work, go to school, who have the ability but are unable because of the way the system works. If they work part-time, financial aid is reduced. Financially, they do better remaining on welfare. In return they give up their dreams and hopes, their souls.

Jean Goldberg, columnist

→1236←

ABSENTEE: A person who fails to show up for work. Absenteeism rises when overtime or speedup is excessive and when workers have too few personal days off to tend to family problems.

Ernest DeMaio, *Words For Workers In Changing Times*, 1993

→1237←

Most of these guys have been working a lot of overtime. They're tired.

Al Woodham, autoworker, on a strike at GM plant over
too much overtime, 1995

→1238←

If too many workers are let go or marginalized into jobs without pension benefits, the capitalist system is likely to collapse slowly in on itself as employers drain it of the workers' funds necessary for new capital investments. In the final analysis, sharing the vast productivity gains of the Information Age is absolutely essential to guarantee the well-being of management, stockholders, labor, and the economy as a whole.

Jeremy Rifkin

✦1239✦

It is ridiculous to call this an industry. This is not. This is rat eat rat, dog eat dog. I'll kill 'em before they kill me. You're talking about the American way of survival of the fittest.

Ray Kroc, chairman of McDonald's, attributed

✦1240✦

I think we ought to bring in 10 of the people who have been downsizing IBM, Xerox, General Motors; ask them exactly how to apply it, and go for a goal of dramatically fewer federal employees, just as there are dramatically fewer middle-management people at those other places. That would save over five years a dramatic amount of money.

Congressman Newt Gingrich, NBC interview, 2/171993

✦1241✦

I think there's a loyalty crisis in the U.S. The average company loses half its customers in five years, half its employees in four years, and half its investors in less than one year. People don't understand the devastating costs of churn. A lot of management pundits say there's no loyalty in our future. I would say there's no future without loyalty.

Frederick F. Reichheld, author, consultant, on corporate
downsizing in the 1990s

✦1242✦

Profits are up, productivity is up, executive compensation is up, and the stock market is up; worker wages and health benefits and pensions are down. America is becoming edgier, angrier, and meaner. Until we ease the growing gaps in work, wages, and wealth, we will see more militia movements, more bombings, more hate crimes, and more of the quiet anguish of Americans losing their sense of a common destiny and a common purpose.

John J. Sweeney, 12/15/1995

✦1243✦

Our 'national security' is better served by having more Americans who can produce critical technologies on American soil than by having American companies hire foreign citizens to do it abroad.

Robert Reich

Reprinted with permission, courtesy ©Patrick Hardin.

→1244←

If leanness-meanness goes on too long and American optimism finally dies, workers may one day fill the streets again. There will be no FDR to rescue capitalism. A new counterculture can grow, this one not besotted by drugs and narcissism. American business will find out how very mean life can get.

[Abraham Michael] A.M. Rosenthal, journalist, *New York Times* editor, columnist, 1960 Pulitzer Prize for international reporting, *New York Times*, 1994

→1245←

We seem to be living in an age when there are a lot of people who want to get all they can, can all they get, and then sit on the can.

Benjamin Hooks

✦1246✦

It seems that unions became less powerful in this country when their leaders were no longer men who smoked cigars.

Mark Russell

✦1247✦

If this country can't absorb another thirty to forty-thousand people and try to find some way for them to make a living, then I feel that, in a sense, we are denying our heritage. We are denying the history, the background, the traditions of this country as a haven for the oppressed, for the people who are in trouble.

George Meany, on legal immigration

✦1248✦

The destitute are not coming; the elderly are not coming. We're primarily getting young men who are aggressive, in good health, and who are hard workers. So we're finding that many employers want to hire them.

Lionel J. Castillo, U.S. Commissioner of Immigration and Naturalization Service, on illegal aliens entering the U.S., 1978

✦1249✦

American capitalism no longer has any use for 40% of the population. They're now superfluous human beings.

Staughton Lynd, labor lawyer, author, 1994

✦1250✦

Without organized resistance to the exploitation of our human and national resources, the welfare of all is placed in jeopardy. Labor has been the focus of this resistance, and the study of the history of working people—both in defeat as well as in history—provides a basis for optimism and courage.

William Cahn, *A Pictorial History of American Labor*, 1972

✦1251✦

We've all heard the lines: unions are outdated. Working people needed unions at one point, but not any more. Employers are decent today; they treat their people OK. And for those who don't, the government provides protections. ... Bull! ... Today's decent employers are decent because unions *force them* to be decent.

Richard J. Perry, 1991

✦1252✦

The challenges change. So do the tools needed to meet them. But one thing cannot change—the conception of trade unionism as morally clean in a way that no business is. Business is profit; the union is idealism, commitment, service. Without the faith of our members, we lose what we have built. That will not happen to our union.

David Dubinsky

✦1253✦

The country has extraordinary strengths in its educated labor force. Literally one-fourth of the labor force of this country is today classified as managerial and professional. There's no other country in the world that has as many.

Daniel Bell

✦1254✦

That you can actually grow up in this country and know nothing about the terrible state of workplace relations is a tremendous indictment of our education system. Where do people go after education? To work. And yet, our kids are so ill prepared for the work world that they know nothing about their rights.

Elaine Bernard

✦1255✦

The peculiar thing is, labor has more resources today than it ever had in the thirties. The white-collar anti-union stereotype is over; schoolteachers, nurses, flight attendants—all organizing. All labor leadership needs now is strategy, imagination, and guts.

Victor Reuther, 1988, in *The Great Divide*, 1988

✦1256✦

If you are working class, you still have dreams and ambitions.

Roseanne Barr, comedienne, actress, on the success of her television show, *Roseanne*

✦1257✦

My interest is in the future because I am going to spend the rest of my life there.

Charles F. Kettering

✦1258✦

The future is in labor's strong, rough hands.

Mother Jones, *The Autobiography of Mother Jones*, 1925

Chapter 16

Team Concept

→1259←

Unions need capitalism like a fish needs water.

David Dubinsky, attributed

→1260←

It is clear that recognition of the proper position of labor and the worker in the production process demands various adaptations in the sphere of the right to ownership.

Pope John Paul II, 1981

→1261←

Until labor and capital join hands and recognize their interest is a common interest ... there can be no progress.

John Davison Rockefeller (1839-1937), industrialist, oil
monopolist, founded Standard Oil, philanthropist

→1262←

Every citizen should have a voice in the conduct of the business or industry which is carried on by means of his labour and the satisfaction of knowing that his labour is directed to the well-being of the community.

William Temple, *Christianity and the Social Order*

→1263←

Labor and capital were two arms of industry, the proper functioning of which could best be secured by cooperation, which in turn could best be promoted by administering their interests together.

Oscar S. Straus, Secretary of Commerce (1906-1908), Theodore
Roosevelt Administration, 1906

→1264←

The first word is trust. I've always believed in cooperation. You need to work to make that company profitable. No union person wants to see a company go out of business.

Joseph Faherty

❖1265❖

We must emphasize and give prominence to the primacy of man in the production process.

Pope John Paul II, in his papal letter, *Laborem Exercens*, 9/1981

❖1266❖

If a worker performs a task 320 times a day, five days a week, for 16 years—no one is more of an expert than this worker. In 16 years, I have never been consulted once about this task qualitatively or quantitatively.

Attributed to Martin Douglas, UAW worker

❖1267❖

Most of the people on your shop floor manage their own lives quite well. They make major purchases, hire and fire help, lead civic organizations and churches, balance their checkbooks and raise their kids, all without a single manager looking over their shoulder. What happens when they walk in the door of your company? Do these people suddenly become stupid or incapable? Of course not!

Darrel W. Ray, work team management expert

❖1268❖

American workers just won't accept regimentation anymore. We are going to have to give workers a piece of the action and stop treating them like children, or, even worse, like machines with nothing to contribute to their jobs but their bodies.

Rex Reed, AT&T

❖1269❖

Participation and cooperation are designed to increase profits and benefits, while collective bargaining is about how to divide benefits.

John T. Joyce, International Union of Bricklayers and Allied Craftsmen (IUBAC), credited

❖1270❖

Bargaining has neither friends nor relations.

Benjamin Franklin

❖1271❖

Genuine, meaningful worker participation must have collective bargaining at its core.

John T. Joyce

→1272←

Bargaining is a participation sport; there are no neutral spectators.

Jesse Prosten, vice president UFCW, in *Out of the Jungle*, 1968

→1273←

Competition brings out the best in products and the worst in people.

David Sarnoff (1891-1971), broadcasting executive

→1274←

We live in a business culture that exalts competition. ... When business as usual means everyone for himself, caring labor seeks to have everyone for himself, caring labor seeks to have everyone take responsibility for the good of the community. Although cooperation, compassion and altruism are equally present in both genders, in this culture we allot such characteristics to women, and then ban them from the marketplace.

Linda Weltner, writer, *Boston Globe*

→1275←

I'm trying hard to find common denominators. Because I seriously doubt there will be any world here if we don't find some way to talk with people we disagree with.

Pete Seeger, folk singer, songwriter, social activist

→1276←

A solid contract, is, in a very real sense, another Emancipation Proclamation.

A. Philip Randolph

→1277←

A good contract with a good union is good business.

John T. Dunlop, 1980

→1278←

Unions can recapture lost membership only if they become a positive force in creating an environment that permits employers to remain competitive. If unions drop their traditional adversarial stance, management must also.

Felix G. Rohatyn, investment banker

→1279←

We're partners with labor because we can't imagine a future without them.

National Steel Corp. advertisement

❧1280❧

The corporation has finally admitted that they need our cooperation as much as we need their jobs.

> David J. Fitzmaurice, IUE president, on IUE-GM national
> agreement, 1996/1997

❧1281❧

What do you have to talk about arsenals for if you want to have peace talks?

> Stephen P. Yokich, president, UAW, on successful contract talks
> without publicity, 1996

❧1282❧

Our membership didn't elect us to go there and strike. Our membership elected us to go out there and get an agreement and bring it back to them, and they'll make the final approval.

> Stephen Yokich, on the success of negotiations
> with General Motors

❧1283❧

You know, Ford Motor Company once said they'd rather shut their doors than recognize our union. But in time, they did. And in time, that proved to be the best decision for both the company and the workers.

> Walter Reuther, in *Cesar Chavez: Autobiography of La Causa*, 1975

❧1284❧

If a company is in trouble, it can always sit down and talk with us. We don't ever intend to drive a company out of business and never have.

> James Kane, president, UE, on protecting wages and jobs

❧1285❧

Chrysler could not have saved and would not [now] exist, had it not been for the sacrifices and the investment of time and deferred wages that the United Auto Workers provided.

> Lane Kirkland, citing to Congress how concession bargaining has
> aided failing industries

❧1286❧

Unionism seldom, if ever, uses such power as it has to insure better work; almost always it devotes a large part of that power to safeguarding bad work.

> H.L. Mencken, *Prejudices, Third Series*, 1922

❧1287❧

No one likes to negotiate for the incompetent worker.

Professor B.J. Widick, Columbia University, in *Industrial Relations*

❧1288❧

This contract opens a new chapter in American Labor relations and clearly signals a move for us in a new direction—away from confrontation and toward cooperation, away from our adversarial past and toward a new alliance aimed at maintaining a competitive leadership in our product and assuring job security for all our employees.

Fred Warren, GM official, commenting on UAW contract
containing major union concessions

❧1289❧

Once you dissipate the militancy and the cohesiveness of working people, you destroy the primary strength of labor unions. ... Our strength comes from our members, and these programs are designed explicitly to dissipate that strength.

William Burrus, referring to employee-involvement programs of
labor-management relations, 1996

❧1290❧

Employee-management cooperation is designed to weaken collective action through the subterfuge of fake empowerment. Cooperation by its definition means compromise—and all that a labor leader has to trade off is workers' knowledge, labor and jobs.

William Burrus

❧1291❧

There is absolutely no evidence in history that cooperating with the employer does unions any good. ... There are just conflicting interests.

William Burrus

❧1292❧

Negotiations are a euphemism for capitulation if the shadow of power is not cast across the bargaining table.

George Shultz

❧1293❧

Stop the CON-cessation game.

Slogan on leaflets, protesting UAW giveback negotiations, 1982

Reprinted with permission, courtesy ©Patrick Hardin.

→1294←

Compromise, but always compromise upward. ... You must never just stay on a level, you've got to move. ... You can't giddy'p by saying whoa.

Esther Peterson (1906-1997), labor organizer, consumer advocate

→1295←

Everything is possible at the bargaining table.

Tom O'Connor, communications director, AFSCME, 1993

→1296←

It's a pretty good rule to work with anyone who will work with you.

John L. Lewis, in *Men Who Lead Labor*, 1937

→1297←

The failure to reach agreement is the problem of management and labor.

Robert J. Brown, Under Secretary of Labor,
Carter Administration, 1978

❧1298❧

The big issue in labor-management relations today is not who can survive a strike, but who can survive, without blinking, the arbitrator's bill.

Thomas Geoghegan, *Which Side Are You On?*, 1991

❧1299❧

Arbitration is a funny business. Sometimes everything goes wrong, and other times everything goes right.

Steve Albanese, business agent, on the unpredictability of arbitrated decisions, 1996

❧1300❧

Arbitration is like a lawsuit in drag.

Thomas Geoghegan

❧1301❧

There must be a partnership of government, business and labor.

Lane Kirkland

❧1302❧

You can't ask unions to walk hand in hand into the unknown land of worker participation while going full-speed ahead with union-busting anti-labor programs. There has to be greater acceptance of unions in this country.

Glen Watts, president,
Communication Workers of America (CWA)

❧1303❧

My view is that the other side of the coin is more appropriate; namely, that management should cooperate with the workers to find ways to enhance the human dignity of labor and to tap the creative resources of each human being in developing a more satisfying worklife, with emphasis on worker participation in the decision-making process.

Irving Bluestone, vice president, UAW, 1976

❧1304❧

Without unions, which means without independence or power, these cooperative programs are hollow attempts to pacify workers' desire for a real voice on the job. The result is that these efforts rarely rise much above free doughnuts and happy talk.

Tom Juravich and Kate Bronfenbrenner, labor educators,
organizers, on employee-involvement programs

✦1305✦

I want very much to cooperate in consensus building and problem solving, but management can't expect cooperation when the hand it puts around my shoulder also has a knife in it.

Glen Watts

✦1306✦

A man who won't meet his men halfway is a goddamn fool.

Mark Hanna (1837-1904) industrialist, republican politician,
advocate of close business-government ties, Senator
(R-Ohio, 1897-1904), 1894

✦1307✦

There are some men who, in a 50-50 proposition, insist on getting the hyphen, too.

Lawrence J. Peter

✦1308✦

We have learned from long, hard experience that undue faith in cooperation and employer benevolence is a road to nowhere. We will continue to reach out to new workers, encourage innovations at the job site and the bargaining table and work cooperatively with employers who truly desire harmonious relations. But we will always ultimately rely on our collective strength.

Arthur Osborne

✦1309✦

Management's definition of being competitive is the reduction of jobs. The union's definition should be the expansion of jobs and the creation of a product that workers are proud to produce. How can labor leaders ask that workers cooperate in their own demise? This cooperative theory is academic gibberish.

William Burrus

✦1310✦

The buzzwords in manufacturing are quality circles, quality groups, quality teams, work teams, etc. They are updated versions of group bonus plans in which earnings were based on exceeding production quotas. Group members monitor each other to maximize production and earnings.

Ernest DeMaio, *Words For Workers In Changing Times*, 1993

✦1311✦

I have found a way of getting workers to increase production, take less pay, spy on their fellow workers and think it is for their own good. How do you do it? ... I get them to form a Quality Circle.

William Winpisinger

✦1312✦

We do not ask to be a partner in management, to be, most likely, the junior partner in success and the senior partner in failure. We do not want to blur in any way the distinction between the respective roles of labor and management in the plant.

Thomas Donahue, 1976

"We're not unsatisfied with your work, Henderson; but the firm's decided to experiment with some of the newer approaches to Human Resource Management."

Reprinted with permission, courtesy ©Patrick Hardin.

✤1313✤

After you wrestle the employee to the ground, pin him down three times—then you say, let's cooperate.

Thomas Donahue, on employee strength regarding employee cooperation

✤1314✤

If you don't have the independent voice for workers, then you have something else. You have something that pretends to be a new workplace.

Thomas Donahue, stressing that union representation is essential with labor-management partnership

✤1315✤

Without strong and effective unions representing the workers, cooperation by labor easily degenerates into the cooperation of a 'company union,' rubber-stamping the management program. It becomes a facade. At best, cooperation—when only one side has real authority—reverts to a form of paternalism.

Monsignor George G. Higgins, *Organized Labor and the Church*, 1993

✤1316✤

Workers rightly reject calls for less adversarial relationships when they are a smoke screen for demands that labor make all the concessions. For a partnership to be genuine, it must be a two-way street, with creative initiative and a willingness to cooperate on all sides.

U.S. Bishops, *Pastoral Letter*, 1986

✤1317✤

I always thought that 'in good faith' meant not only a fair wage for services rendered but faith in the idea of an uneasy but real community that exists between people, between management and labor, when some kind of mutual parity, dignity, and respect can be achieved.

Bruce Springsteen

✤1318✤

While it may seem appropriate for academics and journalists to lecture the trade union movement on the need to abandon a confrontational approach, our very real problem is finding employers, public or private, who wish to deal cooperatively with us.

Thomas Donahue

✦1319✦

No American should make the mistake of thinking that employers today are any more benevolent or compassionate or concerned than employers a century ago. Business is in business to make *money,* not to create decent, safe jobs. If employers were out to do good, they'd be running social service agencies.

Richard J. Perry

✦1320✦

[T]hose responsible for business enterprises are responsible to society for the economic and ecological effects of their operations. They have an obligation to consider the good of persons and not only the increase of profits.

Roman Catholic Catechism segment

✦1321✦

Business interests and their Neanderthal buddies in Congress would love to get rid of unions altogether. Wonderful—then the exploiters among us wouldn't have even the threat of unionization to worry about. ... If companies don't want unions, let them create the kind of workplaces that make unions irrelevant and unnecessary. That isn't hard at all—a fact that seems to escape too many American managers.

John Case, business editor, *Inc.* magazine

Chapter 17

The Sporting Life

➔1322↢

I got a million dollars worth of free advice and a very small raise.

> Edward Raymond "Eddie" Stanky (1917-1999), baseball
> infielder, after negotiating a contract with Branch Rickey, general
> manager, Brooklyn Dodgers, 1945

➔1323↢

Baseball as you know it now and as I knew it then was two different things. It was just pitiful. We had no association, we were making no money, and every time we went into the boss's office, we had to kind of crawl in and beg for a few dollars more. You have to understand that to know why someone would do what I did.

> Curtis Charles "Curt" Flood (1938-1997), St. Louis Cardinals
> centerfielder, artist, whose challenge of baseball's reserve clause
> essentially led to labor liberation of professional athletes

➔1324↢

It is essential to understand that battles are in the hearts of man.

> Vincent Thomas Lombardi (1913-1970), football coach, Green
> Bay Packers (1959-1968) and Washington Redskins (1969)

➔1325↢

I believe any system that produces that result violates my basic right as a citizen and is inconsistent with the laws of the United States.

> Curt Flood, protesting being bought or sold (traded) as property
> regardless of his wishes

➔1326↢

He [Curt Flood] set the stage for the overturning of the reserve clause.

> William Dekova "Bill" White, former player,
> National League president (1989-1994)

→ **Curt Flood**, 1938-1997, Houston, Texas

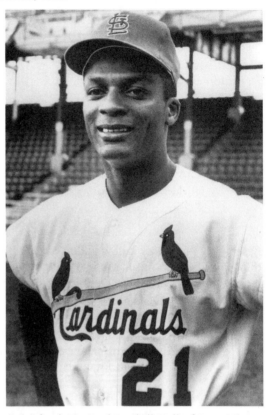

Curt Flood. National Baseball Hall of Fame Library, Cooperstown, N.Y.

In the off-season of 1969, Curt Flood, the St. Louis Cardinals centerfielder for the past 12 years, learned that he had been traded to the Philadelphia Phillies. That December he met with baseball Commissioner Bowie Kuhn, requesting to become a free agent. He then wrote the commissioner, formally objecting to the trade on the grounds that he was not a piece of property to be bought and sold against his wishes. His request was denied under baseball's reserve clause, which bound a player to his club. Flood sued, sitting out the 1970 season. He returned to baseball in 1971 with the Washington Senators, but after being ostracized by his new teammates, he quit baseball altogether after only 18 days into the season. Flood ended his career with a .293 batting average, seven gold gloves, and two World Series championships.

Curt Flood's case was eventually heard by the Supreme Court, which ruled against him on 6/19/1972. But baseball was changed by his case and, in 1976, pitcher Andy Messersmith became baseball's first free agent, gaining freedom to negotiate his contract with any team. Curt Flood lost his case, but his cause was won. Professional athletes unionized, and they now enjoy the fruits of free agency as well as the traditional protections unions furnish their members. ←

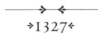

→1327←

I don't want to be a nigger on that man's plantation.

Rodney Cline "Rod" Carew, Minnesota Twins (black) all-star infielder, on becoming a free agent, leaving former owner Cal Griffith, 1978, in *A Whole Different Ball Game*, 1991

✦1328✦

Baseball is the only profession I know of where management dumps money on the players and calls us greedy for taking it. There is no other business that does this—and then calls us spoiled, rich and whiny for taking it. MGM gives a lot of money to Frank Sinatra, but no one doesn't expect him to take it.

Curt Flood

✦1329✦

It doesn't hurt to ask for more than you expect to get. Don't be afraid to climb those golden stairs.

James Alan "Jim" Bouton, former New York Yankees baseball pitcher, television sportswriter, author, *Ball Four Plus Ball Five*, 1981

✦1330✦

Why not? I had a better year than he did.

George Herman "Babe" Ruth, baseball outfielder, when asked how he felt about his new $80,000 contract being higher than President Hoover's salary

✦1331✦

Based on contribution to society, baseball players are grossly overpaid. Teachers, policemen, and firemen should get more money. But we live in a society that says a man is worth what someone is willing to pay him. Is Robert Redford worth $3 million a picture? Is Barbara Streisand worth $5 million a song? Evidently somebody thinks so. In baseball, the income is there; the only question is who's going to get it. My position is that while the players don't deserve all that money, the owners don't deserve it even more.

Jim Bouton

✦1332✦

And when is it against the law in America to make money for possessing a special skill? Sylvester Stallone signs for $12 million a movie, no problem. Elizabeth Taylor, Joan Collins sign for millions, no one says boo. They don't possess a fingernail's worth of talent compared to professional ballplayers.

Ron Rapaport, sports columnist, in *The Great Divide*, 1988

✦1333✦

We're entertainers, and the sky's the limit, brother, when you can make the money.

Wade Anthony Boggs, baseball infielder, defending the players' strike

→1334←

Baseball's greatest blue-collar, punch in/punch out standard.

> Peter Gammons, baseball sports analyst,
> on the Pete Rose all-time hit record

→1335←

The working man's ballet.

> Baseball, as described by Ralph Fasanella

→1336←

You're right, I am overpaid. But you're the dummy who paid to watch me.

> Olden Polynice, National Basketball Association (NBA) center, to
> a fan who yelled that his initials stand for "overpaid," 2/24/1999

→1337←

The strike cost more than just money. Vin Baker and the other players have had a period of inactivity and unemployment. Unemployment is terrifying to people.

> Dr. Joyce Diane Brothers, psychologist, columnist, television
> personality, speculating that the trauma of the NBA lockout might
> be the root of Baker's free-throw difficulties, after the all-star
> forward missed his first 18 attempts and had made only
> seven for 42, 3/3/1999.

→1338←

If the club is losing $15 million, how come there are so many buyers out there willing to invest $85 million—$100 million for the franchise?

> Thomas Michael Glavine, Atlanta Braves baseball pitcher, player
> representative during baseball strike, 1994

→1339←

Either they're not telling people the truth, or the people buying these teams are in it to lose money. Disney isn't in it to lose money. ITT isn't in it to lose money.

> Cam Neeley, hockey player, on National Hockey League (NHL)
> wage dispute, 1994

❧1340❧

I read sportswriters who lament the players' 'decline of loyalty' to teams, fans, and cities, but I never read accusations of disloyalty against the owners when they trade a team's favorite players (or for that matter move entire, long-established teams to bigger markets). Loyalty, as conceived by many writers, is a one-way street; players apparently owe loyalty to their clubs, but when their clubs trade them or sell them for cash, or simply fire them, that's ok—because it's business. And as we all know, loyalty has no place in business.

> Marvin Miller, Major League Baseball Players' Association
> attorney and founder, Major League Baseball Players' Association,
> *A Whole Different Ball Game*, 1991

❧1341❧

Organized baseball is a monopoly. Its practices are in restraint of trade.

> Marvin Miller, *A Whole Different Ball Game*, 1991

❧1342❧

Owners do with their tickets what they say players have no right to do with their talents—charge what the markets will pay.

> George Will

❧1343❧

If you're not fired with enthusiasm, you'll be fired with enthusiasm.

> Vince Lombardi

❧1344❧

I like my players to be married and in debt.

> Ernest "Mr. Cub" Banks, baseball coach, former Chicago Cubs
> shortstop and first baseman, National League Most Valuable
> Player (1958 and 1959)

❧1345❧

I don't like my intelligence insulted by telling me this is the Detroit Tigers.

> [George Lee] Sparky Anderson, manager of the Detroit Tigers, on
> replacement players

❧1346❧

I won't represent any guy who is a replacement. If one says he's just trying to make a little money, I'll tell him, 'Call up UPS [United Parcel Service] and get a job.'

> Alan Hendricks, players' agent

✦1347✦

After the strike ends, they'll be tossed out quicker than yesterday's newspaper.

Alan Hendricks, on replacement players during strike

✦1348✦

What is a strike but a withholding of services? The only difference is that individual holdouts are ignored and ineffective. ... But unified group action can never be ignored. A strike is a weapon that sometimes must be used, but only as a last resort, much like going to war.

Marvin Miller, *A Whole Different Ball Game*, 1991

✦1349✦

The only thing a salary cap does is to guarantee that they will make profits whether they put a good team on the field or not. It takes a lot of the risk out of running your organization.

Tom Glavine, 1994

✦1350✦

Why did the issue of greed only enter the picture when the players finally got a fairer slice of the pie? Lest we forget, that pie became bigger *because* of the players' unionizing efforts.

Marvin Miller

✦1351✦

Owners have individual selfish interest. Each owner, given the chance, would be inclined to do what is best for him, not for the common good, not for the game, certainly not for the fan.

Dick Young, sportswriter,
on the major league baseball strike, 1994

✦1352✦

All commissioners are controlled by the owners.

Marvin Miller

✦1353✦

The safest way to gauge baseball disputes is to assume the owners are wrong. You usually will be right.

George Will

→1354←

I think the fans are important, but they're no different than any other consumers inconvenienced and annoyed, but that doesn't give the fans the right to say the players may not protect themselves.

Marvin Miller, on fan anger over baseball strikes

→1355←

The baseball strike really isn't about baseball; it's about unions. ... There isn't a labor organization in America that doesn't envy the Major League Players Association, the most successful union in history. In their high profile union busting, the baseball owners are standing in for management in general. If the Players Association goes down, any union in America can be broken. Not in years has any strike had such historical importance.

David Lenson, former union president

→1356←

Through a national hidden-ball trick, Reagan and his cohorts managed to deflect attention from themselves to government bureaucrats, always-handy scapegoats, and to ordinary working people who dared demand their share of the loot. In short, they turned the people against themselves—hence the anger at the ballplayers, the vast majority of whom, after all, are poor or middle class folks who made good.

Neal Gabler, writer, on fan anger during baseball strike

→1357←

I think that the labor movement is the only viable force in the country that could create the kind of nonviolent revolution that we need.

Dick Young, on the major league baseball strike, 1994

→1358←

It's not about money. We want the right to be able to go where we want when we're free (agents) ... Whether I have a million or no dollars, I'm going to treat people the same way—with respect. Money can't buy happiness and love, and I got that right now.

Kenneth Wade Hill, Anaheim Angels baseball pitcher, during
baseball strike, 1994

✦1359✦

The players' strike contained a large ingredient of the opposite of greed—sacrifice for the benefit of strangers. Many players who struck absorbed financial losses they will never recoup. They did so to preserve a compensation system—won for them by the sacrifices of earlier strikes—many of the benefits of which will accrue to players who are not yet in the major leagues, or even professional baseball.

George Will

✦1360✦

This is either a threat to be ignored, or an offer to be accepted.

Sandy Alderson, executive vice president for baseball operations, responding to the major league umpires' near-unanimous (57 of 66 members) decision to resign on 9/1/1999 in an effort to prevent a lockout and force meaningful contract negotiations before their current contract expired, 7/17/1999

✦1361✦

It might be our cheapest. solution.

Sandy Alderson, commenting on the possibility of accepting the umpires' resignations and replacing them with less experienced umpires, 7/17/1999

✦1362✦

That typifies the smugness and the arrogance that has led us to where we are [at an impasse in contract negotiations].

Richie Phillips, counsel and leader of Major League Umpires Association, 7/17/1999

✦1363✦

They say we're too confrontational. Yes, we are. But we have to be.

Terry Tata, National League (NL) umpire, 8/3/1999

✦1364✦

I feel totally betrayed by the umpires who left the union, quit my family, put us in this situation.

Bill Hohn, one of 22 major league baseball umpires, who had resigned, effective 9/1/1999, and were fired beforehand, 8/3/1999 (27 umpires broke union solidarity by not resigning or by withdrawing resignations by 7/25/1999)

→1365←
The strategy was flawed from the beginning.
> John Hirschbeck, American League (AL) umpire, one of 23
> American League umpires who broke solidarity, 8/3/1999

→1366←
Because of them, we've lost our solidarity. We've lost our strength. That's not Richie's fault.
> Terry Tata, on why the umpires' job action failed, 9/1/1999

→1367←
He took me from nowhere to the dream house. I've got two kids in private school and two others in college. I have a beautiful house. I have a great life.
> Eric Gregg, NL umpire, after losing his job, on his continuing
> support for Richie Phillips for the many concessions won for
> umpires over two decades of his leadership, 9/1/1999

→1368←
We smoked them.
> Howard Ganz, attorney for major league baseball, on the outcome
> of the umpires' job action, 9/1/1999

→1369←
We want a union that is run by umpires and advised by attorneys.
> John Hirschbeck, commenting after major league umpires voted 57
> to 35 to form a new union, effectively ousting Richie Phillips as
> counsel and leader for the umpires' union, 11/30/1999

→1370←
It's a great honor being the highest U.S. player drafted. I don't feel pressure. Pressure is when you don't have a job and have six kids to feed.
> Tim Connolly, hockey player, after being drafted by the NHL New
> York Islanders, 7/1999

→1371←
The real superstar is a man or woman raising six kids on a $150 a week.
> Spencer Haywood, NBA all-star forward (In 1970, Haywood
> challenged the NBA rule that prevented players from signing contracts
> prior to the graduation of their college class. Under the guise that the
> NBA wanted young players to finish their education, the rule amount-
> ed to a four-year college farm system for the NBA in which the players
> were not paid. In *Spencer Haywood* vs. *The National Basketball Association*,
> 1971, the Supreme Court declared the NBA rule illegal, paving the way
> for players to sign at any age under the "early entry rule.")

About the Author

Peter Bollen is a native of Lynn, Massachusetts, where he lives with his wife, Ellen, and where he did much of the research for this book. He belongs to the American Postal Workers Union, Communication Workers of America, National Writers Union, and the Postal Press Association.

After completing his military obligation in the U.S. Navy, Bollen worked several jobs including printing pressman, meatpacker, lettercarrier, postal clerk, and freelance writer. Bollen authored *A Handbook of Great Labor Quotations*, published by Hillside Books in 1983, and *Nuclear Voices*, published by Highland/Hillside Books in 1986. He is the award-winning editor of the *Northeast News Service*, a union trade journal.

In 1990, Congress enacted an *honoraria ban*, in effect barring federal employees from earning income from freelance writing. As a postal (federal) employee, a lawsuit was initiated on Bollen's behalf by the New England Legal Foundation. Bollen's case was eventually heard by the Supreme Court (*United States of America et.* al v. *National Treasury Employees Union et.* al respondents, 1995), where the ban was successfully overturned (2/22/1995) on First Amendment challenges.

All federally employed freelance writers owe a significant debt of gratitude to the New England Legal Foundation, particularly to lead counsel Stephen Ostrach. With the assistance of attorneys Todd Brilliant and Emily Livingston, their arguments were upheld through the federal courts, the Court of Appeals, and the High Court during a five-year ordeal.

Alex Beam, columnist of the *Boston Globe,* and Representative Barney Frank (D-Mass.) also played important roles in this case: Alex Beam wrote supportive columns that publicized the unfairness of the ban; Representative Frank responded directly to Bollen's protests and successfully forged passage of a congressional motion to amend the honoraria ban. Because of these collective efforts, federal employees once again enjoy the same creative and journalistic freedoms as other Americans.

About the Author

Selected Bibliography

Alinsky, Saul. *Rules For Radicals*. New York, Random House. 1971.
John L. Lewis: An Unauthorized Biography. New York, G.P. Putnam's. 1949.
Reveille For Radicals. University of Chicago Press. 1945.

Allen, Steve. *Reflections*. New York, Prometheus Books. 1994.

Andrews, Robert. *Columbia Dictionary of Quotations*. New York, Columbia University Press. 1993.

Balliet, Lee. *Survey of Labor Relations*. Washington, D.C., BNA Books. 1987.

Bennet, Jr. Lerone. *What Manner of Man—A Biography of Martin Luther King, Jr.* Boulder, Colo., Johnson Publishing Co. 1964.

Bimba, Anthony. *History of the Working Class*. New York, International Publishers. 1927.

Bollen, James. *The Colonial Strike*. Boston, AFT 189 & Local 616, UPWA. 1975.

Bollen, Peter. *A Handbook of Great Labor Quotations*. Lynn, Mass., Hillside Books. 1983.

Bouton, Jim. *Ball Four Plus Ball Five*. New York, Stein & Day. 1981.

Boyer, Richard O. and Herbert Morais. *Labor's Untold Story*. New York, Cameron Associates. 1955.

Brecher, Jeremy. *Strike!* Boston, South End Press. 1983.

Brill, Steven. *The Teamsters*. New York, Simon & Schuster. 1978.

Brooks, Thomas R. *Toil and Trouble*. New York, Dell Publishing. 1964.

Bufe, Charles. *The Heretic's Handbook of Quotations*. Tucson, Ariz., See Sharp Press. 1988.

Cahn, William. *The Lawrence Strike of 1912—The Bread & Roses Strike*. New York, Pilgrim Press.1954, 1980.
A Pictorial History of American Labor. New York, Crown. 1972.

Cannon, Jimmy. *Nobody Asked Me*, But. New York, Holt, Rinehard, Winston. 1978.

Carruth, Gorton and Ehrlich, Eugene. *The Giant Book of American Quotations*. New York, Gramercy Books. 1988.

Chomsky, Noam. *Keeping the Rabble In Line*. Monroe, Maine, Common Courage Press. 1994.

Cooke, Alistair. *Alistair Cooke's America*. New York, Alfred A. Knopf. 1973.

Cuomo, Mario. *Reason To Believe*. New York, Simon & Schuster. 1995.

DeMaio, Ernest. *Words For Workers In Changing Times*. Salem, Mass., Deschamps Printing & DeMaio. 1993.

Dickson, Paul. *The New Official Rules*. Reading, Mass., Addison-Wesley. 1989.

Dubinsky, David and A.H. Raskin. *A Life With Labor*. New York, Simon & Schuster. 1977.

Dunn, Robert. *The Palmer Raids*. New York, Labor Research Association. 1948.

Ehrenreich, Barbara. *The Worst Years of Our Lives*. New York, Pantheon. 1990.

Ehrlich, Eugene and DeBruhl, Marshall. *International Thesaurus of Quotations, Revised and Updated*. New York, Harper Perennial. 1996

Erlich, Mark. *With Our Hands*. Philadelphia, Temple University Press. 1986.

Fine, Sidney. *Labor History, Vol. 18, No. 3*. Editorial Board, Tamiment Institute. University of Michigan. (No date.)

Fink, Gary M. *Biographical Dictionary of American Labor Leaders*. New York, Greenwood Press. 1974.

Finks, P. David. *The Radical Vision of Saul Alinsky*. New York, Paulist Press. 1984.

Flynn, Elizabeth Gurley. *I Speak My Own Piece*. New York, Masses & Mainstream.1955.

Foner, Philip S. *Women and the American Labor Movement*. New York, The Free Press. 1982.
The Industrial Workers of the World. New York, International Publishers. 1965.
History of the Labor Movement in the United States. New York, International Publishers. 1947.

Fowke, Edith and Glazer, Joe. *Songs of Work and Protest*. Mineola, N.Y., Dover. 1973.

Frank, Leonard R. *Random House Webster's Quotationary*. New York, Random House. 1998.

Friedman, Clara H. *Between Labor and Management*. New York, Twayne. 1955.

Friedman, Murray, Ed. *Overcoming Middle Class Rage*. Philadelphia, Westminster Press. 1971.

Galbraith, John Kenneth. *A Life In Our Times*. Boston, Houghton Mifflin. 1981.
Annals Of An Abiding Liberal. Boston, Houghton Mifflin. 1979.

Gentry, Curt. *Frame Up*. New York, W.W. Norton. 1967.

Geoghegan, Thomas. *Which Side Are You On?* New York, Farrar, Straus, Giroux. 1991.

Georgianna, Daniel with Roberta Hazen Aaronson. *The Strike of '28*. New Bedford, Mass., Spinner Publications. 1993.

Gilpin, Toni, Gary Isaac, Dan Letwin and Jack McKivigan. *On Strike For Respect: The Clerical and Technical Workers' Strike at Yale University*. Chicago, Charles H. Kerr. 1988.

Ginger, Ray. *The Bending Cross*. New Brunswick, N. J., Rutgers University Press. 1949.

Gompers, Samuel. *Seventy Years of Life and Labor, an Autobiography*. New York, E.P. Dutton. 1925.

Gould, Jean and Lorena Hickok. *Labor's Rugged Individualist*. New York, Dodd, Mead. 1972.

Green, Gilbert. *What's Happening To Labor?* New York, International Publishers. 1976.

Green, James R. *Workers' Struggles, Past and Present: "A Radical America"* Reader. Philadelphia, Temple University Press. 1983.
The World of the Worker. New York, Hill and Wang. 1980.

Green, Jonathon. *The Book of Political Quotes*. New York, McGraw-Hill. 1982.

Hanrahan, John D. *Government For Sale*. Washington, D.C., AFSCME. 1977.

Harris, Leon. *Upton Sinclair—American Rebel*. New York, Thomas Crowel. 1975

Higgins, George G. Monsignor, with William Bole. *Organized Labor and the Church*. New York, Paulist Press. 1993.

Horwitt, Sanford D. *Let Them Call Me Rebel*. New York, Alfred A. Knopf. 1989.

Humphrey, Hubert H. *The Education of a Public Man*. New York, Doubleday. 1976.

Hymowitz, Carol and Michael Weissman. *History of Women in America.* New York, Bantam. 1978.

James, Simon. *A Dictionary of Economic Quotations.* Totwa, N. J., Rowman & Allanheld. 1984.

Jones, Mary Harris. *The Autobiography of Mother Jones, Pittston Strike Commemorative Edition,* Chicago, Charles H. Kerr. 1990.

Josephson, Matthew. *The Robber Barons.* New York, Harcourt, Brace, World. 1934, 1962.

Kahn, Albert E. *High Treason.* New York, The Hour. 1950.

Kaplan, Justin. *Lincoln Steffens.* New York, Simon & Schuster. 1974.

King, Jr., Martin Luther. *Where Do We Go From Here: Chaos or Community.* New York, Harper & Row. 1967.

LaBotz, Dan. *A Troublemaker's Handbook.* Detroit, Labor Notes. 1991.

Larrowe, Charles P. *Harry Bridges—The Rise and Fall of Radical Labor in the United States.* New York, Lawrence Hill & Co. 1972.

Lash, Joseph P. *Eleanor: The Years Alone.* New York, Signet. New American Library. 1972.

Levitan, Sar A. *Blue Collar Workers.* New York, McGraw-Hill. 1971.

Levitt, Martin Jay. *Confessions of a Union Buster.* New York, Crown. 1993.

Levy, Jacques. *Cesar Chavez. Autobiography of La Causa.* New York, W.W. Norton. 1975.

Lichtenstein, Nelson. *The Most Dangerous Man In Detroit.* New York, Basic Books. 1995.

Madison, Charles A. *Critics & Crusaders—A Century of American Protest.* New York, Holt, 1948.

Manchester, William. *The Glory and the Dream.* Boston, Little Brown & Co., 1974.

Marshall, Ray. *Unheard Voices.* New York, Basic Books. 1987.

Matles, James and James Higgins. *Them and Us.* Englewood Cliffs, N. J., Prentice Hall. 1974.

McFeely, William S. *Frederick Douglass.* New York, W.W. Norton. 1991.

McGuckin, Henry. *Memoirs of a Wobbly.* Chicago, Charles H. Kerr. 1987.

Meltzer, Milton. *Bread and Roses: The Struggle of American Labor.* New York, Alfred A. Knopf. 1967.

Mill Hunk Herald Staff—Worker Writer Anthology. *Overtime–Punchin' Out With the Mill.* HunkMill Hunk Herald. Albuquerque, N..M., West End Press & Piece of the Hunk Publishers, Inc. 1990.

Miller, Marvin. *A Whole Different Ballgame.* New York, Birch Lane Press. 1991.

Minton, Bruce and John Stuart. *Men Who Lead Labor.* New York, Birch Lane Press. 1991.

Morris, Richard B. *The U.S. Dept. of Labor Bicentennial History of the American Laborer.* Washington, D.C., Government Printing Office. (No date.)

Mortimer, Wyndham. *Organize: My Life As A Union Man.* Boston, Beacon Press. 1971.

Murphy, Edward F. *Webster's Treasury of Relevant Quotations.* New York, Greenwich House. 1978.

Murray, R. Emmett. *The Lexicon of Labor.* New York, The New Press, 1998.

Nelson, Kevin. *Baseball's Greatest Quotes.* New York, Firestone Books. 1982.

O'Connor, Tom & Associates. *Newtwit!* New York, Doubleday. 1995.

Orear, Leslie and Stephen H. Diamond. *Out of the Jungle.* Chicago, Hyde Park Press. 1968.

Pelling, Henry. *American Labor.* Chicago, University of Chicago. 1960.

Peter, Lawrence J. *Peter's People.* New York, Tower Books. 1979.

Pivan, Frances Fox and Richard A. Cloward. *Regulating the Poor: The Function of Public Welfare*. New York, Random House. 1971.

Reuther, Victor. *The Brothers Reuther*. Boston, Houghton Mifflin. 1976.

Riley, Dorothy Winbush. *My Soul Looks Black, 'Less I Forget*. New York, Harper Collins. 1993.

Robinson, Archie. *George Meany and His Times*. New York, Simon & Schuster. 1982.

Roboff, Sari. *Boston's Labor Movement*. Boston, The Boston 200 Corporation. 1977.

Russell, Bertrand. *In Praise of Idleness*. London, Unwin. 1970.

Schneiderman, Rose and Lucy Goldthwaite. *All For One*. Middlebury, Vt., Paul S. Erikson. 1967.

Schwartz, Robert M. *Your Rights On The Job*. Boston, Labor Guild of Boston. 1983.

Seldes, George. *The Great Thoughts*. New York, Ballantine. 1985.
The Great Quotations. Seacaucus, N.J., Lyle Stuart. 1960.
Freedom of the Press. New York, Bobbs-Merrill. 1935.

Shostak, Arthur B. *For Labor's Sake*. New York, University Press of America. 1995.
Robust Unionism. New York, ILR Press. 1991.

Smith, Page. *Dissenting Opinions*. San Francisco, North Point Press. 1984.

Sullivan, George and Barbara Lagowski. *The Sports Curmudgeon*. New York, Warner Books. 1993.

Sward, Keith. *The Legend of Henry Ford*. New York, Rinehart & Co. 1948.

Terkel, Studs. *The Great Divide*. New York, Pantheon. 1988.
American Dreams: Lost and Found. New York, Pantheon. 1980.
Working. New York, Avon Books. 1974.

Tsongas, Paul. *The Road From Here— Liberalism and Realities in the 1980s*. New York, Alfred A. Knopf. 1981.

Uphoff, Walter H. Kohler. *On Strike— Thirty Years of Conflict*. Boston, Beacon Press. 1967.

Vorse, Mary Heaton. *Labor's New Millions*. New York, Modern Age Books. 1938.

Walsh, John and Garth Mangum. *Labor Struggle in the Post Office*. New York, M.E. Sharp. 1992.

Wechsler, James A. *Labor Baron—A Portrait of John L. Lewis*. New York, William Morrow. 1944.

Weinberg, Arthur. *Attorney for the Damned*. New York, Simon & Schuster. 1957.

Wertheimer, Barbara Mayer. *We Were There*. New York, Pantheon. 1977.

Winoker, Jon. *The Portable Curmudgeon Redux*. New York, Dutton. 1992.

Yessne, Peter. *Quotations From Mayor Daley*. New York, Pocket Books. 1969.

Resource Directory

For more complete records of labor periodicals and literature, comprehensive records are maintained at the George Meany Memorial Archives Library, 10000 N. Hampshire Avenue, Silver Springs, MD 20903 and at other institutions and universities specializing in labor studies.

———————→ ←———————

AFL-CIO News. Monthly. Michael Byrne, Ed., 815 Sixteenth St. NW, Washington, DC 20036.

AFSCME Public Employee. Bimonthly. Jeff Rubin, Ed., AFSCME, AFL-CIO, 1625 L. St. NW, Washington, DC 20036.

The American Postal Worker. Monthly. Moe Biller, President/Ed., 1300 L. St. NW, Washington, DC 20005.

The American Prospect. Bimonthly. Robert Kuttner, Paul Starr, Eds., The American Prospect. P.O. Box 383080, Cambridge, MA 02238.

America @ Work. Monthly. Tula Connell, Ed., AFL-CIO Public Affairs Dept., Rm. 209, 815 Sixteenth St. NW, Washington, DC 20006.

American Writer. Monthly. Marcy Rein, Ed., National Writers Union/UAW, 113 University Place, New York, NY 10003.

Bay State Employee-AFSCME Council 93. Monthly. Tom Brophy, Ed., AFSCME Council 93, 8 Beacon St., Boston, MA 02108.

Boston Globe. Daily. Matthew V. Storin, Ed., 135 Morrissey Blvd., Boston, MA 02107.

The Boston Globe Magazine. Weekly. Evelynne Kramer, Ed., Globe Newspaper Co., P.O. Box 2378, Boston, MA 02107.

The Builders. Monthly. Building and Construction Trades Dept., AFL-CIO, Rm. 603, 815 Sixteenth St. NW, Washington, DC 20006.

Business Week. Weekly. Stephen D. Shepherd, Ed., The McGraw-Hill Companies Bldg., 1221 Avenue of the Americas, New York, NY 10020.

The 480-481 Communicator. Monthly. Paul Felton, Ed., Communicator, 810 Livernois, Ferndale, MI 48220.

CWA News. Monthly. John Cusick, Ed., Communications Workers of America, 501 - 3rd St., NW Washington, DC 20001.

Daily Evening Item. Daily. Alan Kort, Ed., Daily Evening Item, P.O. Box 951, Lynn, MA 01903.

Detroit Sunday Journal. Weekly. Staff, The Detroit Sunday Journal, 3100 E. Jefferson, Detroit, MI 48207.

Dollars and Sense. Bimonthly. Marc Breslow, Betsy Reed, Eds., Dollars and Sense, 1 Summer St., Somerville, MA 02143.

Federal Times. Weekly. Staff, c/o Editor, 6883 Commercial Dr., Springfield, VA 22159.

The Federationist. Monthly. AFL-CIO Publication (Former). Lane Kirkland, 815 Sixteenth St. NW, Washington, DC 20036.

In These Times. Biweekly. James Weinstein, Ed., 2040 N. Milwaukee Ave., Chicago, IL 60647.

ILCA Reporter, Monthly. Jim Earp, President, ILCA AFL-CIO, 815 Sixteenth St. NW, Washington, DC 20006.

Iowa Postal Worker-APWU. Monthly. Lance Coles, President, Iowa Postal Worker, Box 539, Des Moines, IA 50302.

IUE Electrical Union News. Monthly. Rick Casilli, Ed., IUE Local 201, 100 Bennett St., Lynn, MA 01905.

Label Letter. Bimonthly. Charlie Mercer, Ed., Union Label & Service Trades Dept., AFL-CIO, 815 Sixteenth St. NW, Washington, DC 20006.

Labor Life Newsletter. Monthly. Fr. Edward Boyle, Ed., Catholic Labor Guild, 883 Hancock St., Quincy, MA 02169.

Labor Notes. Monthly. Jim West, Ed., Labor Education and Research Project, 7435 Michigan Ave., Detroit, MI 48210.

Labor Party Advocate. Monthly. Bob Kasen, Ed., Labor Party Advocate, P.O. Box 53177, Washington, DC 20009.

Labor's Heritage. Quarterly. Stuart B. Kaufman, Ed., Labor's Heritage, 10000 New Hampshire Ave., Silver Springs, MD 20903.

Liberal Opinion Week. Weekly. Syndicated commentary. Living History, Inc., 108 East 5th St., Vinton, IA 52349.

Los Angeles Times. Times Mirror Square, Los Angeles, CA 90053

Lynn Sunday Post. Weekly. Jim Malone, Ed., Sunday Post, 152 Sylvan St., Danvers, MA 01923.

Maritime Newsletter. Monthly. Michael Sacco, President, Maritime Newsletter, Rm. 210, 815 Sixteenth St. NW, Washington, DC 20006.

Mother Jones. Monthly. Jeffrey Klein, Ed., Mother Jones, 731 Market. St., San Francisco, CA 94103.

The Nation. Weekly. Victor Navasky, Editorial Dir., 72 Fifth Ave., New York, NY 10011.

New York Times Book Review. Weekly. 229 W. 43rd St., New York, NY 10036.

Newsweek. Weekly. 444 Madison Ave., New York, NY 10022.

Northeast News Service-APWU. Monthly. Peter Bollen, Ed., NENS, P.O. Box 601, Lynnfield, MA 01940.

The Northern Light-APWU. Monthly local journal. Rick Oswald, Ed., The Northern Light, P.O. Box 581216, Minneapolis, MN 55458.

North Shore Sunday. Weekly. Taylor Armerding, Ed., North Shore Sunday, 152 Sylvan St., Danvers, MA 01923.

The PA Perspective. Periodically. Bill Altier, Ed., Princeton Associates, Inc., P.O. Box 820, Buckingham, PA 18912.

Parade Magazine. Weekly. Walter Anderson, Ed., 711 Third Ave., New York, NY 10017.

People's Culture. Quarterly. Fred Whitehead, Ed., Box 5334, Kansas City, KS 66119.

Playboy. Monthly. Hugh Hefner, Ed., Publisher, Playboy, Playboy Bldg., 919 N. Michigan Ave., Chicago, IL 60611.

Postal Press Newsletter-APWU. Quarterly. Tony Carobine, President/Ed., APWU *National Press Association*, P.O. Box 888, Iron Mountain, MI 49801.

The Progressive. Monthly. Matthew Rothschild, Ed., The Progressive, 409 E. Main St., Madison, WI 53703.

Racine Labor. Weekly. John Nelander, Ed., The Racine Labor, 1840 Sycamore Ave., Racine, WI 53406.

Rough Draft. Monthly, Elinor Craig, Ed., National Writers Union-Boston Local, 650 Beacon St., 4th Fl., Boston, MA 02215.

Solidarity. Monthly. Dave Elsila, Ed., United Auto Workers, 8000 E. Jefferson, Detroit, MI 48214.

The Teamster. Monthly. Ron Carey, Ed., (Former) 25 Louisiana Ave. NW, Washington, DC 20001.

Time. Weekly. Time, Inc., Staff, 75 Rockefeller Plaza, New York, NY 10019.

UA Journal. Monthly. Marvin J. Boede, Gen. President, United Association of Journeymen and Apprentices of the Plumbing and PipeFitting Industry of the United States and Canada. UA Journal, 901 Massachusetts Ave. NW, Washington, DC 20001.

UE News. Monthly. Peter Gilmore, Ed., United, Electrical, Radio and Machine Workers of America (UE), 2400 Oliver Bldg., 535 Smithfield St., Pittsburgh, PA 15222.

UMWA Journal. Monthly. Richard Trumka, United Mine Workers of America, 900 - 15th St. NW, Washington, DC 20005.

The Union Builder of Greater Cincinnati. Monthly. Tom Brimm, Ed., 1216 E. McMillan St., Cincinnati, OH 45206.

Union Plus. Quarterly. Erin Eckles, Ed., Union Privilege, 1125 - 15th St. NW, Washington, DC 20005.

U.S. News & World Report. Weekly. James Fallows, Ed., 2400 N. St. NW, Washington, DC 20037.

The Washington Monthly. Monthly. Charles Peters, Ed., The Washington Monthly, 1611 Connecticut Ave., NW, Washington, DC 20009.

The Washington Post. Daily. Lawrence Meyer, Ed., 1150 - 15th St. NW, Washington, DC 20071.

The Washington Spectator. Monthly. Ben A. Franklin, Ed., The Public Concern Foundation, Inc., London Terrace Station, P.O. Box 20065, New York, NY 10011.

The Word-APWU. Monthly, local journal. Ross Baker, Ed., South Shore Area Local-APWU, P.O. Box 1455, Brockton, MA 02403.

Workers' Education Newsletter. Monthly. Jim Abrams, Exec. Sec., Workers' Education Local 189, P.O. Box 1368, Johnstown, PA 15907.

The Writer. Quarterly. Marcy Rein, Ed., National Writers Union/UAW, 337 - 17th St., #101, Oakland, CA 94612.

Z Magazine. Monthly. Lydia Sargent, Ed., Z Magazine, 18 Millfield St., Woods Hole, MA 02543.

World Wide Web Resource

www.aflcio.org. AFL-CIO main page with many union services, links, and news.

www.laboreducator.org. Includes labor news magazine and weekly *LaborTalk* column by Harry Kelder.

www.labornet.org. Includes a large directory with links to many union web sites.

www.unionlabel.org. Information on the products and countries behind what we buy, AFL-CIO political actions, and boycotts.

www.workingfamilies.com. Provides labor news and online services for labor union members.

List of Photographs, Drawings, and Biographical Briefs

Acronym Glossary and Index

Organizations are indexed here only if they appear as acronyms. Indexing is by quotation numbers or, where indicated, by *page number*. If searching for particular unions, also use key words and the author index.

Author Index

by Name and Keyword

Quotation authors are listed by quotation numbers under their pen or popular names. To shorten the reader's search, a quote may have more than one author entry. For examples, slogans, signs, placards, songs, and organizations can be found under those categories; an "author" can be identified by several key words, such as with the quotation from the preamble to the AFL constitution, which can be found under *preamble, constitution,* or *AFL.*

A

Abel, I.W. 151
Acuna, Roberto 180
Adler, Mortimer 1230
advertisement, Canadian brewer 1189
advertisement, corporate seminar 1189
advertisement, National Steel Corp. 1279
advertisement, strikebreaker protest 282
AFL, preamble to constitution 469
AFL resolution, 1886 795
AFL, slogan 61
AFL song 728
AFL-CIO, Education Dept. 720
AFL-CIO statement, Human Rights 573
AFL-CIO, Massachusetts 327, 520, 720
AFL-CIO, preamble 987
AFL-CIO resolution, 1955 635
AFL-CIO, resolution, 1979 641
Albanese, Joe 316
Albanese, Steve 1299
Alderson, Sandy 1360, 1361
Alewitz, Mike (mural) 484
Alighieri, Dante 605
Alinsky, Saul 116, 172, 310, 365, 384, 389, 394, 420, 431, 435, 441, 647, 992, 993, 994, 996, 997, 998
Allen, Steve 49, 772, 1150
Altgeld, John Peter 362

Alvarez, Adrian 56
American Federation of Labor, 1886 resolution 795
Anderson, Paul 519
Anderson, Robert 762
Anderson, Sparky 1345
Angelou, Maya 3
anonymous 109, 489, 1182
anonymous AFL song 728
anonymous labor leader 957
Anthony, Susan Brownell 587
Arbiter Program, preamble 19
Aristotle 2
Arouet, Francois (Voltaire) 15
Asner, Ed 932, 958, 1183
Auden, W.H. 104
authors, *On Strike For Respect* 456

B

Bachman, Maria 48
Bader, Joe 340
Baer, George 146, 629
Bagley, Sarah 583
Banks, Ernest 1344
banner, Kodak union 265
banner, popular (democracy) 695
banner, popular (without labor) 89
banners, eight-hour day 60, 219
banners, Tompkins Square 60
Barkett, Al 1138
Barnette, Alf 1146

Word and Keyword Index